双语名著无障碍阅读丛书

·经典集锦·

森林王子

The Jungle Book

[英国] 吉卜林 著

王文丽 译

中国出版集团

中译出版社

图书在版编目（CIP）数据

森林王子：英汉对照／（英）吉卜林（Rudyard Kipling）著；王文丽译.
—北京：中译出版社，2018.4
（双语名著无障碍阅读丛书）
ISBN 978-7-5001-5577-5

Ⅰ.①森…　Ⅱ.①吉…　②王…　Ⅲ.①英语－汉语－对照读物　②童话－
作品集－英国－近代　Ⅳ.①H319.4：I

中国版本图书馆CIP数据核字（2018）第 049312 号

出版发行／中译出版社
地　　　址／北京市西城区车公庄大街甲4号物华大厦6层
电　　　话／(010) 68359827；　68359303（发行部）；　53601537（编辑部）
邮　　　编／100044
传　　　真／(010) 68357870
电子邮箱／book@ctph.com.cn
网　　　址／http://www.ctph.com.cn

总 策 划／张高里
策划编辑／胡晓凯
责任编辑／李　颖　范祥镇

封面设计／潘　峰
排　　版／北京竹页文化传媒有限公司
印　　刷／山东泰安新华印务有限责任公司
经　　销／新华书店

规　　格／710毫米×1000毫米　1/16
印　　张／19.5
字　　数／309千字
版　　次／2018年4月第一版
印　　次／2018年4月第一次

ISBN 978-7-5001-5577-5　定价：35.00元

多年以来，中译出版社有限公司（原中国对外翻译出版有限公司）凭借国内一流的翻译和出版实力及资源，精心策划、出版了大批双语读物，在海内外读者中和业界内产生了良好、深远的影响，形成了自己鲜明的出版特色。

二十世纪八九十年代出版的英汉（汉英）对照"一百丛书"，声名远扬，成为一套最权威、最有特色且又实用的双语读物，影响了一代又一代英语学习者和中华传统文化研究者、爱好者；还有"英若诚名剧译丛""中华传统文化精粹丛书""美丽英文书系"，这些优秀的双语读物，有的畅销，有的常销不衰反复再版，有的被选为大学英语阅读教材，受到广大读者的喜爱，获得了良好的社会效益和经济效益。

"双语名著无障碍阅读丛书"是中译专门为中学生和英语学习者精心打造的又一品牌，是一个新的双语读物系列，具有以下特点：

选题创新——该系列图书是国内第一套为中小学生量身打造的双语名著读物，所选篇目均为教育部颁布的语文新课标必读书目，或为中学生以及同等文化水平的社会读者喜闻乐见的世界名著，重新编译为英汉（汉英）对照的双语读本。这些书既给青少年读者提供了成长过程中不可或缺的精神食粮，又让他们领略到原著的精髓和魅力，对他们更好地学习英文大有裨益；同时，丛书中入选的《论语》《茶馆》《家》等汉英对照读物，亦是热爱中国传统文化的中外读者所共知的经典名篇，能使读者充分享受阅读经典的无限乐趣。

无障碍阅读——中学生阅读世界文学名著的原著会遇到很多生词和文化难点。针对这一情况，我们给每一本读物原文中的较难词汇和不易理解之处都加上了注释，在内文的版式设计上也采取英汉（或汉英）对照方式，扫清了学生阅读时的障碍。

优良品质——中译双语读物多年来在读者中享有良好口碑，这得益于作者和出版者对于图书质量的不懈追求。"双语名著无障碍阅读丛书"继承了中译双语读物的优良传统——精选的篇目、优秀的译文、方便实用的注解，秉承着对每一个读者负责的精神，竭力打造精品图书。

愿这套丛书成为广大读者的良师益友，愿读者在英语学习和传统文化学习两方面都取得新的突破。

目录 CONTENTS

目录
CONTENTS

Rudyard Kipling

Mowgli's Brothers

Now Rann the Kite brings home the night
That Mang the Bat sets free —
The herds are shut in byre[1] *and hut*
For loosed till dawn are we.
This is the hour of pride and power,
Talon and tush and claw.
Oh, hear the call! — Good hunting all
That keep the Jungle Law!

Night-Song in the Jungle

It was seven o'clock of a very warm evening in the Seeonee hills when Father Wolf woke up from his day's rest, scratched himself, **yawned**[2], and spread out his paws one after the other to get rid of the sleepy feeling in their tips. Mother Wolf lay with her big gray nose dropped across her four tumbling, squealing cubs, and the moon shone into the mouth of the cave where they all lived. "Augrh!" said Father Wolf. "It is time to hunt again." He was going to **spring**[3] down hill when a little shadow with a **bushy**[4] tail crossed the **threshold**[5] and **whined**[6]: "Good luck go with you, O Chief of the Wolves. And good luck and strong white teeth go with noble children that they may never

毛格利的兄弟们

① byre ['baiə] *n.* [英国英语] 牛栏,牛棚,牛舍

黑夜被蝙蝠芒恩释放,
又被鸢鹰兰恩带回了家。
牧群被关进棚里,
因为我们会游荡到天明。
现在是用我们的利爪和尖牙
显示荣耀和力量的时刻。
噢,听听这嚎叫——祝所有
遵守丛林法则的兽众打猎顺利!

——丛林夜之歌

② yawn [jɔːn] *v.* 打呵欠

③ spring [spriŋ] *v.* 跳,跃起

④ bushy ['buʃi] *a.* 毛茸茸的
⑤ threshold ['θreʃhəuld] *n.* 门口,入口
⑥ whine [wain] *v.* 发牢骚

　　思翁尼群山,一个非常暖和的傍晚,狼爸爸睡了一天,醒来时已经七点钟了。他挠挠痒痒,打个哈欠,把爪子一个个地舒展开来,好赶走残留在爪尖儿的睡意。狼妈妈还躺着,她那大大的灰鼻子枕在四个狼崽儿身上,他们还站立不稳,不时发出尖叫。月光从他们一家住的山洞口照进来。狼爸爸叫道:"嗷呜!该去打猎了。"他正要跳下山坡,一个小小的身影拖着一条毛茸茸的尾巴溜进门,哼哼唧唧地说:"噢,狼王,祝您好运。也祝您尊贵的孩子们享有好运和强壮的白牙,永不忘记这世上还有人忍饥挨饿。"

forget the hungry in this world."

It was the **jackal**①—Tabaqui, the Dish-licker—and the wolves of India **despise**② Tabaqui because he runs about making **mischief**③, and telling tales, and eating **rags**④ and pieces of leather from the village rubbish-heaps. But they are afraid of him too, because Tabaqui, more than anyone else in the jungle, is apt to go mad, and then he forgets that he was ever afraid of anyone, and runs through the forest biting everything in his way. Even the tiger runs and hides when little Tabaqui goes mad, for madness is the most **disgraceful**⑤ thing that can overtake a wild creature. We call it **hydrophobia**⑥, but they call it dewanee—the madness—and run.

"Enter, then, and look," said Father Wolf **stiffly**⑦, "but there is no food here."

"For a wolf, no," said Tabaqui, "but for so mean a person as myself a dry bone is a good feast. Who are we, the Gidur-log [the jackal people], to pick and choose?" He **scuttled**⑧ to the back of the cave, where he found the bone of a **buck**⑨ with some meat on it, and sat cracking the end merrily.

"All thanks for this good meal," he said, licking his lips. "How beautiful are the noble children! How large are their eyes! And so young too! Indeed, indeed, I might have remembered that the children of kings are men from the beginning."

Now, Tabaqui knew as well as anyone else that there is nothing so unlucky as to compliment children to their faces. It pleased him to see Mother and Father Wolf look uncomfortable.

Tabaqui sat still, rejoicing in the mischief that he had made, and then he said spitefully:

"Shere Khan, the Big One, has shifted his hunting grounds. He will hunt among these hills for the next moon, so he has told me."

Shere Khan was the tiger who lived near the Waingunga River, twenty miles away.

"He has no right!" Father Wolf began angrily—"By the Law of the Jungle he has no right to change his quarters without due warning. He will frighten every head of game within ten miles, and I—I have to kill for two, these days."

① jackal ['dʒækɔːl] *n.*【动物】豺，胡狼

② despise [di'spaiz] *v.* 轻视，藐视

③ mischief ['mistʃif] *n.* 恶作剧，捣蛋

④ rag [ræg] *n.* 破布

⑤ disgraceful [dis'greisful] *a.* 丢脸的，丢人现眼的

⑥ hydrophobia [ˌhaidrəu'fəubjə] *n.* 狂犬病

⑦ stiffly ['stifli] *ad.* 生硬地

⑧ scuttle ['skʌtl] *v.* 急促地跑

⑨ buck [bʌk] *n.*【动物】雄鹿

这是豺狗塔巴奇，外号叫作"舔盘子的"。印度的狼都看不起塔巴奇，因为他总是跑来跑去惹是生非，东家长西家短，要不就是从村子的垃圾堆里刨些破布烂皮什么的来吃吃。但是狼也害怕他，因为塔巴奇要比丛林里任何野兽都容易发狂，一发起疯来他就忘了他以前怕过谁，满林子撒野，见什么咬什么。小小的塔巴奇发疯的时候，甚至连老虎也会跑掉躲起来，因为疯病是任何野兽可能遭遇的最丢脸的事儿。我们管这叫狂犬病，他们管它叫"疯癫症"，唯恐避之不及。

狼爸爸冷冰冰地说："进来看看吧，但是这儿可没什么吃的。"

塔巴奇说："对狼来说是没有，不过对像我这样的贱民来说，一根干骨头就称得上大餐了。我们豺族哪有资格挑三拣四？"他屁颠屁颠地跑到山洞后面，找到一根还剩点儿肉的鹿骨头，坐下来高高兴兴地开始大嚼。

他舔舔嘴说："谢谢您的这顿大餐。您的孩子们长得可真好啊，眼睛又大，年纪又轻！当然啦，当然啦，我差点忘了，国王的孩子一开始就不是凡夫俗子啊！"

众所周知，当着孩子的面恭维他们最容易招来厄运。塔巴奇当然也知道，但是他就乐意看见狼爸爸和狼妈妈露出不安的表情。

塔巴奇一动也不动地坐着，欣赏他一手制造的恶作剧，然后充满恶意地说：

"'大个子'希尔汗换猎场了。下个月他就会到这片山里来打食儿，他是这么跟我说的。"

希尔汗是一头老虎，住在二十英里外的瓦因刚加河附近。

"他凭什么！"狼爸爸生气地喊道："按照丛林法则，他没有权利不打招呼就换领地。他会把方圆十英里以内的所有猎物都给吓跑的，可是我——我这些天可得抓两头狼的食物啊。"

"His mother did not call him Lungri [the Lame One] for nothing," said Mother Wolf quietly. "He has been **lame**① in one foot from his birth. That is why he has only killed **cattle**②. Now the villagers of the Waingunga are angry with him, and he has come here to make our villagers angry. They will **scour**③ the jungle for him when he is far away, and we and our children must run when the grass is set alight. Indeed, we are very grateful to Shere Khan!"

"Shall I tell him of your gratitude?" said Tabaqui.

"Out!" snapped Father Wolf. "Out and hunt with **thy**④ master. Thou hast done harm enough for one night."

"I go," said Tabaqui quietly. "Ye can hear Shere Khan below in the thickets. I might have saved myself the message."

Father Wolf listened, and below in the valley that ran down to a little river he heard the dry, angry, snarly, singsong whine of a tiger who has caught nothing and does not care if all the jungle knows it.

"The fool!" said Father Wolf. "To begin a night's work with that noise! Does he think that our buck are like his fat Waingunga **bullocks**⑤?"

"H'sh. It is neither bullock nor buck he hunts to-night," said Mother Wolf. "It is Man."

The whine had changed to a sort of humming **purr**⑥ that seemed to come from every quarter of the compass. It was the noise that bewilders woodcutters and gypsies sleeping in the open, and makes them run sometimes into the very mouth of the tiger.

"Man!" said Father Wolf, showing all his white teeth. "Faugh! Are there not enough **beetles**⑦ and frogs in the tanks that he must eat Man, and on our ground too!"

The Law of the Jungle, which never orders anything without a reason, forbids every beast to eat Man except when he is killing to show his children how to kill, and then he must hunt outside the hunting grounds of his pack or tribe. The real reason for this is that man-killing means, sooner or later, the arrival of white men on elephants, with guns, and hundreds of brown men

① lame [leim] *a.* 瘸的，跛的

② cattle ['kætl] *n.* 牛

③ scour ['skauə] *v.* 荡涤，肃清

④ thy [ðai] *a.* ［古语、诗歌用语］你的

⑤ bullock ['bulək] *n.* 【动物】阉牛

⑥ purr [pə:] *n.* (猫等发出的) 呜呜声

⑦ beetles ['bi:tl] *n.* 【昆虫】甲虫

狼妈妈不动声色地说："他妈妈叫他'朗格里'（意为瘸子），可不是乱叫的。他生下来一条腿就瘸了，所以他只杀牛。他把瓦因刚加河一带的村民都给惹恼了，现在又要来招惹咱这儿的村民。到时候他一走了之，村民们会到丛林里来四下搜他。等他们把草都烧起来，我们和孩子就只好逃命了。那我们可真得要好好感谢希尔汗呢！"

"要不要我向他转达一下你们的谢意？"塔巴奇说。

狼爸爸一声怒吼："滚！出去陪你的主子打猎去！你已经搅得我们一个晚上不得安生了。"

塔巴奇轻声嘟囔："我走，不过，你能听见希尔汗就在底下的灌木丛里。早知道我就不来传话儿了。"

狼爸爸听了听，的确，从下面通向一条小溪的山谷里，传来了老虎干巴巴的、气急败坏、唱经一样的嚎叫。他什么也没逮着，也毫不在乎整个丛林都知道他一无所获。

狼爸爸说："这个笨蛋！晚上的捕猎刚开始动静就这么大，他以为我们这儿的雄鹿跟他瓦因刚加河那儿的肥阉牛一样蠢吗？"

狼妈妈说："嘘——今晚他想猎的既不是阉牛也不是雄鹿，而是人。"

老虎的哀嚎变成了一种低沉的呜呜声，好像从四面八方传来。正是这种声音让露宿的樵夫和吉普赛人惊恐不安，慌不择路地逃跑，有时偏偏一头撞进老虎那张大嘴里。

"人！"狼爸爸喊道，气得龇出一口白牙。"呸！难道池塘里的甲虫和青蛙还不够他吃，他还想吃人，而且是在我们的地盘上！"

丛林法则的每一条都是有道理的，它规定任何野兽都不得吃人，除非是为了给幼崽演示如何捕杀猎物，而且还必须是在自家猎场或者本部落领地之外。至于说为什么，当然是因为一旦杀了人，迟早会招来带着猎枪、骑着大象的白人，还有成百上千敲锣打鼓、放着鞭炮、

with **gongs**[1] and rockets and torches. Then everybody in the jungle suffers. The reason the beasts give among themselves is that Man is the weakest and most defenseless of all living things, and it is **unsportsmanlike**[2] to touch him. They say too—and it is true—that man-eaters become **mangy**[3], and lose their teeth.

The purr grew louder, and ended in the full-throated "Aaarh!" of the tiger's charge.

Then there was a howl—an untigerish howl—from Shere Khan. "He has missed," said Mother Wolf. "What is it?"

Father Wolf ran out a few paces and heard Shere Khan **muttering**[4] and mumbling savagely as he tumbled about in the **scrub**[5].

"The fool has had no more sense than to jump at a woodcutter's campfire, and has burned his feet," said Father Wolf with a **grunt**[6]. "Tabaqui is with him."

"Something is coming uphill," said Mother Wolf, **twitching**[7] one ear. "Get ready."

The bushes rustled a little in the thicket, and Father Wolf dropped with his **haunches**[8] under him, ready for his leap. Then, if you had been watching, you would have seen the most wonderful thing in the world—the wolf checked in mid-spring. He made his bound before he saw what it was he was jumping at, and then he tried to stop himself. The result was that he shot up straight into the air for four or five feet, landing almost where he left ground.

"Man!" he snapped. "A man's cub. Look!"

Directly in front of him, holding on by a low branch, stood a naked brown baby who could just walk—as soft and as dimpled a little atom as ever came to a wolf's cave at night. He looked up into Father Wolf's face, and laughed.

"Is that a man's cub?" said Mother Wolf. "I have never seen one. Bring it here."

A Wolf accustomed to moving his own cubs can, if necessary, mouth an egg without breaking it, and though Father Wolf's jaws closed right on the child's back not a tooth even scratched the skin as he laid it down

① gong [gɔŋ] *n.* 铜锣，锣

② unsportsmanlike [ˌʌnˈspɔːtsmənlaik] *a.* 没有运动道德的

③ mangy [ˈmeindʒi] *a.* 患疥癣的；下贱的，卑鄙的

④ mutter [ˈmʌtə] *v.* 低声说

⑤ scrub [skrʌb] *n.* 灌木

⑥ grunt [grʌnt] *n.* （表示不满、轻蔑等的）哼声，咕哝

⑦ twitch [twitʃ] *v.* 抽动

⑧ haunch [hɔːntʃ] *n.* [常用复数]（动物的）腰腿部

举着火炬的棕人。那样的话丛林里所有的生灵都会遭殃。野兽之间流传的说法是人是所有生物中最弱小也最缺乏自卫能力的，所以进攻人类就未免显得没有风度。他们还说不能碰人是因为吃了人的动物会长癣，还会掉牙；当然事实也的确如此。

老虎的咕噜声越来越大，最终变成一声洪亮的"啊呜"，这是表示进攻的咆哮。

接着希尔汗又发出一声嚎叫，却没了虎啸的威风。狼妈妈听了说："他没得手。这是怎么了？"

狼爸爸跑出去几步远，听到希尔汗一边在灌木丛里跌跌撞撞，一边发出气急败坏的咕哝声。

狼爸爸哼了一声："这个笨蛋也太没脑子了，居然扑到樵夫的篝火上，把自个儿的脚丫子给烫伤了。现在塔巴奇跟着他呢。"

"有什么东西到山坡上来了。准备好。"狼妈妈说着，一只耳朵抖了抖。

灌木丛传来轻微的沙沙声，狼爸爸用后腿蹲下，准备随时扑向来者。接着——如果你在场的话，你会看到世界上最奇妙的一件事情——狼跳到一半又收住了。他还没看清他的目标就跳了起来，然后又想办法停下来。结果就是他直跃到空中大概四到五英尺高，然后又几乎原地落下。

狼爸爸突然喊道："人！是人的崽子。看！"

只见狼爸爸正前方站着一个浑身光溜溜的棕色小孩儿，他手里攀着一根低矮的枝条，将将会走路的样子——有史以来还从未有过这么软乎乎的还带酒窝儿的小东西在夜里来到狼窝呢。他抬起头看着狼爸爸的脸，笑了。

狼妈妈说："这是人的小崽儿吗？我还从没见过呢。把它带过来。"

叼惯了幼崽的狼，必要时能口含鸡蛋而不破。所以狼爸爸虽然紧紧地咬住了小孩的背部，可是当他把小孩放在狼崽中间的时候，他的牙齿连孩子的一丝皮

among the cubs.

"How little! How naked, and—how bold!" said Mother Wolf softly. The baby was pushing his way between the cubs to get close to the warm hide. "Ahai! He is taking his meal with the others. And so this is a man's cub. Now, was there ever a wolf that could boast of a man's cub among her children?"

"I have heard now and again of such a thing, but never in our **Pack**① or in my time," said Father Wolf. "He is altogether without hair, and I could kill him with a touch of my foot. But see, he looks up and is not afraid."

The moonlight was blocked out of the mouth of the cave, for Shere Khan's great **square**② head and shoulders were thrust into the entrance. Tabaqui, behind him, was squeaking: "My lord, my lord, it went in here!"

"Shere Khan does us great honor," said Father Wolf, but his eyes were very angry. "What does Shere Khan need?"

"My **quarry**③. A man's cub went this way," said Shere Khan. "Its parents have run off. Give it to me."

Shere Khan had jumped at a woodcutter's campfire, as Father Wolf had said, and was furious from the pain of his burned feet. But Father Wolf knew that the mouth of the cave was too narrow for a tiger to come in by. Even where he was, Shere Khan's shoulders and forepaws were cramped for **want**④ of room, as a man's would be if he tried to fight in a **barrel**⑤.

"The Wolves are a free people," said Father Wolf. "They take orders from the Head of the Pack, and not from any **striped**⑥ cattle-killer. The man's cub is ours—to kill if we choose."

"Ye choose and ye do not choose! What talk is this of choosing? By the bull that I killed, am I to stand nosing into your dog's **den**⑦ for my fair **dues**⑧? It is I, Shere Khan, who speak!"

The tiger's roar filled the cave with thunder. Mother Wolf shook herself clear of the cubs and sprang forward, her eyes, like two green moons in the darkness, facing the blazing eyes of Shere Khan.

"And it is I, Raksha [The Demon], who answers. The man's cub is mine,

肤也没划破。

狼妈妈轻轻地说："他多小啊，光溜溜的，可是又——多么胆大！"小孩挤到狼崽中间想要靠近狼妈妈温暖的皮毛。"啊哈！他跟其他孩子一起吃起来了。这么说来，人的幼崽就长这样啊。真是的，有哪头狼敢说自己还奶过人的幼崽呢？"

狼爸爸说："我以前偶尔也听说过这种东西，可在咱们群里我这辈子还从来没看见过。他一丝儿毛都没有，我的爪子轻轻碰他一下就能弄死他。可是你看，他抬着头，居然一点儿也不害怕。"

洞口的月光被挡住了，原来希尔汗把他的大方脑袋和肩膀挤了进来。塔巴奇紧跟在他后面，尖叫着说："大人，大人，它跑到里面去了！"

狼爸爸两眼冒火，说："希尔汗大人光临寒舍，真是我们的荣幸。请问大人有何贵干？"

希尔汗说："我来找我的猎物。一个人的小崽子到这边来了。它的父母跑掉了。把它给我吧。"

就像狼爸爸之前说的那样，希尔汗扑到一个樵夫的篝火上，烧伤了脚，现在正憋着火呢。但是狼爸爸清楚洞口对老虎来说太小了，他进不来。这会儿，希尔汗的肩头和前爪已经卡在了洞口，施展不开，就好像一个人被塞进酒桶还想跟人打架一样。

狼爸爸说："我们狼是自由的民族，只听从狼族首领的命令，长着条纹、只敢抓牛来吃的家伙可不配向我们发号施令。人崽儿是我们的，就是要杀，也得我们说了算。"

"你们说了算！这是什么话？就凭我杀死的那些公牛，难道还得要我钻到你们的狗窝里来寻摸我应得的东西？现在可是我，希尔汗在说话呢！"

老虎的咆哮声响彻山洞。狼妈妈动了动，把身上的幼崽们抖落下来，一下子跳了出来，她的双眼好像黑暗中的两轮碧月，直直地瞪着希尔汗喷火的眼睛。

"现在是我，拉克沙（意为魔鬼），在跟你说话。

① pack [pæk] n. 一伙

② square [skwɛə] a. 方的

③ quarry ['kwɔri] n. 猎物

④ want [wɔnt] n. 缺乏，缺少

⑤ barrel ['bærəl] n. 桶，大木桶

⑥ striped [straipt] a. 有斑纹的，有条纹的

⑦ den [den] n.（野生动物的）洞窟

⑧ due [dju:] n. 应得物，应得（或应付）的东西

Lungri—mine to me! He shall not be killed. He shall live to run with the Pack and to hunt with the Pack; and in the end, look you, hunter of little naked cubs—frog-eater—fish-killer—he shall hunt thee! Now get hence, or by the Sambhur that I killed (I eat no starved cattle), back thou goest to thy mother, burned beast of the jungle, lamer than ever thou camest into the world! Go!"

Father Wolf looked on amazed. He had almost forgotten the days when he won Mother Wolf in fair fight from five other wolves, when she ran in the Pack and was not called The Demon for compliment's sake. Shere Khan might have faced Father Wolf, but he could not stand up against Mother Wolf, for he knew that where he was she had all the advantage of the ground, and would fight to the death. So he backed out of the cave mouth growling, and when he was clear he shouted:

"Each dog barks in his own yard! We will see what the Pack will say to this fostering of man-cubs. The cub is mine, and to my teeth he will come in the end, O bush-tailed thieves!"

Mother Wolf threw herself down **panting**① among the cubs, and Father Wolf said to her gravely: "Shere Khan speaks this much truth. The cub must be shown to the Pack. Wilt thou still keep him, Mother?"

"Keep him!" she **gasped**②. "He came naked, by night, alone and very hungry; yet he was not afraid! Look, he has pushed one of my babes to one side already. And that lame **butcher**③ would have killed him and would have run off to the Waingunga while the villagers here hunted through all our **lairs**④ in revenge! Keep him? Assuredly I will keep him. Lie still, little frog. O thou Mowgli—for Mowgli the Frog I will call thee—the time will come when thou wilt hunt Shere Khan as he has hunted thee."

"But what will our Pack say?" said Father Wolf.

The Law of the Jungle **lays down**⑤ very clearly that any wolf may, when he marries, withdraw from the Pack he belongs to. But as soon as his cubs are old enough to stand on their feet he must bring them to the Pack Council, which

朗格里，人崽儿是我的，我一个人的！谁也不许杀他。他会活下去，和狼群一起奔跑、捕食；你等着吧，你这个只敢抓身无寸缕的幼崽、吃蛙捕鱼的'杀手'总有一天会被他杀掉！你马上给我滚蛋，要不然的话，以我杀死的水鹿起誓——我可不吃什么饿死的家畜——你这个丛林里挨火烧的家伙，瘸着腿爬回你娘那儿去，比你从娘胎里出来的时候还要瘸！滚！"

狼爸爸看呆了。他都差点儿忘了当年他可是跟五头公狼狠狠打了一架才赢得狼妈妈的芳心，那时她被狼群叫作"魔鬼"可不是浪得虚名。希尔汗也许能斗斗狼爸爸，但是狼妈妈他可不敢，因为他明白狼妈妈占尽地利，而且会豁出命来跟他干。所以他只好低吼着退出洞口。他一出去就咆哮起来："强龙不压地头蛇！你要养人崽子，我们就看看狼群怎么说吧。这只崽儿是我的，他迟早会落进我嘴里，你们这些大尾巴贼！"

狼妈妈喘着粗气倒下来，趴在幼崽中间，狼爸爸严肃地对她说："希尔汗这一点说得倒是没错。我们得让狼群看看人崽。孩子他妈，你还是想要养他吗？"

她喘着气说："养啊！他来的时候可是光溜溜的，独自个儿，饿着肚子，在大晚上来的，但是一点也不害怕！看，他已经把我的一个宝宝挤到一边儿去了。那个瘸腿的屠夫差点就杀了他，然后逃回瓦因刚加河去，而这儿的村民为了报复就会闯进我们的家来翻个底朝天。养他？我当然要养了。小青蛙，躺下来别动了。哦，你这个毛格利，你就像青蛙一样，所以我要叫你毛格利。总有一天，你会像今天希尔汗追杀你一样追杀他的。"

狼爸爸说："可是咱们狼群会怎么说呢？"

丛林法则规定得很清楚，当一头狼婚配时，可以退出之前所属的狼群。但是一旦他的幼崽大到可以独自站立，他就必须把他们带到每逢月圆之夜召开的族群议会上让其他狼认识他们。被察看后的幼崽就可以自由来去，

① pant [pænt] v. 气喘

② gasp [gɑːsp] v. 喘，喘气，喘息

③ butcher ['butʃə] n. 屠杀者，残杀者

④ lair [leə] n. 兽穴，兽巢

⑤ lay down 规定，制定

is generally held once a month at full moon, in order that the other wolves may identify them. After that **inspection**① the cubs are free to run where they please, and until they have killed their first buck no excuse is accepted if a grown wolf of the Pack kills one of them. The punishment is death where the murderer can be found; and if you think for a minute you will see that this must be so.

Father Wolf waited till his cubs could run a little, and then on the night of the Pack Meeting took them and Mowgli and Mother Wolf to the Council Rock—a hilltop covered with stones and **boulders**② where a hundred wolves could hide. Akela, the great gray Lone Wolf, who led all the Pack by strength and **cunning**③, lay out at full length on his rock, and below him sat forty or more wolves of every size and color, from badger-colored **veterans**④ who could handle a buck alone to young black three-year-olds who thought they could. The Lone Wolf had led them for a year now. He had fallen twice into a wolf trap in his youth, and once he had been beaten and left for dead; so he knew the manners and customs of men. There was very little talking at the Rock. The cubs tumbled over each other in the center of the circle where their mothers and fathers sat, and now and again a senior wolf would go quietly up to a cub, look at him carefully, and return to his place on noiseless feet. Sometimes a mother would push her cub far out into the moonlight to be sure that he had not been overlooked. Akela from his rock would cry: "Ye know the Law—ye know the Law. Look well, O Wolves!" And the anxious mothers would **take up**⑤ the call: "Look—look well, O Wolves!"

At last—and Mother Wolf's neck **bristles**⑥ lifted as the time came—Father Wolf pushed "Mowgli the Frog," as they called him, into the center, where he sat laughing and playing with some **pebbles**⑦ that glistened in the moonlight.

Akela never raised his head from his paws, but went on with the **monotonous**⑧ cry: "Look well!" A **muffled**⑨ roar came up from behind the rocks—the voice of Shere Khan crying: "The cub is mine. Give him to me. What have the Free People to do with a man's cub?" Akela never even twitched his ears. All he said was: "Look well, O Wolves! What have the Free People to

① inspection [in'spekʃən] *n.*
检查,检验

② boulder ['bəuldə] *n.* (大)
卵石,圆石

③ cunning ['kʌniŋ] *n.* 狡猾,
狡诈

④ veteran ['vetərən] *n.* 老
手,富有经验的人

⑤ take up 接着讲,接下去
说

⑥ bristle ['brisl] *n.* (动物
的) 短而硬的毛,刚毛

⑦ pebble ['pebl] *n.* 卵石,
石子

⑧ monotonous [mə'nɔtənəs]
a. (声音) 单调的,无
抑扬顿挫的

⑨ muffle ['mʌfl] *v.* 使 (声
音) 低沉

直到他们独立猎杀第一头雄鹿之前,狼群里的任何一头成年狼都不得以任何借口杀死他们。否则,只要凶手被抓住,就会被处以死刑。只要你稍微动动脑筋就会明白,这样规定是很有必要的。

等到狼崽刚刚会跑了,狼爸爸就在族群议会召开的那天晚上带着他们和毛格利还有狼妈妈一起来到议会岩,这个山顶上全是石头,大大小小,可供一百只狼藏身。狼群的首领阿凯拉是一头体型庞大的灰色"独狼",拥有超群的力量和智慧。他在属于自己的那块岩石上舒展身子趴下来,在他下方坐着四十来只大小不同、毛色各异的狼,他们中有的是能独立对付雄鹿的、毛色跟獾一样的老狼,还有的是自认为能对付雄鹿的、三岁左右的年轻黑狼。独狼成为他们的首领已有一年了。他年轻时曾两次坠入捕狼的陷阱,还有一次差点被打死,所以他对人类的手段和习惯了如指掌。现在议会岩上几乎鸦雀无声。一些狼父狼母围成一个圈子坐着,他们的幼崽在圈子中间翻滚打闹。时不时地一头老狼会静悄悄地走上前去细细打量某只幼崽,然后再蹑足回到自己的位置上。有时一个母亲会把自己的幼崽远远地推到月光下,以免他被漏看了。阿凯拉则会在他的宝座上高喊:"你们知道法则——你们知道法则。看仔细了,所有的狼民!"而焦虑的母亲们则会跟着喊:"看啊,看仔细了,所有的狼民!"

终于,轮到人崽了,狼妈妈颈项上的鬃毛都竖了起来,狼爸爸把"青蛙毛格利"——他们这么叫他——推到了中间。他坐在那儿一边笑一边玩着被月亮照得闪闪发光的小石头。

阿凯拉的头压根没从爪子上抬起来,他继续重复着单调的叫喊:"看仔细了!"但是从岩石背后传来被压低了的吼声,那是希尔汗在嚷嚷:"这只崽子是我的。把他给我。自由的狼族跟人崽儿有什么关系?"阿凯拉压根连耳朵都没动弹一下。他只是说:"看仔细了,狼民!别人的命令

do with the orders of any save the Free People? Look well!"

There was a chorus of deep growls, and a young wolf in his fourth year flung back Shere Khan's question to Akela: "What have the Free People to do with a man's cub?" Now, the Law of the Jungle lays down that if there is any **dispute**[①] as to the right of a cub to be accepted by the Pack, he must be spoken for by at least two members of the Pack who are not his father and mother.

"Who speaks for this cub?" said Akela. "Among the Free People who speaks?" There was no answer and Mother Wolf got ready for what she knew would be her last fight, if things came to fighting.

Then the only other creature who is allowed at the Pack Council—Baloo, the sleepy brown bear who teaches the wolf cubs the Law of the Jungle: old Baloo, who can come and go where he pleases because he eats only nuts and roots and honey—rose upon his hind quarters and grunted.

"The man's cub—the man's cub?" he said. "I speak for the man's cub. There is no harm in a man's cub. I have no gift of words, but I speak the truth. Let him run with the Pack, and be entered with the others. I myself will teach him."

"We need yet another," said Akela. "Baloo has spoken, and he is our teacher for the young cubs. Who speaks besides Baloo?"

A black shadow dropped down into the circle. It was Bagheera the Black **Panther**[②], **inky**[③] black all over, but with the panther markings showing up in certain lights like the pattern of watered silk. Everybody knew Bagheera, and nobody cared to cross his path; for he was as cunning as Tabaqui, as bold as the wild buffalo, and as **reckless**[④] as the wounded elephant. But he had a voice as soft as wild honey dripping from a tree, and a skin softer than **down**[⑤].

"O Akela, and ye the Free People," he purred, "I have no right in your assembly, but the Law of the Jungle says that if there is a doubt which is not a killing matter in regard to a new cub, the life of that cub may be bought at a price. And the Law does not say who may or may not pay that price. Am I right?"

跟自由民有什么关系？看仔细了！"

狼群响起了一片低沉的吼声，一只四岁的小狼把希尔汗的问题又问了一遍："自由民和人的幼崽有什么关系？"根据丛林法则的规定，族群里若有人不同意接纳某只幼崽，那必须有至少两名族群成员为这只幼崽辩护，而且辩护者还不能是幼崽的父母。

① dispute [dis'pju:t] *n.* 争论，辩论

阿凯拉问道："谁来为这只幼崽说话？自由民中有谁发言吗？"没人回答。狼妈妈做好了最后一搏的准备，如果一切最终不得不诉诸武力的话。

这时，唯一被允许参加狼群议会的非族群成员，老爱犯困的棕熊巴鲁——老巴鲁负责教狼崽丛林法则，他享有来去自由的权利，因为他只吃坚果、根茎和蜂蜜——站了起来，哼哼着发话了："人崽——真是人崽？我来为人崽说话。人崽又没什么害处。我嘴笨，但是我说的是实话。让他和狼群一起奔跑吧，让他和其他幼崽一起加入进来。我会亲自教他的。"

阿凯拉说："我们还需要一个辩护者。巴鲁替他申辩了，他是我们狼崽的老师。除了巴鲁之外，还有谁愿意发言？"

一个黑色的身影跳进了圈子。那是黑豹巴格伊尔拉，他全身漆黑，但是在特定的光线下会显出豹纹，就像波纹绸一样。所有人都认识巴格伊尔拉，但是谁也不敢挡他的道，因为他像塔巴奇一样狡猾，像野牛一样勇猛，又像受伤的大象一样毫无畏惧。可是他的嗓子却轻柔得像野蜂蜜从树上滴落下来一样，他的毛皮呢，则比羽绒还要柔软。

② panther ['pænθə] *n.*【动物】豹
③ inky ['iŋki] *a.* 似墨的，漆黑的
④ reckless ['reklis] *a.* 鲁莽的
⑤ down [daun] *n.*（小鸟的）绒毛，柔毛，软毛

他轻轻地说："噢，阿凯拉，还有自由民，我无权干涉你们的集会，但是根据丛林法，如果对如何处置一只新的幼崽有争议，但又没有严重到非得处死这只幼崽的话，那可以有人出价买下这只幼崽的命。至于谁能买谁不能买，丛林法却没有规定。我说得对吗？"

"Good! Good!" said the young wolves, who are always hungry. "Listen to Bagheera. The cub can be bought for a price. It is the Law."

"Knowing that I have no right to speak here, I ask your leave."

"Speak then," cried twenty voices.

"To kill a naked cub is shame. Besides, he may make better sport for you when he is grown. Baloo has spoken in his behalf. Now to Baloo's word I will add one bull, and a fat one, newly killed, not half a mile from here, if ye will accept the man's cub according to the Law. Is it difficult?"

There was a **clamor**[①] of scores of voices, saying: "What matter? He will die in the winter rains. He will **scorch**[②] in the sun. What harm can a naked frog do us? Let him run with the Pack. Where is the bull, Bagheera? Let him be accepted." And then came Akela's deep bay, crying: "Look well—look well, O Wolves!"

Mowgli was still deeply interested in the pebbles, and he did not notice when the wolves came and looked at him one by one. At last they all went down the hill for the dead bull, and only Akela, Bagheera, Baloo, and Mowgli's own wolves were left. Shere Khan roared still in the night, for he was very angry that Mowgli had not been handed over to him.

"Ay, roar well," said Bagheera, under his whiskers, "for the time will come when this naked thing will make thee roar to another **tune**[③], or I know nothing of man."

"It was well done," said Akela. "Men and their cubs are very wise. He may be a help in time."

"Truly, a help in time of need; for none can hope to lead the Pack forever," said Bagheera.

Akela said nothing. He was thinking of the time that comes to every leader of every pack when his strength goes from him and he gets **feebler**[④] and feebler, till at last he is killed by the wolves and a new leader comes up—to be killed in his turn.

"Take him away," he said to Father Wolf, "and train him as **befits**[⑤] one of

"好啊，好啊！"年轻的狼都叫起来，他们总是饥肠辘辘。"就听巴格伊尔拉的吧。让谁来买下人崽吧。这可是丛林法说的。"

"我知道我本无权在此发言，所以恳请各位允许。"

二十个声音叫道："说吧。"

"杀死一只光身子的幼崽并不光彩。等他长大了，你们再捕猎他也许更有意思。巴鲁已经替他辩护了。现在除了巴鲁的话，我再加上一头公牛，这可是我刚杀死的一头肥牛，就在离这儿不到半英里的地方，只要你们愿意遵守法则的规定接受人崽。这对你们来说并不困难吧？"

几十个声音一下子闹哄哄地响起来："这有什么大不了的呢？他反正会被冬雨冻死，要不就是被太阳晒死。一只光身子的青蛙还能伤害我们吗？让他和狼群一起跑吧。巴格伊尔拉，那头公牛在哪儿？接纳人崽吧。"然后阿凯拉发出低沉的嗥叫："看仔细了——看仔细了，狼民！"

毛格利还在专心致志地玩着石头，他并没有注意到一头接一头的狼走过来审视他。终于他们都跑下山去享用那头死牛了，只有阿凯拉、巴格伊尔拉、巴鲁和收养毛格利的一家子留了下来。希尔汗还在夜色里咆哮，因为毛格利没有交还给他，他非常生气。

巴格伊尔拉的声音从胡须下传出来："啊，使劲儿叫吧，我可知道这个光溜溜的小东西总有一天会让你鬼哭狼嚎的，要不我就算跟人类白打交道了。"

阿凯拉说："这件事情总算圆满解决了。人和人的幼崽都是很聪明的。他将来会派上用场的。"

"肯定的，在你需要他的时候会帮上忙。谁也不能指望永远领导狼群呀。"巴格伊尔拉说。

阿凯拉什么也没说。他在想着每一个狼群的领袖都会遇到的那一天，当他失去力量，变得越来越虚弱的时候，其他狼会将他杀死，然后选出一个新的领袖——终有一天，这个新领袖也会被杀死。

他对狼爸爸说："把他带走吧，像培养一个自由民

① clamor ['klæmə] n. 喧闹，叫嚷

② scorch [skɔ:tʃ] v. 烧焦，烤焦

③ tune [tju:n] n. 声调，语调

④ feeble ['fi:bl] a. 软弱的，虚弱的，无力的

⑤ befit [bi'fit] v. 与……相当

the Free People."

And that is how Mowgli was entered into the Seeonee Wolf Pack for the price of a bull and on Baloo's good word.

Now you must be content to skip ten or eleven whole years, and only guess at all the wonderful life that Mowgli led among the wolves, because if it were written out it would fill ever so many books. He grew up with the cubs, though they, of course, were grown wolves almost before he was a child. And Father Wolf taught him his business, and the meaning of things in the **jungle**①, till every **rustle**② in the grass, every breath of the warm night air, every note of the owls above his head, every scratch of a bat's **claws**③ as it **roosted**④ for a while in a tree, and every splash of every little fish jumping in a pool meant just as much to him as the work of his office means to a business man. When he was not learning he sat out in the sun and slept, and ate and went to sleep again. When he felt dirty or hot he swam in the forest pools; and when he wanted honey (Baloo told him that honey and **nuts**⑤ were just as pleasant to eat as raw meat) he climbed up for it, and that Bagheera showed him how to do. Bagheera would lie out on a branch and call, "Come along, Little Brother," and at first Mowgli would cling like the **sloth**⑥, but afterward he would fling himself through the branches almost as boldly as the gray ape. He took his place at the Council Rock, too, when the Pack met, and there he discovered that if he stared hard at any wolf, the wolf would be forced to drop his eyes, and so he used to stare for fun. At other times he would pick the long **thorns**⑦ out of the **pads**⑧ of his friends, for wolves suffer terribly from thorns and **burs**⑨ in their coats. He would go down the hillside into the cultivated lands by night, and look very curiously at the villagers in their huts, but he had a mistrust of men because Bagheera showed him a square box with a drop gate so cunningly hidden in the jungle that he nearly walked into it, and told him that it was a trap. He loved better than anything else to go with Bagheera into the dark warm heart of the forest, to sleep all through the **drowsy**⑩ day, and at night see how Bagheera did his killing. Bagheera killed right and left

那样好好训练他。"

　　这就是毛格利加入思翁尼狼群的经过，多亏巴鲁替他说好话，再加上一头公牛的命，他才被族群接纳了。

　　现在你也许乐意跳过十来年的时光，只靠猜测去想象毛格利在狼群中度过的那些精彩岁月，因为如果把它们全都写下来，那得写出好多好多的书了。他和狼崽一起长大，但是他们显然比毛格利长得快，他还没变成一个孩童，他们就已经差不多成年了。狼爸爸教他打猎，还教会他认识丛林里的所有事物，直到他对一切了如指掌，就像一个商人熟悉自己办公室的一切事务一样。他知道草丛的每一次响动、温暖的晚风每一次吹拂意味着什么，也知道头顶的夜枭发出的每个叫声、停在枝头的蝙蝠每一次拨拉爪子又代表着什么，还清楚池塘里的小鱼儿每次蹦出水面是为了什么。学习以外的时间，他会坐在太阳底下打盹儿，吃完饭再接着睡过去。当他觉得身上脏了或者热了，他会到森林的水塘里去游个泳；当他想吃蜂蜜的时候——巴鲁教过他蜂蜜和坚果就跟生肉一样好吃——他就会爬上去取，就像巴格伊尔拉教过他的那样。巴格伊尔拉会趴在一个树枝上对他喊："来呀，小兄弟。"而他呢，刚开始的时候还像树懒一样紧紧地抓着，后来就学会跟灰猿似的在树枝间大胆地纵身跳跃。狼群开会的时候，他在议会岩上也有了一席之地。在那儿，他发现只要自己紧紧盯着一头狼，对方就会不得不垂下眼眸，所以他就总这样盯着玩儿。有时，他会帮自己的朋友挑出脚掌里的长刺，因为狼的毛皮经常粘上荆棘和刺果，深受其苦。他还会在夜间溜下山跑到农田里去，好奇地观察茅屋里的村民，但是他并不信任人类，因为巴格伊尔拉曾经给他看过一个方盒子，那个盒子极其巧妙地隐藏在丛林里，上面有一个会掉下来关闭的门，他差点儿就走进去了，巴格伊尔拉告诉他那就是陷阱。他最爱干的事莫过于跟着巴格伊尔拉钻进丛林幽暗温暖的深处饱饱地睡上一整天，到晚上的时候再看巴格伊尔

① jungle ['dʒʌŋgl] n.（热带）植丛，丛林

② rustle ['rʌsl] n. 沙沙声，窸窣声

③ claw [klɔ:] n.（动物的）爪，脚爪

④ roost [ru:st] v. 栖息

⑤ nut [nʌt] n. 坚果

⑥ sloth [sloθ] n.【动物】树懒

⑦ thorn [θɔ:n] n. 刺，棘

⑧ pad [pæd] n. 某些动物的爪垫，肉趾（指在手指的末节或动物的下方的脂肪组织块）

⑨ bur [bə:] n.【植物】刺果（植物）

⑩ drowsy ['drauzi] a. 昏昏欲睡的

as he felt hungry, and so did Mowgli — with one exception. As soon as he was old enough to understand things, Bagheera told him that he must never touch cattle because he had been bought into the Pack at the price of a bull's life. "All the jungle is **thine**①," said Bagheera, "and thou canst kill everything that thou art strong enough to kill; but for the sake of the bull that bought thee thou must never kill or eat any cattle young or old. That is the Law of the Jungle." Mowgli obeyed faithfully.

And he grew and grew strong as a boy must grow who does not know that he is learning any lessons, and who has nothing in the world to think of except things to eat.

Mother Wolf told him once or twice that Shere Khan was not a creature to be trusted, and that some day he must kill Shere Khan. But though a young wolf would have remembered that advice every hour, Mowgli forgot it because he was only a boy — though he would have called himself a wolf if he had been able to speak in any human **tongue**②.

Shere Khan was always crossing his path in the jungle, for as Akela grew older and feebler the lame tiger had come to be great friends with the younger wolves of the Pack, who followed him for **scraps**③, a thing Akela would never have allowed if he had dared to push his authority to the proper **bounds**④. Then Shere Khan would **flatter**⑤ them and wonder that such fine young hunters were content to be led by a dying wolf and a man's cub. "They tell me," Shere Khan would say, "that at Council ye dare not look him between the eyes." And the young wolves would growl and bristle.

Bagheera, who had eyes and ears everywhere, knew something of this, and once or twice he told Mowgli in so many words that Shere Khan would kill him some day. Mowgli would laugh and answer: "I have the Pack and I have thee; and Baloo, though he is so lazy, might strike a blow or two for my sake. Why should I be afraid?"

It was one very warm day that a new **notion**⑥ came to Bagheera — born of something that he had heard. Perhaps Ikki the **Porcupine**⑦ had told him; but he

拉怎么狩猎。巴格伊尔拉打猎毫无顾忌，只要饿了，就开杀。毛格利也是这样，想杀什么就杀什么，但是有一样例外。他刚懂事的时候，巴格伊尔拉就告诉他永远不许碰人养的牛，因为是靠一头牛的命才换来他被狼群接纳的资格。巴格伊尔拉对他说："丛林里的一切都是你的，只要是你力之所及，任你猎杀；但是因为你的命是牛换来的，你永远不能杀牛或吃牛，无论老幼。这就是丛林法则。"毛格利严格遵守了巴格伊尔拉的教诲。

他长得越来越强壮结实，一个男孩儿，只要他从没意识到自己是在学东西，然后成天只想着吃，那就会长成这样。

狼妈妈有一两次曾经告诉他不要相信希尔汗，而且有一天他得杀了希尔汗。要是一头小狼，可能会把这个叮咛时时刻刻牢记在心，毛格利却忘记了，因为他只是个小孩儿——不过他要是会说人话，他肯定会管自己叫狼。

他在丛林里常常碰到希尔汗。随着阿凯拉年纪变老，身体日渐虚弱，这只瘸腿老虎和年轻一些的狼成了好朋友，让他们跟在自己后面捡点残渣剩饭。要是阿凯拉敢于对他们严加管教的话，是绝对不会允许他们这么干的。希尔汗奉承这些狼，说他想不通为什么像他们这样又年轻又厉害的猎手怎么会臣服于一只快要死了的老狼和一只人崽子。希尔汗说："我听说在狼族议会上你们都不敢直视他的眼睛。"这些年轻的狼就会炸起毛咆哮起来。

巴格伊尔拉消息灵通，听说了这件事情，曾经费尽唇舌警告毛格利要小心希尔汗可能会对他下手。毛格利却笑着回答："我有族群，又有你，还有巴鲁，虽然他太懒了，但好歹也会替我打几下子。我有什么好怕的呢？"

有一天，天气非常暖和，巴格伊尔拉和毛格利正待在丛林深处。这时，巴格伊尔拉想出了一个新点子，灵

① thine [θain] *pron.* 你的东西

② tongue [tʌŋ] *n.* 语言

③ scrap [skræp] *n.* ［复数］残羹剩饭
④ bound [baund] *n.* ［常用复数］范围，领域
⑤ flatter ['flætə] *v.* 恭维

⑥ notion ['nəuʃən] *n.* 怪诞的想法
⑦ porcupine ['pɔːkjupain] *n.* 【动物】豪猪

said to Mowgli when they were deep in the jungle, as the boy lay with his head on Bagheera's beautiful black skin, "Little Brother, how often have I told thee that Shere Khan is thy enemy?"

"As many times as there are nuts on that palm," said Mowgli, who, naturally, could not count. "What of it? I am sleepy, Bagheera, and Shere Khan is all long tail and loud talk — like Mao, the Peacock."

"But this is no time for sleeping. Baloo knows it; I know it; the Pack know it; and even the foolish, foolish deer know. Tabaqui has told thee too."

"Ho! ho!" said Mowgli. "Tabaqui came to me not long ago with some **rude**① talk that I was a naked man's cub and not fit to **dig**② pig-nuts. But I caught Tabaqui by the tail and swung him twice against a palm-tree to teach him better manners."

"That was foolishness, for though Tabaqui is a mischief-maker, he would have told thee of something that concerned thee closely. Open those eyes, Little Brother. Shere Khan dare not kill thee in the jungle. But remember, Akela is very old, and soon the day comes when he cannot kill his buck, and then he will be leader no more. Many of the wolves that looked thee over when thou wast brought to the Council first are old too, and the young wolves believe, as Shere Khan has taught them, that a man-cub has no place with the Pack. In a little time thou wilt be a man."

"And what is a man that he should not run with his brothers?" said Mowgli. "I was born in the jungle. I have obeyed the Law of the Jungle, and there is no wolf of ours from whose paws I have not pulled a thorn. Surely they are my brothers!"

Bagheera **stretched**③ himself at full length and half shut his eyes. "Little Brother," said he, "feel under my jaw."

Mowgli put up his strong brown hand, and just under Bagheera's silky chin, where the giant **rolling**④ muscles were all hid by the glossy hair, he came upon a little **bald**⑤ spot.

"There is no one in the jungle that knows that I, Bagheera, carry that

感来自他听说过的一件事情，或许是豪猪伊吉告诉他的。他对此时枕在他漂亮的黑色皮毛上的毛格利说："小兄弟，我跟你说过多少次希尔汗是你的敌人？"

毛格利说："好多次，就跟那棵棕榈树上的果子一样多。"当然啦，他不会计数，所以才这么说。"那又怎样？我困得很，巴格伊尔拉，希尔汗不过就是尾巴长，嗓门大罢了——就跟孔雀摩尔一样嘛。"

"现在可不是睡觉的时候。巴鲁知道，我知道，狼群也知道，哪怕是笨得不得了的鹿也知道。塔巴奇也跟你这样说过呀。"

毛格利说："哈哈！塔巴奇前段时间来找我说了些混话，说什么我是个光身子的人崽，连挖花生都不配。我抓住他的尾巴，把他甩到棕榈树上砸了两次，好让他懂点儿规矩。"

"你这样做可不明智。虽然塔巴奇不干好事，但是他说的跟你可是大有关系。睁开眼睛，小兄弟。希尔汗不敢在丛林里杀死你。但是记住，阿凯拉已经很老了，很快他就再也无法杀死雄鹿，那时他就不再是头狼了。当初你被带到议会上，那些审视过你的狼很多也都老了。年轻的狼听信了希尔汗的谗言，认为人崽不应该待在狼群里。要不了多久你就会长成一个大人。"

毛格利说："长成大人又怎样，就不能和兄弟们一起奔跑了吗？我是在丛林里出生的。我遵守丛林法则，我还替狼群里所有的狼拔过爪子里的刺。他们当然都是我的弟兄！"

巴格伊尔拉伸长了身子，半闭上眼睛。他说："小兄弟，来摸摸我的下巴下面。"

毛格利举起他有力的棕色的手，去摸巴格伊尔拉丝般光滑的下巴，在光亮的毛发下面藏着大块大块的肌肉，在那儿，他摸到了一个小小的秃斑。

"丛林里没人知道我巴格伊尔拉身上有这块印记

① rude [ru:d] *a.* 粗鲁的
② dig [dig] *v.*（如用铲或其他工具或用手、爪、动物的口、鼻部等）掘，挖掘

③ stretch [stretʃ] *v.* 伸开，展开，伸展
④ rolling ['rəuliŋ] *a.* 起伏的，高低不平的
⑤ bald [bɔ:ld] *a.*（土地、山等）光秃秃的，无树的

mark — the mark of the collar; and yet, Little Brother, I was born among men, and it was among men that my mother died — in the cages of the king's palace at Oodeypore. It was because of this that I paid the price for thee at the Council when thou wast a little naked cub. Yes, I too was born among men. I had never seen the jungle. They fed me behind bars from an **iron**[①] **pan**[②] till one night I felt that I was Bagheera — the Panther — and no man's plaything, and I broke the silly lock with one blow of my paw and came away. And because I had learned the ways of men, I became more terrible in the jungle than Shere Khan. Is it not so?"

"Yes," said Mowgli, "all the jungle fear Bagheera — all except Mowgli."

"Oh, thou art a man's cub," said the Black Panther very **tenderly**[③]. "And even as I returned to my jungle, so thou must go back to men at last — to the men who are thy brothers — if thou art not killed in the Council."

"But why — but why should any wish to kill me?" said Mowgli.

"Look at me," said Bagheera. And Mowgli looked at him steadily between the eyes. The big panther turned his head away in half a minute.

"That is why," he said, shifting his paw on the leaves. "Not even I can look thee between the eyes, and I was born among men, and I love thee, Little Brother. The others they hate thee because their eyes cannot meet **thine**[④]; because thou art wise; because thou hast pulled out thorns from their feet — because thou art a man."

"I did not know these things," said Mowgli **sullenly**[⑤], and he frowned under his heavy black eyebrows.

"What is the Law of the Jungle? Strike first and then give tongue. By thy very carelessness they know that thou art a man. But be wise. It is in my heart that when Akela misses his next kill — and at each hunt it costs him more to **pin**[⑥] the buck — the Pack will turn against him and against thee. They will hold a jungle Council at the Rock, and then — and then — I have it!" said Bagheera,

——那是项圈留下的斑痕。可是，小兄弟，我其实是在人类中间出生的，我母亲也是在人类中间死去的——在笼子里，就在乌德珀尔的国王宫殿那儿。正因为这样，在你还是个没长毛的小崽儿时，我才在狼族议会上买下了你的性命。是的，我也是在人中间降生的。我以前从没见过丛林。人们把我关在笼子里，用铁盘喂我吃东西。直到有一天晚上我意识到我是巴格伊尔拉——黑豹——而不是人的玩意儿时，我就一爪子砸碎了那把愚蠢的锁，跑掉了。正因为我学会了人类的那些手段，我在丛林里才变得比希尔汗还可怕。不是吗？”

毛格利说："是的，整个丛林都害怕巴格伊尔拉，只有毛格利不怕。"

黑豹非常温柔地说："噢，你可是个人崽儿啊。所以就像我回到丛林里来，你最终也必须回到人类那儿去，回到你的人类兄弟那儿——如果你没有在狼族议会上被杀死的话。"

毛格利问道："可是为什么？为什么会有狼想要杀我呢？"

巴格伊尔拉说："看着我。"毛格利稳稳地注视着他的双眼。半分钟后大黑豹就把头转开了。

他把爪子从树叶上挪了一下，说："这就是为什么。就算是我也不能直视你的眼睛。我可是生在人类中间的，我还爱你呢，小兄弟。他们恨你是因为他们无法和你对视，因为你聪明，还因为你帮他们拔过爪子上的刺——因为你是一个人。"

毛格利郁闷地说："我过去不知道这些事情。"他又粗又黑的眉毛都皱了起来。

"丛林法则怎么说的来着？先打了再说话。正是因为你这样粗心大意的，他们知道你只是个人。所以放聪明点，我心里清楚着呢，等到阿凯拉逮不住猎物的时候——现在每次狩猎他制服雄鹿都越来越费劲——狼群就会反对他，还有你。他们会在议会岩上召开丛林大会，

① iron ['aiən] a. 铁的
② pan [pæn] n. 盘子

③ tenderly ['tɛndəli] a. 温和地

④ thine [ðain] pron. 你的东西，你的

⑤ sullenly ['sʌlənli] ad. 不高兴地，绷着脸，忧郁地

⑥ pin [pin] v. 牵制，钳制

leaping up. "Go thou down quickly to the men's huts in the valley, and take some of the Red Flower which they grow there, so that when the time comes thou mayest have even a stronger friend than I or Baloo or those of the Pack that love thee. Get the Red Flower."

By Red Flower Bagheera meant fire, only no creature in the jungle will call fire by its proper name. Every beast lives in deadly fear of it, and invents a hundred ways of describing it.

"The Red Flower?" said Mowgli. "That grows outside their **huts**① in the **twilight**②. I will get some."

"There speaks the man's cub," said Bagheera proudly. "Remember that it grows in little pots. Get one swiftly, and keep it by thee for time of need."

"Good!" said Mowgli. "I go. But art thou sure, O my Bagheera"—he slipped his arm around the **splendid**③ neck and looked deep into the big eyes—"art thou sure that all this is Shere Khan's doing?"

"By the Broken Lock that freed me, I am sure, Little Brother."

"Then, by the Bull that bought me, I will pay Shere Khan full tale for this, and it may be a little over," said Mowgli, and he bounded away.

"That is a man. That is all a man," said Bagheera to himself, lying down again. "Oh, Shere Khan, never was a blacker hunting than that frog-hunt of thine ten years ago!"

Mowgli was far and far through the forest, running hard, and his heart was hot in him. He came to the cave as the evening mist rose, and drew breath, and looked down the valley. The cubs were out, but Mother Wolf, at the back of the cave, knew by his breathing that something was troubling her frog.

"What is it, Son?" she said.

"Some bat's chatter of Shere Khan," he called back. "I hunt among the plowed fields tonight," and he plunged downward through the bushes, to the stream at the bottom of the valley. There he checked, for he heard the yell of the Pack hunting, heard the **bellow**④ of a hunted Sambhur, and the **snort**⑤ as

到那时——到那时——我知道了！"巴格伊尔拉说着跳了起来。"快，你到下面山谷里，到人的茅屋那儿去，拿些他们种在那里的红花，这样到时候你就会有一个强大的朋友，甚至比我、巴鲁或者狼群里任何爱你的那些狼都要强大。去取红花吧。"

巴格伊尔拉说的红花就是火，只不过丛林里的动物都不知道它真正的名字。所有野兽都怕火怕得要死，所以想出了不下一百种叫法来指代它。

毛格利说："红花？就是黄昏时开在他们茅屋外面的那个吗？我会去拿一些的。"

巴格伊尔拉骄傲地说："这才是人恳该说的话嘛。记住，它就长在那种小罐子里。动作麻利点，拿到了就放在你身边以备万一。"

毛格利说："好的！我去。但是，噢，我的巴格伊尔拉，你确信——"他一边说着一边搂住黑豹那漂亮的脖子，深深地看着对方的大眼睛——"你确定这都是希尔汗搞的鬼？"

"凭那把解放了我的破锁起誓，我确定，小兄弟。"

"那好吧，凭那头赎了我的公牛起誓，我会跟希尔汗好好算算这笔账的，说不定还会跟他多要点呢。"毛格利说完就一蹦一跳地走开了。

"这才像个人样嘛，完完全全的一个人。"巴格伊尔拉自言自语地说着又躺了下来。"啊，希尔汗，你十年前那场抓青蛙的闹剧可是最最倒霉的一次捕猎啦！"

毛格利已经在森林里跑出很远很远了，他拼命地奔跑着，心情无比迫切。夜晚的薄雾升起时，他来到山洞前，吸了一口气，顺着山谷望下去。小狼们不在家，但是山洞里面的狼妈妈听见毛格利的呼吸声就知道她的小青蛙遇上烦心事了。

她问："怎么了，孩子？"

他回头喊道："有人说了些希尔汗的事儿。今天晚上我要去耕地里打猎。"说完他就猛扑下去，穿过灌木丛，来到谷底的溪流旁边。在那儿他停了下来，因为他听见

① hut [hʌt] n.（避雨）茅屋，（简陋的）小屋
② twilight ['twailait] n. 黄昏

③ splendid ['splendid] a. 极好的，绝妙的

④ bellow ['beləu] n.（公牛、象等的）吼叫声
⑤ snort [snɔ:t] n. 鼻息声

the buck turned at bay. Then there were **wicked**①, bitter howls from the young wolves: "Akela! Akela! Let the Lone Wolf show his strength. Room for the leader of the Pack! Spring, Akela!"

The Lone Wolf must have sprung and missed his hold, for Mowgli heard the snap of his teeth and then a yelp as the Sambhur knocked him over with his forefoot.

He did not wait for anything more, but **dashed**② on; and the yells grew fainter behind him as he ran into the croplands where the villagers lived.

"Bagheera spoke truth," he panted, as he **nestled**③ down in some cattle **fodder**④ by the window of a hut. "To-morrow is one day both for Akela and for me."

Then he pressed his face close to the window and watched the fire on the **hearth**⑤. He saw the husbandman's wife get up and feed it in the night with black **lumps**⑥. And when the morning came and the mists were all white and cold, he saw the man's child pick up a **wicker**⑦ pot **plastered**⑧ inside with earth, fill it with lumps of red-hot charcoal, put it under his blanket, and go out to tend the cows in the byre.

"Is that all?" said Mowgli. "If a cub can do it, there is nothing to fear." So he strode round the corner and met the boy, took the pot from his hand, and disappeared into the mist while the boy howled with fear.

"They are very like me," said Mowgli, blowing into the pot as he had seen the woman do. "This thing will die if I do not give it things to eat"; and he dropped **twigs**⑨ and dried bark on the red stuff. Halfway up the hill he met Bagheera with the morning **dew**⑩ shining like moonstones on his coat.

"Akela has missed," said the Panther. "They would have killed him last night, but they needed thee also. They were looking for thee on the hill."

"I was among the plowed lands. I am ready. See!" Mowgli held up the fire-pot.

① wicked ['wikid] a. 顽皮
的，淘气的

② dash [dæʃ] v. 飞奔，急奔

③ nestle ['nesl] v. 安卧，舒
适地躺

④ fodder ['fɔdə] n.（喂养
牛、马、羊的）粗饲料，
秸秆

⑤ hearth [hɑːθ] n. 壁炉，壁
炉炉床

⑥ lump [lʌmp] n. 块

⑦ wicker ['wikə] n.（尤指
编制篮、筐等的）树枝
或藤条

⑧ plaster ['plɑːstə] v. 涂以
灰泥

⑨ twig [twig] n. 细枝，嫩
枝

⑩ dew [djuː] n. 露水，露

了狼群围猎时的叫喊，听到了被追捕的水鹿发出的嘶吼，以及被团团围住时喷出的鼻息声。接着听到那些年轻的狼恶毒而尖刻地叫嚷着："阿凯拉，阿凯拉！让独狼显显威风！让开，给狼王腾出地儿来！跳啊，阿凯拉！"

独狼肯定跳起来了，但是扑了个空，因为毛格利听到他的牙齿合上时咔嚓一声，水鹿用前蹄把他踢开，独狼发出一声痛苦的尖叫。

毛格利没有再听下去，而是继续往前跑，他身后传来的呼喊声越来越弱，最后他跑进了村民们住的庄稼地。

他趴在茅屋窗下的饲料堆上，喘着气对自己说："巴格伊尔拉说得没错，明天对我和阿凯拉来说都是生死攸关的一天。"

他把脸紧贴在窗户上，望着灶膛里的火。他看见农夫的老婆在夜里起来往火里添上一些黑块块儿。黎明来到，升起白白的冰冷的晨雾，他又看见农夫的孩子捡起一个里层是陶土、外层是柳条编的罐子，往里面装满了一块块火红的木炭，放在自己的大披风下面，然后出去照看牛棚里的奶牛。

毛格利说："这样就行了吗？如果一个人崽子都能做到，那就没什么可怕的。"他几步绕过屋角，碰上那个男孩，从他手里抢过罐子就跑进雾里不见了，把那个孩子吓得直叫唤。

毛格利学着农妇的样子往罐子里吹气，一边自言自语地说："他们长得跟我真像。要是我不给它吃点东西的话，这玩意儿会死的。"于是他往那红红的东西上丢了一些小树枝和干树皮。在半山腰上，他遇见了巴格伊尔拉，黑豹的皮毛间缀着晨露，好像闪闪发光的月光石。

黑豹说："阿凯拉失手了。他们本来昨天夜里就要杀了他，可是他们还想把你也一块儿干掉。他们一直在山上找你呢。"

"我去了耕田里。我都准备好了，看！"毛格利举起火罐。

"Good! Now, I have seen men thrust a dry branch into that stuff, and presently the Red Flower blossomed at the end of it. Art thou not afraid?"

"No. Why should I fear? I remember now — if it is not a dream — how, before I was a Wolf, I lay beside the Red Flower, and it was warm and pleasant."

All that day Mowgli sat in the cave **tending**① his fire pot and dipping dry branches into it to see how they looked. He found a branch that satisfied him, and in the evening when Tabaqui came to the cave and told him rudely enough that he was wanted at the Council Rock, he laughed till Tabaqui ran away. Then Mowgli went to the Council, still laughing.

Akela the Lone Wolf lay by the side of his rock as a sign that the leadership of the Pack was open, and Shere Khan with his following of scrap-fed wolves walked to and fro openly being flattered. Bagheera lay close to Mowgli, and the fire pot was between Mowgli's knees. When they were all gathered together, Shere Khan began to speak — a thing he would never have dared to do when Akela was in his **prime**②.

"He has no right," whispered Bagheera. "Say so. He is a dog's son. He will be frightened."

Mowgli sprang to his feet. "Free People," he cried, "does Shere Khan lead the Pack? What has a tiger to do with our leadership?"

"Seeing that the leadership is yet open, and being asked to speak —" Shere Khan began.

"By whom?" said Mowgli. "Are we all jackals, to **fawn**③ on this cattle butcher? The leadership of the Pack is with the Pack alone."

There were yells of "Silence, thou man's cub!" "Let him speak. He has kept our Law"; and at last the seniors of the Pack **thundered**④: "Let the Dead Wolf speak." When a leader of the Pack has missed his kill, he is called the Dead Wolf as long as he lives, which is not long.

Akela raised his old head **wearily**⑤: —

"Free People, and ye too, jackals of Shere Khan, for twelve seasons I have led ye to and from the kill, and in all that time not one has been trapped or

"太好了！嗯，我以前看见人类往那里面插一根干树枝，然后枝头马上就开出红花来。你难道不害怕吗？"

"不怕，我为什么要害怕呢？我现在想起来了——如果不是我做梦的话——在我当狼以前，我就躺在红花边上，又暖和又舒服。"

那天整整一天毛格利都坐在洞里照看他的火罐，把一根又一根的干树枝伸进去，瞧一瞧烧得怎么样，最后才找到一根让他满意的树枝。到了晚上，塔巴奇跑来毫不客气地跟他说要他到议会岩去一趟。他笑啊笑，笑得塔巴奇落荒而逃。接着，毛格利去了议会岩，依旧大笑着。

独狼阿凯拉躺在自己的石座旁，表示狼王的位子已经空出来了。希尔汗呢，带着那帮捡他剩饭吃的狗腿子们走来走去，毫不掩饰地接受他们的奉承。毛格利身边趴着巴格伊尔拉，两个膝盖中间放着那个火罐子。当所有人都到齐了，希尔汗就开始说话了——这要是在从前阿凯拉当头狼的时候，他可不敢这么干。

巴格伊尔拉轻轻地说："他没有权利发言。你就这么说吧。他不过是个狗娘养的，他会被吓住的。"

毛格利一跃而起，喊道："自由民们，难道现在是希尔汗在领导狼群吗？一只老虎凭什么当我们的头儿？"

"狼王的位子不是还空着吗，我呢，就被请来说两句——"希尔汗刚开了个头，毛格利就打断他："谁请你了？难道我们都成了豺狗，得要拍你这个牛屠夫的马屁不成？狼王谁来当只能狼群说了算。"

狼群里爆发出一片喊声，有的叫"闭嘴吧，你这个人崽子！"有的嚷"让他说吧，他一向遵守我们的法则。"终于，资格老的那些狼齐声怒吼："让死狼说话！"当狼王打猎失手时，他就被称作"死狼"，直到他真的死去，不过那通常也要不了多久。

阿凯拉疲倦地抬起他年迈的头颅："自由民们，还有你们，希尔汗的狗腿子们，我带领你们捕猎，来来回回已经有十二个年头了。在这么长的时间里，从没有一

① tend [tend] v. 照顾，照料

② prime [praim] n. 壮年

③ fawn [fɔːn] v. 卑躬屈膝，阿谀奉承

④ thunder ['θʌndə] v. 大声吼叫

⑤ wearily ['wiərili] ad. 疲倦地

maimed[1]. Now I have missed my kill. Ye know how that plot was made. Ye know how ye brought me up to an untried buck to make my weakness known. It was cleverly done. Your right is to kill me here on the Council Rock, now. Therefore, I ask, who comes to make an end of the Lone Wolf? For it is my right, by the Law of the Jungle, that ye come one by one."

There was a long **hush**[2], for no single wolf cared to fight Akela to the death. Then Shere Khan roared: "Bah! What have we to do with this toothless fool? He is **doomed**[3] to die! It is the man-cub who has lived too long. Free People, he was my meat from the first. Give him to me. I am weary of this man-wolf **folly**[4]. He has troubled the jungle for ten seasons. Give me the man-cub, or I will hunt here always, and not give you one bone. He is a man, a man's child, and from the **marrow**[5] of my bones I hate him!"

Then more than half the Pack yelled: "A man! A man! What has a man to do with us? Let him go to his own place."

"And turn all the people of the villages against us?" clamored Shere Khan. "No, give him to me. He is a man, and none of us can look him between the eyes."

Akela lifted his head again and said, "He has eaten our food. He has slept with us. He has driven game for us. He has broken no word of the Law of the Jungle."

"Also, I paid for him with a bull when he was accepted. The worth of a bull is little, but Bagheera's honor is something that he will perhaps fight for," said Bagheera in his gentlest voice.

"A bull paid ten years ago!" the Pack **snarled**[6]. "What do we care for bones ten years old?"

"Or for a **pledge**[7]?" said Bagheera, his white teeth **bared**[8] under his lip. "Well are ye called the Free People!"

"No man's cub can run with the people of the jungle," howled Shere Khan. "Give him to me!"

"He is our brother in all but blood," Akela went on, "and ye would kill

① maim [meim] v. 使负重
伤

② hush [hʌʃ] n. 安静，寂静

③ doom [du:m] v. 命定，注
定（尤指遭厄运）

④ folly ['fɔli] n. 愚笨，愚蠢

⑤ marrow ['mærəu] n. 髓，
骨髓

⑥ snarl [snɑ:l] v.（犬等）
叫，咆哮

⑦ pledge [pledʒ] n. 誓约，
誓言

⑧ bare [bɛə] v. 使暴露

头狼掉进过陷阱或者受伤变成残废。这次我失手了。这是怎么回事你们心里有数。你们故意把我引来捉一只初生的雄鹿，好暴露我的弱点。你们这一手玩儿得漂亮。现在，你们有权利在这议会岩上杀死我。那么，我想问问，谁愿意来结束独狼的性命？因为按照丛林法则，我也有权利跟你们一个一个地决斗。"

过了很久也没人说话，因为没有哪头狼愿意和阿凯拉单挑。希尔汗吼起来："呸！咱们跟这个牙齿都掉光了的废物说什么说？他早晚都会死！那个人崽，才是活得太久了。自由民们，他早就该被我吃了。把他还给我吧。这不人不狼的蠢玩意儿早把我给烦透了。他已经在丛林里折腾了十年了。把人崽给我，要不然我就一直在你们这儿捕猎，一根骨头也不给你们留。他是个人，一个人的崽子，我打骨子里恨他！"

一大半的狼都开始叫起来："人！人！人跟我们有什么干系？让他滚回他自己的地盘去！"

希尔汗不满地说："回去干什么？好让村里所有的人都来跟咱们作对吗？不，还是把他给我吧。他是一个人，咱们谁敢直视他的眼睛啊！"

阿凯拉又一次抬起头说："可是他和我们同吃同睡，还替我们追赶猎物。他可从没违反过任何一条丛林法则。"

巴格伊尔拉用他最最轻柔的声音说道："再说了，当初为了让狼群接受他，我也付了一头公牛的代价啊。虽说一头牛不值什么，但是我巴格伊尔拉为了荣誉倒说不定愿意豁出去打一仗。"

狼群嘶喊道："十年前付的一头牛！我们凭什么要为十年的老骨头买账？"

"那为了你们的誓言呢？好嘛，怪不得你们叫作自由民哪！"巴格伊尔拉说着，亮出他的白牙。

希尔汗吼着说："人崽不配和丛林之民一起奔跑。把他给我！"

阿凯拉接着说："总之他是我们的兄弟，只不过血

him here! In truth, I have lived too long. Some of ye are eaters of cattle, and of others I have heard that, under Shere Khan's teaching, ye go by dark night and snatch children from the villager's doorstep. Therefore I know ye to be cowards, and it is to cowards I speak. It is certain that I must die, and my life is of no worth, or I would offer that in the man-cub's place. But for the sake of the Honor of the Pack,—a little matter that by being without a leader ye have forgotten,—I promise that if ye let the man-cub go to his own place, I will not, when my time comes to die, bare one tooth against ye. I will die without fighting. That will at least save the Pack three lives. More I cannot do; but if ye will, I can save ye the shame that comes of killing a brother against whom there is no fault—a brother spoken for and bought into the Pack according to the Law of the Jungle."

"He is a man—a man—a man!" snarled the Pack. And most of the wolves began to gather round Shere Khan, whose tail was beginning to **switch**[1].

"Now the business is in thy hands," said Bagheera to Mowgli. "We can do no more except fight."

Mowgli stood upright—the fire pot in his hands. Then he stretched out his arms, and yawned in the face of the Council; but he was furious with rage and sorrow, for, wolflike, the wolves had never told him how they hated him. "Listen you!" he cried. "There is no need for this dog's **jabber**[2]. Ye have told me so often tonight that I am a man (and indeed I would have been a wolf with you to my life's end) that I feel your words are true. So I do not call ye my brothers any more, but sag [dogs], as a man should. What ye will do, and what ye will not do, is not yours to say. That matter is with me; and that we may see the matter more plainly, I, the man, have brought here a little of the Red Flower which ye, dogs, fear."

He flung the fire pot on the ground, and some of the red coals lit a **tuft**[3] of dried **moss**[4] that flared up, as all the Council drew back in terror before the leaping flames.

Mowgli **thrust**[5] his dead branch into the fire till the twigs lit and crackled,

缘不同，可是你们却要在这儿杀死他！说真的，我也活够了。你们现在有的连牛都吃，我听说还有的竟然在希尔汗的教唆下摸黑去村民家偷小孩。所以，我知道你们都是些懦夫，我下面的话也就是对懦夫说的。我肯定是要死的，我的性命也没什么价值，要不然我就会拿它去换人崽的命。但是为了族群的荣誉——当然了，你们现在没了领袖也就忘了有荣誉这回事了——我承诺，只要你们让人崽回到他的应属之地，那么等到我注定该死的那一天，我绝不会动你们一根毫毛。我情愿毫不反抗就去死。那样至少能让族群少损失三条性命。除此之外，我也做不了更多的了；但是如果你们愿意，我可以使你们免于背负残杀无辜兄弟的骂名，他可是按照法规、经过申辩、缴过赎金，被族群堂堂正正接纳进来的。"

狼群嘶吼着："他是个人——人——人！"绝大多数狼开始聚拢到希尔汗身边，他也开始摇晃起尾巴来。

巴格伊尔拉对毛格利说："现在该你作决定啦。除了战斗我们别无选择。"

毛格利站得笔直，手里捧着火罐。然后他伸开双臂，对着族群大会打了个呵欠；但其实他内心悲愤交加，因为这些狼从没告诉过毛格利他们多么恨他，他们天性如此。毛格利喊道："你们听着！没有必要像狗一样地乱吠。今天晚上你们已经无数次地说过我是人（我本来是愿意一辈子和你们一起做狼的），所以我觉得你们说得没错。我也不再把你们看作我的弟兄，而是像人那样，管你们叫'傻格'（意为狗）。现在，你们要做什么，不做什么，你们说了可不算。那得由我来决定。为了让大家更明白地认识到这一点，我，作为人，拿来了一些你们这些狗害怕的红花。"

他把火罐扔到地上，几块通红的炭把一簇干苔藓点燃了，火苗一跃而起，整个狼族都吓得往后退，好躲开那跳跃的火焰。

毛格利把他选的那根枯树枝插进火里，等到上面的

① switch [switʃ] v. 甩动（尾巴等）

② jabber ['dʒæbə] n. 莫名其妙的话

③ tuft [tʌft] n.（头发、羽毛、草等的）一簇，一束，一丛
④ moss [mɔs] n.【植物】苔藓
⑤ thrust [θrʌst] v. 猛推

and whirled it above his head among the cowering wolves.

"Thou art the master," said Bagheera in an undertone. "Save Akela from the death. He was ever thy friend."

Akela, the grim old wolf who had never asked for mercy in his life, gave one **piteous**① look at Mowgli as the boy stood all naked, his long black hair tossing over his shoulders in the light of the blazing branch that made the shadows jump and **quiver**②.

"Good!" said Mowgli, staring round slowly. "I see that ye are dogs. I go from you to my own people — if they be my own people. The jungle is shut to me, and I must forget your talk and your companionship. But I will be more merciful than ye are. Because I was all but your brother in blood, I promise that when I am a man among men I will not betray ye to men as ye have betrayed me." He kicked the fire with his foot, and the sparks flew up. "There shall be no war between any of us in the Pack. But here is a debt to pay before I go." He strode forward to where Shere Khan sat **blinking**③ stupidly at the flames, and caught him by the tuft on his chin. Bagheera followed in case of accidents. "Up, dog!" Mowgli cried. "Up, when a man speaks, or I will set that coat ablaze!"

Shere Khan's ears lay flat back on his head, and he shut his eyes, for the blazing branch was very near.

"This cattle-killer said he would kill me in the Council because he had not killed me when I was a cub. Thus and thus, then, do we beat dogs when we are men. Stir a **whisker**④, Lungri, and I ram the Red Flower down thy gullet!" He beat Shere Khan over the head with the branch, and the tiger whimpered and whined in an **agony**⑤ of fear.

"Pah! Singed jungle cat — go now! But remember when next I come to the Council Rock, as a man should come, it will be with Shere Khan's **hide**⑥ on my head. For the rest, Akela goes free to live as he pleases. Ye will not kill him, because that is not my will. Nor do I think that ye will sit here any longer, lolling out your tongues as though ye were somebodies, instead of dogs whom I

细枝都点燃了，开始噼啪作响，他便举起树枝在头顶挥舞，周围的群狼全都缩成了一团。

巴格伊尔拉低声地说："现在你说了算，救救阿凯拉吧。他一直都是你的朋友。"

阿凯拉这作风严厉的老狼，一辈子也没向谁求过饶，但是现在却可怜兮兮地看着毛格利。男孩全身赤裸，黑黑的长发披散在肩头，手里的树枝火光熊熊，在地上投下不断颤动跳跃的阴影。

毛格利慢慢地扫视了周围一圈，说道："好！我知道你们都是狗。我会离开你们回到我自己的族群——如果他们真的是我的自己人的话。丛林对我关上了大门，我也必须忘记过去同你们的交谈和你们的陪伴。但是我会比你们仁慈。因为我曾经和你们亲如兄弟，我发誓，等我回到人类中间去做一个人时，我不会像你们出卖过我那样把你们出卖给人。"他踢踢火堆，弄得火星四溅开来。"我不会和狼群开战。但是在我走之前有一笔账得好好算算。"他一步跨到希尔汗跟前，一把揪住他下巴上的毛，而那老虎还蹲在那儿傻傻地看着火焰直眨眼。巴格伊尔拉跟在毛格利后面以防不测。毛格利喊道："起来，狗！起来，人在跟你说话呢。否则我就把你这身毛给烧了！"

希尔汗的双耳后折贴在了脑袋上，眼睛也闭上了，因为熊熊燃烧的树枝近在咫尺。

"这个牛屠夫说他要在大会上杀了我，因为当初我还小的时候他没能杀死我。那么这样，这样，我们人就是这样打狗的。朗格利，你只要敢动一根胡子，我就把红花塞到你的喉咙里去！"他用树枝抽打希尔汗的脑袋，老虎害怕得发出阵阵呜咽声。

"呸！你这焦毛大猫——现在滚吧！但是记住，下次等我作为一个人，再来到议会岩时，我会在头上披着希尔汗的皮来。至于你们，阿凯拉可以随他喜欢自由地活着，你们不能杀他，因为我不允许。我也不想让你们再在这里坐着，伸着舌头好像什么大人物似的，其实你

① piteous ['pitiəs] *a.* 可怜的

② quiver ['kwivə] *v.* 颤抖

③ blink [bliŋk] *v.* 眨着眼睛看

④ whisker ['wiskə] *n.* （动物的）须

⑤ agony ['ægəni] *n.* （精神上或肉体上极度的）痛苦

⑥ hide [haid] *n.* 兽皮

drive out—thus! Go!" The fire was burning furiously at the end of the branch, and Mowgli struck right and left round the circle, and the wolves ran howling with the sparks burning their fur. At last there were only Akela, Bagheera, and perhaps ten wolves that had taken Mowgli's part. Then something began to hurt Mowgli inside him, as he had never been hurt in his life before, and he caught his breath and sobbed, and the tears ran down his face.

"What is it? What is it?" he said. "I do not wish to leave the jungle, and I do not know what this is. Am I dying, Bagheera?"

"No, Little Brother. That is only tears such as men use," said Bagheera. "Now I know thou art a man, and a man's cub no longer. The jungle is shut indeed to thee **henceforward**①. Let them fall, Mowgli. They are only tears." So Mowgli sat and cried as though his heart would break; and he had never cried in all his life before.

"Now," he said, "I will go to men. But first I must say farewell to my mother." And he went to the cave where she lived with Father Wolf, and he cried on her **coat**②, while the four cubs howled miserably.

"Ye will not forget me?" said Mowgli.

"Never while we can follow a trail," said the cubs. "Come to the foot of the hill when thou art a man, and we will talk to thee; and we will come into the **croplands**③ to play with thee by night."

"Come soon!" said Father Wolf. "Oh, wise little frog, come again soon; for we be old, thy mother and I."

"Come soon," said Mother Wolf, "little naked son of mine. For, listen, child of man, I loved thee more than ever I loved my cubs."

"I will surely come," said Mowgli. "And when I come it will be to lay out Shere Khan's hide upon the Council Rock. Do not forget me! Tell them in the jungle never to forget me!"

The **dawn**④ was beginning to break when Mowgli went down the hillside alone, to meet those **mysterious**⑤ things that are called men.

们不过就是一群狗，被我赶跑的狗——就像这样！滚！"树枝的顶端燃烧着熊熊的火焰，毛格利朝周围东打一下西打一下，火星烧着了群狼的毛皮，吓得他们嗥叫着四下逃窜。最后只剩下阿凯拉和巴格伊尔拉，还有十来只站在毛格利这边的狼。这时，毛格利的身体里好像有个地方开始疼痛，他从没这样疼过，疼得气都喘不上来，他抽泣着，眼泪沿着脸颊流下来。

他说："这是什么？这是什么？我不想离开丛林，我也不知道这是什么东西。我是要死了吗，巴格伊尔拉？"

巴格伊尔拉说："不是的，小兄弟。那不过是眼泪，只有人才会用的东西。现在我知道你已经是个男人，不再是个人崽了。从今以后丛林确确实实不再对你敞开。你就让它流吧，毛格利。那不过是眼泪罢了。"于是毛格利坐下大哭起来，哭得好像心都要碎了，他这辈子还从没这样哭过。

他说："好吧，我会到人类那儿去。但是首先我得去跟妈妈告别。"他回到狼妈妈和狼爸爸住的山洞，扑倒她怀里大哭一场，四头狼崽也在一边哀哀地叫。

毛格利问："你们不会忘了我吧？"

狼崽都说："永远不会，只要我们还会辨别踪迹。等你当了人，你就到山脚下来，我们会和你说话；晚上我们会到田里去找你玩儿。"

狼爸爸说："快点来！哦，聪明的小青蛙，快点回来，因为你的妈妈和我，我们都老了。"

狼妈妈也说："快点回来，我光溜溜的小儿子。你听着，人娃娃，我爱你超过爱自己的孩子。"

毛格利说："我肯定会来的。等我回来，我会把希尔汗的皮晾在议会岩上。别忘了我！告诉丛林里的其他动物，永远也别忘了我！"

天亮了，毛格利一个人走下山坡，去找那些被称作人的神秘的生灵。

① henceforward ['hens'fɔ:wəd] *ad.* 今后

② coat [kəut] *n.* 皮毛，兽皮

③ cropland ['krɔp,lænd] *n.* 田地，耕地，农田

④ dawn [dɔ:n] *n.* 黎明，拂晓

⑤ mysterious [mi'stiəriəs] *a.* 神秘的

Hunting-Song of the Seeonee Pack

As the dawn was breaking the Sambhur belled
    Once, twice and again!
And a **doe**[①] leaped up, and a doe leaped up
From the pond in the wood where the wild deer **sup**[②].
This I, **scouting**[③] alone, **beheld**[④],
    Once, twice and again!

As the dawn was breaking the Sambhur belled
    Once, twice and again!
And a wolf stole back, and a wolf stole back
To carry the word to the waiting pack,
And we sought and we found and we bayed on his track
    Once, twice and again!

As the dawn was breaking the Wolf Pack yelled
    Once, twice and again!
Feet in the jungle that leave no mark!

西翁尼狼群的狩猎之歌

① doe [dəu] n.【动物】雌
鹿, 雌羚羊
② sup [sʌp] v. 小口地唱
③ scout [skaut] v. 寻找
④ beheld [bi'held]
v.（behold 的过去式和
过去分词）见到, 注意
到

天光破晓, 水鹿低鸣,
一声, 两声, 三声!
鹿群饮水的池塘边
一头又一头的小鹿纵身跃起。
在林中独自侦察的我看见了
一次, 两次, 三次!

天光破晓, 水鹿低鸣,
一声, 两声, 三声!
一只狼偷偷溜回来, 一只狼偷偷溜回来,
给等待的狼群捎个信儿,
我们寻啊, 找啊, 沿着他的足迹叫啊,
一次, 两次, 三次!

天空在破晓, 狼群在喊叫,
一声, 两声, 三声!
没在丛林留下一个脚印!

Eyes that can see in the dark—the dark!
Tongue—give tongue to it! **Hark**[1]! O hark!
　　Once, twice and again!

① hark [hɑːk] v. [主要用于
祈使句] 听,倾听,注意
听

眼睛在黑夜中看得清——黑夜!

喉咙——放开喉咙喊吧! 听啊! 听啊!

一声, 两声, 三声!

Kaa's Hunting

His spots are the joy of the Leopard: his horns are the Buffalo's pride.

Be clean, for the strength of the hunter is known by the gloss of his hide.

*If ye find that the Bullock can **toss**① you, or the heavy-browed Sambhur can **gore**②;*

Ye need not stop work to inform us: we knew it ten seasons before.

***Oppress**③ not the cubs of the stranger, but **hail**④ them as Sister and Brother,*

*For though they are little and **fubsy**⑤, it may be the Bear is their mother.*

"There is none like to me!" says the Cub in the pride of his earliest kill;

But the jungle is large and the Cub he is small. Let him think and be still.

Maxims of Baloo

All that is told here happened some time before Mowgli was turned out of the Seeonee Wolf Pack, or revenged himself on Shere Khan the tiger. It was in the days when Baloo was teaching him the Law of the Jungle. The big, serious, old brown bear was delighted to have so quick a **pupil**⑥, for the young wolves will only learn as much of the Law of the Jungle as applies to their own pack

蟒蛇卡的狩猎

猎豹以他的斑点为乐，野牛以他的双角为荣。

要保持清洁，猎手的毛皮是否光滑说明他的能力大小。

如果你发现小公牛能把你扔出去，眉毛浓重的水鹿能用角顶伤你，

不用专门停下工作来告诉我们：早在十年前我们就已知道啦。

不要欺负陌生的幼崽，要叫他们"兄弟"或"姊妹"，

因为他们虽然又小又胖，却很有可能是熊的孩子。

第一次杀死猎物时，幼崽都会骄傲地大喊"谁也没有我这么厉害！"

但是丛林如此广袤，而幼崽如此渺小。让他好好静静地思考。

——巴鲁的格言

我们接下来要讲的故事发生在毛格利被赶出西翁尼狼族之前，他也还没有去找老虎希尔汗报仇。那时他还在跟着巴鲁学习丛林法则。块头巨大、生性严肃的老棕熊很喜欢这个敏捷的学生，因为其他的小狼只肯学习跟他们自己族群相关的丛林法，一旦会背诵猎歌就会逃之

① toss [tɔs] v. 扔，抛
② gore [gɔ:] v.（长角动物）用角（或獠牙）抵，刺

③ oppress [ə'pres] v. 压迫，压制
④ hail [heil] v. 向……欢呼
⑤ fubsy ['fʌbzi] a.［英国方言］肥胖的

⑥ pupil ['pjupəl] n. 门生，弟子

and tribe, and run away as soon as they can repeat the Hunting Verse—"Feet that make no noise; eyes that can see in the dark; ears that can hear the winds in their lairs, and sharp white teeth, all these things are the marks of our brothers except Tabaqui the Jackal and the Hyaena whom we hate." But Mowgli, as a man-cub, had to learn a great deal more than this. Sometimes Bagheera the Black Panther would come **lounging**① through the jungle to see how his pet was getting on, and would purr with his head against a tree while Mowgli recited the day's lesson to Baloo. The boy could climb almost as well as he could swim, and swim almost as well as he could run. So Baloo, the Teacher of the Law, taught him the Wood and Water Laws: how to tell a rotten branch from a sound one; how to speak politely to the wild bees when he came upon a **hive**② of them fifty feet above ground; what to say to Mang the Bat when he disturbed him in the branches at midday; and how to warn the water-snakes in the pools before he splashed down among them. None of the Jungle People like being disturbed, and all are very ready to **fly at**③ an intruder. Then, too, Mowgli was taught the Strangers' Hunting Call, which must be repeated aloud till it is answered, whenever one of the Jungle-People hunts outside his own grounds. It means, translated, "Give me leave to hunt here because I am hungry." And the answer is, "Hunt then for food, but not for pleasure."

All this will show you how much Mowgli had to learn by heart, and he grew very tired of saying the same thing over a hundred times. But, as Baloo said to Bagheera, one day when Mowgli had been **cuffed**④ and run off in a temper, "A man's cub is a man's cub, and he must learn all the Law of the Jungle."

"But think how small he is," said the Black Panther, who would have **spoiled**⑤ Mowgli if he had had his own way. "How can his little head carry all thy long talk?"

"Is there anything in the jungle too little to be killed? No. That is why I teach him these things, and that is why I hit him, very softly, when he forgets."

"Softly! What dost thou know of softness, old Iron-feet?" Bagheera grunted.

① lounge [laundʒ] v. 闲荡，闲逛

② hive [haiv] n. 蜂团，蜂群

③ fly at 猛扑，猛烈攻击

④ cuff [kʌf] v. 用巴掌打，掌击，掴

⑤ spoil [spɔil] v. 娇惯坏，宠坏

天天。猎歌是这么唱的："我们的爪子悄无声息，我们的双眼能穿透黑暗，我们的耳朵能捕捉巢穴里的微风，我们的牙齿又白又尖利。这些都是我们弟兄的标志，除了我们讨厌的土狼、鬣狗——塔巴奇"。但是毛格利作为一个人崽要学的东西远远超出这些。有时黑豹巴格伊尔拉会穿过丛林来看看他的小宝贝学习进展如何。他会一边把脑袋靠在树上打呼噜，一边听着毛格利给巴鲁背诵当天学习的课程。这男孩爬树跟游泳一样棒，游泳又几乎跟跑步一样棒。所以法则教师巴鲁就教给了他跟森林和水域相关的法则：比如如何辨别腐朽的树枝和结实的树枝；如果在离地五十英尺高的地方遇见了一群野蜂，该如何跟他们礼貌地打招呼；如果中午的时候打扰了在叶子间休息的蝙蝠芒恩该怎么说话；在跳进池塘之前又该怎么提醒底下的水蛇避开。丛林的民众没有谁愿意受惊扰，一有入侵者，都会在第一时间发动攻击。所以毛格利也学了"外来者的求猎呼号"，凡是丛林居民，无论谁离开自己的地盘打猎时都必须大声重复这个呼号，直到得到应答。如果把它翻成人的语言，那就是"请允许我在此狩猎，因为我饥肠辘辘"。回答则是"只可猎取食物，不可以此取乐"。

我说这些是让你明白毛格利需要用心记住多少东西，而且要把一件事情翻来覆去念上一百遍，他烦得不行了。但是就像巴鲁跟巴格伊尔拉说的那样，"人崽就是人崽，他必须学会所有的丛林法则"。他说这话时，毛格利刚因为挨了一巴掌气呼呼地跑掉了。

黑豹说："可是想想他还这么小呢。他那小脑袋怎么能装下你那些长篇大论呢？"要是让巴格伊尔拉来带孩子，他肯定会把毛格利给惯坏了不可。

"丛林里有什么东西会因为太小而不被杀吗？没有。所以我才要教他这些事情，所以他记不住的时候，我才打他，轻轻地打一下。"

"轻轻地！你这老铁掌，你知道什么叫轻轻地？"

"His face is all **bruised**① today by thy—softness. Ugh."

"Better he should be bruised from head to foot by me who love him than that he should come to harm through ignorance," Baloo answered very earnestly. "I am now teaching him the Master Words of the Jungle that shall protect him with the birds and the Snake People, and all that hunt on four feet, except his own pack. He can now **claim**② protection, if he will only remember the words, from all in the jungle. Is not that worth a little beating?"

"Well, look to it then that thou dost not kill the man-cub. He is no tree trunk to sharpen thy **blunt**③ claws upon. But what are those Master Words? I am more likely to give help than to ask it"—Bagheera stretched out one paw and admired the steel-blue, ripping-chisel **talons**④ at the end of it—"still I should like to know."

"I will call Mowgli and he shall say them—if he will. Come, Little Brother!"

"My head is ringing like a bee tree," said a **sullen**⑤ little voice over their heads, and Mowgli slid down a tree trunk very angry and **indignant**⑥, adding as he reached the ground: "I come for Bagheera and not for thee, fat old Baloo!"

"**That is all one to me**⑦," said Baloo, though he was hurt and grieved. "Tell Bagheera, then, the Master Words of the Jungle that I have taught thee this day."

"Master Words for which people?" said Mowgli, delighted to show off. "The jungle has many tongues. I know them all."

"A little thou knowest, but not much. See, O Bagheera, they never thank their teacher. Not one small wolfling has ever come back to thank old Baloo for his teachings. Say the word for the Hunting-People, then—great scholar."

"We be of one blood, ye and I," said Mowgli, giving the words the Bear

① bruise [bru:z] v. 使（皮肉）青肿，使受瘀伤

② claim [kleim] v. 要求（应得权利）

③ blunt [blʌnt] a. 钝的，不锋利的

④ talon ['tælən] n.［常作复数］（尤指猛禽的）爪

⑤ sullen ['sʌlən] a. 愠怒的，不高兴的

⑥ indignant [in'dignənt] a. 愤怒的，愤慨的

⑦ that is all one to me 对我来说都一样

巴格伊尔拉不满地嘟囔着："今天他的脸都肿了，就因为你那'轻轻的'一下。哼！"

巴鲁非常认真地回答道："他就是从头到脚都被我打肿了也比他因为无知而闯祸强，我这才叫爱他。我现在教他的是丛林密语，能够保护他不受任何东西的伤害，不管是鸟、蛇，还是靠四条腿打猎的走兽，除了他自己的族群以外。现在只要他能记住这些话，他就能免受丛林里任何动物的伤害。为了这个挨点打又算得了什么呢？"

"呵呵，那你就小心点别把人崽给打死咯。他可不是你拿来磨磨钝爪子的树干啊。话说回来，密语到底是什么啊？一向都是别人来求我帮忙，我还从来没求过别人呢。不过，了解一下也不坏啊。"巴格伊尔拉一边说着，一边伸出一只脚，欣赏着脚尖上那闪着金属般亮光、像细长凿一样锋利的爪子。

"我叫毛格利来说给你听吧，如果他愿意的话。来吧，小兄弟！"

他们头顶上传来一个小小的、闷闷不乐的声音："我这头还在嗡嗡响呢，就跟住了蜜蜂的空心树一样。"毛格利抱着满腹的委屈和怒火从树干上滑下来，踩到地上时还加了一句："我是为了巴格伊尔拉才来的，可不是为了你，胖子老巴鲁！"

"为谁来都一样。来吧，给巴格伊尔拉念念我今天教你的丛林密语。"巴鲁说是这么说，其实心里还是挺难过的。

"哪一族的密语呢？丛林里有那么多语言。我可全都知道。"毛格利说着，很高兴有个机会能卖弄一下。

"你才知道一点点而已，哪有多少。你看看，巴格伊尔拉，他们从来都不知道感谢老师。没有哪头小狼回来感谢过老巴鲁的教诲。好吧，大学者，你就说说捕猎族的密语吧。"

"你和我，我们拥有共同的血缘。"毛格利用熊的

accent which all the Hunting People use.

"Good. Now for the birds."

Mowgli repeated, with the Kite's whistle at the end of the sentence.

"Now for the Snake-People," said Bagheera.

The answer was a perfectly indescribable **hiss**[①], and Mowgli kicked up his feet behind, clapped his hands together to applaud himself, and jumped on to Bagheera's back, where he sat sideways, drumming with his heels on the glossy skin and making the worst faces he could think of at Baloo.

"There—there! That was worth a little bruise," said the brown bear tenderly. "Some day thou wilt remember me." Then he turned aside to tell Bagheera how he had begged the Master Words from Hathi the Wild Elephant, who knows all about these things, and how Hathi had taken Mowgli down to a pool to get the Snake Word from a water-snake, because Baloo could not pronounce it, and how Mowgli was now reasonably safe against all accidents in the jungle, because neither snake, bird, nor beast would hurt him.

"No one then is to be feared," Baloo **wound up**[②], patting his big furry stomach with pride.

"Except his own tribe," said Bagheera, under his breath; and then aloud to Mowgli, "Have a care for my ribs, Little Brother! What is all this dancing up and down?"

Mowgli had been trying to make himself heard by pulling at Bagheera's shoulder fur and kicking hard. When the two listened to him he was shouting at the top of his voice, "And so I shall have a tribe of my own, and lead them through the branches all day long."

"What is this new folly, little dreamer of dreams?" said Bagheera.

"Yes, and throw branches and dirt at old Baloo," Mowgli went on. "They have promised me this. Ah!"

"Whoof!" Baloo's big paw **scooped**[③] Mowgli off Bagheera's back, and as the boy lay between the big fore-paws he could see the Bear was angry.

口音念了一遍所有捕猎族都会的密语。

"好。现在说说鸟类用的。"

毛格利念了一遍，句尾带上了鸢鹰特有的口哨。

巴格伊尔拉说："现在该蛇族了。"

① hiss [his] *n.* 嘶嘶声

回答他的是一声完全无法形容的咝咝声。毛格利往后踢踢脚，又给自己鼓掌喝彩，还跳到巴格伊尔拉的背上，侧坐着用脚后跟在黑豹光滑的皮毛上敲着鼓点，一边还对着巴鲁做出各种各样他能想出来的最最难看的鬼脸。

棕熊温柔地说："好了，好了，能念成这样，受点轻伤完全值得嘛。总有一天你会记得我的。"说完，他转过脸去跟巴格伊尔拉说起他是怎么去求野象哈提教他这些密语的，对这一类事情哈提可是了如指掌。因为巴鲁不会蛇族密语，所以哈提又带着毛格利到池塘边去向一条水蛇请教。现在毛格利在丛林里可以说是几乎来去无碍了，因为无论鸟、蛇，还是走兽都不会伤害他。

② wind up 结束（讲话等）

"再也不用害怕谁了。"巴鲁总结说，骄傲地拍了拍他那毛茸茸的大肚皮。

"除了他自己的族群，"巴格伊尔拉低声接了一句，又提高嗓门对毛格利说道："小兄弟，小心我的肋骨！这么跳上跳下的干吗啊？"

为了让黑豹和棕熊听他说话，毛格利刚才一直在拉扯巴格伊尔拉肩膀上的毛，还使劲儿踢他。等他们俩注意听时，他放声大喊："这样我就会有我自己的一个部落了，我可以带着他们成天在树上跑来跑去。"

巴格伊尔拉问："这又是什么新把戏啊，小小梦想家？"

毛格利接着说："对，还要冲老巴鲁扔树枝和泥巴。他们都跟我说好了。啊！"

③ scoop [sku:p] *v.*（敏捷地）抱起，搂起

"噗——"巴鲁的大掌一下把毛格利从巴格伊尔拉的背上扯下来。当男孩儿朝天躺在大大的熊掌之间时，他看出来棕熊发火了。

"Mowgli," said Baloo, "thou hast been talking with the Bandar-log—the Monkey People."

Mowgli looked at Bagheera to see if the Panther was angry too, and Bagheera's eyes were as hard as **jade**① stones.

"Thou hast been with the Monkey People—the gray **apes**②—the people without a law—the eaters of everything. That is great **shame**③."

"When Baloo hurt my head," said Mowgli (he was still on his back), "I went away, and the gray apes came down from the trees and had pity on me. No one else cared." He snuffled a little.

"The pity of the Monkey People!" Baloo snorted. "The **stillness**④ of the mountain stream! The cool of the summer sun! And then, man-cub?"

"And then, and then, they gave me nuts and pleasant things to eat, and they—they carried me in their arms up to the top of the trees and said I was their blood brother except that I had no tail, and should be their leader some day."

"They have no leader," said Bagheera. "They lie. They have always lied."

"They were very kind and **bade**⑤ me come again. Why have I never been taken among the Monkey People? They stand on their feet as I do. They do not hit me with their hard paws. They play all day. Let me get up! Bad Baloo, let me up! I will play with them again."

"Listen, man-cub," said the Bear, and his voice rumbled like thunder on a hot night. "I have taught thee all the Law of the Jungle for all the peoples of the jungle—except the Monkey-Folk who live in the trees. They have no law. They are **outcasts**⑥. They have no speech of their own, but use the stolen words which they overhear when they listen, and **peep**⑦, and wait up above in the branches. Their way is not our way. They are without leaders. They have no **remembrance**⑧. They boast and chatter and pretend that they are a great people about to do great affairs in the jungle, but the falling of a nut turns their minds to laughter and all is forgotten. We of the jungle have no dealings with them. We do not drink where the monkeys drink; we do not go where the monkeys go; we

① jade [dʒeid] *n.* 玉石，翡翠
② ape [eip] *n.* 黑猩猩，大猩猩，猩猩
③ shame [ʃeim] *n.* 耻辱，无耻行为

④ stillness ['stilnis] *n.* 静止，不动

⑤ bade [bæd] *v.*（bid 的一种过去式）邀请

⑥ outcast ['autkɑːst] *n.* 被（家庭或社会）遗弃者，被逐出者
⑦ peep [piːp] *v.*（表示埋怨、抗议等）嘀咕
⑧ remembrance [ri'membrəns] *n.* 回忆

巴鲁说："毛格利，你一直在跟邦达－罗格——猴民来往呢。"

毛格利看看巴格伊尔拉，想知道黑豹是否也在生气，只见巴格伊尔拉的眼睛变得像翡翠一样又冷又硬。

"你跟猴民混在一起，那些灰猿——什么都吃——无法无天，真是丢脸！"

毛格利（还仰面躺着）说："巴鲁那会儿把我的头打伤了，我就跑掉了。然后那些灰猿就从树上下来安慰我。除了他们，谁也不管我。"他轻轻地抽了一下鼻子。

巴鲁哼了一声，说："猴民的怜悯！就跟说山溪也会静止，夏日也会清凉一样！后来呢，人崽子？"

"后来，后来，他们就给我吃坚果还有别的好吃的，他们还——还用胳膊夹着我把我带到树顶上去了。他们说我跟他们同宗，只不过没有尾巴，还说我有一天会当他们的头领。"

巴格伊尔拉说："他们根本没有头领。他们在撒谎。他们总是撒谎。"

"可是他们对我很好，还让我再去玩儿。你们怎么从来不带我去猴民那儿呢？他们跟我一样都能直立着。而且他们也不会用硬爪子打我。他们整天都玩儿。让我起来，坏巴鲁，让我起来！我还要去跟他们玩儿。"

棕熊说话了，他的声音像闷热的晚上隆隆的雷声一样。"听着，人崽儿，我已经教过你丛林里所有居民都遵守的丛林法则，但是住在树上的猴族不算，他们不遵守任何法则。他们是被驱逐出去的流浪者。他们连自己的语言都没有，只会在树上偷听、偷看，等着别人说些什么，他们就偷来用。他们和我们走的不是一条路。他们没有首领，也没有记性。他们夸夸其谈，假装自己是一个伟大的民族，要在丛林里干些大事；可是只要一颗坚果落下来，就会让他们哈哈大笑，把什么都忘了。我们丛林各族和他们没有往来。我们不在猴子喝水的地方喝水，不到猴子去的地方去，不在他们打猎的地方打

do not hunt where they hunt; we do not die where they die. Hast thou ever heard me speak of the Bandar-log till today?"

"No," said Mowgli in a whisper, for the forest was very still now Baloo had finished.

"The Jungle-People put them out of their mouths and out of their minds. They are very many, evil, dirty, shameless, and they desire, if they have any fixed desire, to be noticed by the Jungle People. But we do not notice them even when they throw nuts and **filth**① on our heads."

He had hardly spoken when a shower of nuts and twigs spattered down through the branches; and they could hear coughings and howlings and angry jumpings high up in the air among the thin branches.

"The Monkey-People are forbidden," said Baloo, "forbidden to the Jungle-People. Remember."

"Forbidden," said Bagheera, "but I still think Baloo should have warned thee against them."

"I—I? How was I to guess he would play with such dirt. The Monkey People! Faugh!"

A fresh shower came down on their heads and the two **trotted**② away, taking Mowgli with them. What Baloo had said about the monkeys was perfectly true. They belonged to the tree-tops, and as beasts very seldom look up, there was no occasion for the monkeys and the Jungle-People to cross each other's path. But whenever they found a sick wolf, or a wounded tiger, or bear, the monkeys would **torment**③ him, and would throw sticks and nuts at any beast for fun and in the hope of being noticed. Then they would howl and **shriek**④ senseless songs, and invite the Jungle-People to climb up their trees and fight them, or would start **furious**⑤ battles over nothing among themselves, and leave the dead monkeys where the Jungle-People could see them. They were always just going to have a leader, and laws and customs of their own, but they never did, because their memories would not hold over from day to day, and so they compromised things by making up a saying, "What the Bandar-log think now the jungle will

猎，也不在他们死的地方死。今天之前你听我说起过邦达－罗格吗？"

"没有。"毛格利小声地说，因为巴鲁说完话时整个丛林都一片寂静。

"丛林各族不吃他们也不惦记他们。他们数量众多，邪恶、肮脏、无耻。要说他们有什么不变的想法，那就是想得到丛林居民的注意。但是就算他们往我们头上扔干果和垃圾，我们也不会搭理他们。"

他的话还没说完，干果和小树枝就像急雨一般从树上洒落下来，他们还能听见高高的细枝间传来聒噪声、尖叫声和生气地跳来跳去的声音。

巴鲁说："猴民被禁止和丛林各族往来。记住了。"

巴格伊尔拉也说："严禁。但是我还以为巴鲁早就警告过你远离他们呢。"

"我——我吗？我怎么猜得到他会去跟这些垃圾玩儿呢？猴民！呸！"

又是一阵坚果和树枝的急雨，他俩带着毛格利快步走开了。巴鲁说的这些话千真万确。猴民属于树梢，而走兽很少往上看，所以猴民和丛林居民很少有交集。但是无论什么时候，只要猴子们发现一只生病的狼，或者受伤的老虎，抑或棕熊，他们就会折磨他。他们会往任何野兽身上扔树枝或是坚果，只为了引起注意。他们还会尖叫、乱唱一气，想激得丛林族民爬上树去跟他们打一架；要不就是来个窝里斗，莫名其妙地混战一场，然后把打死的猴子尸体丢在丛林族民能看到的地方。他们总是马上就要有个首领，马上就要制定自己的法律和规则了，可是却从来没有实现过，因为他们的记性太短，今天想到的事情明天就忘了。所以他们干脆编了一套说法，叫"邦达－罗格考虑事情总比丛林族民早一步"，这样一来他们就觉得好受多了。虽

① filth [filθ] *n.* 污秽，污物

② trot [trɔt] *v.* 小跑着前进

③ torment [tɔː'ment] *v.* 使烦恼
④ shriek [ʃriːk] *v.* 尖声地叫喊

⑤ furious ['fjuːriəs] *a.* 狂暴的，凶猛的

think later," and that comforted them a great deal. None of the beasts could reach them, but on the other hand none of the beasts would notice them, and that was why they were so pleased when Mowgli came to play with them, and they heard how angry Baloo was.

They never meant to do any more—the Bandar-log never mean anything at all; but one of them invented what seemed to him a brilliant idea, and he told all the others that Mowgli would be a useful person to keep in the tribe, because he could **weave**① sticks together for protection from the wind; so, if they caught him, they could make him teach them. Of course Mowgli, as a **woodcutter's**② child, inherited all sorts of **instincts**③, and used to make little huts of fallen branches without thinking how he came to do it. The Monkey-People, watching in the trees, considered his play most wonderful. This time, they said, they were really going to have a leader and become the wisest people in the jungle—so wise that everyone else would notice and **envy**④ them. Therefore they followed Baloo and Bagheera and Mowgli through the jungle very quietly till it was time for the midday nap, and Mowgli, who was very much ashamed of himself, slept between the Panther and the Bear, resolving to have no more to do with the Monkey People.

The next thing he remembered was feeling hands on his legs and arms— hard, strong, little hands—and then a swash of branches in his face, and then he was staring down through the swaying **boughs**⑤ as Baloo woke the jungle with his deep cries and Bagheera bounded up the trunk with every tooth bared. The Bandar-log howled with triumph and scuffled away to the upper branches where Bagheera dared not follow, shouting: "He has noticed us! Bagheera has noticed us. All the Jungle-People admire us for our skill and our cunning." Then they began their flight; and the flight of the Monkey-People through tree-land is one of the things nobody can describe. They have their regular roads and crossroads, up hills and down hills, all laid out from fifty to seventy or a hundred feet above ground, and by these they can travel even at night if necessary. Two of the strongest monkeys caught Mowgli under the arms and swung off with him

① weave [wi:v] v. 织

② woodcutter ['wud,kʌtə]
n.［美国英语］伐木者，
樵夫

③ instinct ['instiŋkt] n. 本
能

④ envy ['envi] v. 妒忌

⑤ bough [bau] n.【植物学】
树枝（尤指主枝）

然没有什么野兽能抓得住他们，但是也没有什么野兽愿意理睬他们，所以当毛格利找他们玩时，他们才那么兴高采烈，他们也听见巴鲁后来多么生气了。

其实他们本来也没打算再做什么——邦达－罗格从来就没打算过什么。但是他们当中有一个出了个自以为高明的主意，他跟其他猴子说毛格利待在猴族里可能会派上用场，因为他会把树枝编在一起挡风。如果他们抓住了他，就可以让毛格利教他们。当然了，毛格利作为樵夫的后代，继承了各种各样的本能，他曾经用枯枝搭了些小棚子，虽然他也不明白自己怎么就会干那个的。而在林间观察他的猴民呢，觉得他的把戏简直太棒了。猴民说这回他们真的是要有一个头领了，而且从此以后要成为丛林里最聪明的族群，聪明到所有人都会注意甚至嫉妒他们。因此他们悄悄地跟踪巴鲁、巴格伊尔拉和毛格利穿过丛林，直到这三个停下来睡午觉。毛格利睡在黑豹和棕熊中间，他心里非常羞愧，所以下定决心再也不跟猴民有任何来往。

接下来他能记得的就是有好多手——结实的、有力的小手——落在他的腿上、胳膊上，然后是树枝打在脸上，再然后就是他从摇晃的树枝间往下望，那时巴鲁正在发出低沉的呼喊，把整个丛林都给惊醒了，而巴格伊尔拉则露出每一颗獠牙，纵身跃上树干。邦达－罗格发出胜利的呼啸，互相扭打着逃到更高的树枝上，看到巴格伊尔拉再也不敢追上来，他们叫道："他终于注意到我们了！巴格伊尔拉注意到我们了。所有的丛林族民都羡慕我们的技巧和机智。"接下来他们开始飞跃，谁也无法描述出来猴民是怎样在树间飞跃的。他们有惯走的道路和岔道，沿着山脉起起伏伏，全在距离地面五十到七十甚或一百英尺高的地方。如有必要，他们甚至在夜间也能穿行如梭。两只最强壮的猴子抓着毛格利的胳膊，带着他从一个树梢荡到另一个树梢，一蹿就是二十英尺远。要是没带人的话，他们能有现在的两倍那么快；但

through the treetops, twenty feet at a **bound**①. Had they been alone they could
have gone twice as fast, but the boy's weight held them back. Sick and **giddy**②
as Mowgli was he could not help enjoying the wild rush, though the glimpses
of earth far down below frightened him, and the terrible check and **jerk**③ at the
end of the swing over nothing but empty air brought his heart between his teeth.
His escort would rush him up a tree till he felt the thinnest topmost branches
crackle and bend under them, and then with a cough and a **whoop**④ would fling
themselves into the air outward and downward, and bring up, hanging by their
hands or their feet to the lower **limbs**⑤ of the next tree. Sometimes he could see
for miles and miles across the still green jungle, as a man on the top of a **mast**⑥
can see for miles across the sea, and then the branches and leaves would **lash**⑦
him across the face, and he and his two guards would be almost down to earth
again. So, bounding and crashing and whooping and **yelling**⑧, the whole tribe of
Bandar-log swept along the tree-roads with Mowgli their prisoner.

For a time he was afraid of being dropped. Then he grew angry but knew
better than to struggle, and then he began to think. The first thing was to send back
word to Baloo and Bagheera, for, at the pace the monkeys were going, he knew
his friends would be left far behind. It was useless to look down, for he could
only see the topsides of the branches, so he stared upward and saw, far away in
the blue, Rann the Kite balancing and wheeling as he kept watch over the jungle
waiting for things to die. Rann saw that the monkeys were carrying something,
and dropped a few hundred yards to find out whether their load was good to eat.
He whistled with surprise when he saw Mowgli being dragged up to a treetop and
heard him give the Kite call for—"We be of one blood, thou and I." The waves
of the branches closed over the boy, but Rann balanced away to the next tree in
time to see the little brown face come up again. "Mark my trail!" Mowgli shouted.
"Tell Baloo of the Seeonee Pack and Bagheera of the Council Rock."

"In whose name, Brother?" Rann had never seen Mowgli before, though of
course he had heard of him.

"Mowgli, the Frog. Man-cub they call me! Mark my trail!"

① bound [baund] *n.* 跳动，跳跃

② giddy ['gidi] *a.* 头晕的，眩晕的

③ jerk [dʒəːk] *n.* 急促而猛烈的动作

④ whoop [huːp] *n.* 狂叫声

⑤ limb [lim] *n.* 【植物学】大（树）枝

⑥ mast [mɑːst] *n.* 柱，杆

⑦ lash [læʃ] *v.* 鞭打，抽打

⑧ yell [jel] *v.* 呼喊，叫喊

是男孩的体重把他们拖慢了。虽然又是恶心又是头晕，毛格利还是禁不住喜欢这么狂野的跑法，尽管从这么高的地方看下去让他胆战心惊，而且每次在一片虚空中荡出去又突然停下来再往前猛冲，让他的心都吊到嗓子眼了。他的护卫们会带着他一路冲到树顶上，直到那些最细的枝丫被他们的身子压弯了，噼啪作响，然后发出喀喀的吼叫和高呼声，嗖地一下往外、往下荡到空中，接着又用手或脚攀住下一棵树上低一些的树枝把自己给扯上去。有时候他能看见绵延几英里的碧绿丛林，就好像一个人坐在桅杆顶端能够看见广阔的海面。紧接着树枝和叶片会从他脸上横扫过去，他和他的两个护卫又会险些擦到地面。就这样，一路跳着、冲着、荡着、喊着，邦达－罗格的整个族群胁持着他们的囚犯毛格利沿着"树道"呼啸而去。

有那么一会儿，他害怕自己会被扔下去。然后他生起气来，可是也知道最好不要挣扎，再后来他开始思考。他要做的头一桩事就是给巴鲁和巴格伊尔拉送信，因为照猴子们的速度来看，他的朋友们肯定已经被落在后面很远了。往下张望是没有用的，他只能看见树顶。所以他往上看去，只见在高高的碧空中，鸢鹰兰恩来回盘旋，观察丛林里有什么快死的动物。兰恩看见猴子们带着一样东西在跑，就往下降了几百码好看看他们是不是带了什么好吃的玩意儿。当他看见毛格利被拖上一棵树顶时，他惊讶地吹了一声口哨，接着就听见毛格利喊出了鸢鹰的口诀："你和我，我们拥有共同的血缘。"男孩被树枝的波浪给淹没了，但是兰恩稳住身子及时赶到下一棵树的上空，看到他那小小的棕色脸蛋又了冒出来。毛格利大喊道："记住我的踪迹！去告诉西翁尼狼族的巴鲁和议会岩的巴格伊尔拉。"

"是谁托我带话儿啊，兄弟？"兰恩以前从没见过毛格利，尽管他当然听说过他。

"毛格利，青蛙毛格利。他们也管我叫人崽！记住

The last words were shrieked as he was being swung through the air, but Rann nodded and rose up till he looked no bigger than a speck of dust, and there he hung, watching with his telescope eyes the swaying of the treetops as Mowgli's **escort**① whirled along.

"They never go far," he said with a chuckle. "They never do what they set out to do. Always **pecking at**② new things are the Bandar-log. This time, if I have any eye-sight, they have pecked down trouble for themselves, for Baloo is no fledgling and Bagheera can, as I know, kill more than goats."

So he rocked on his wings, his feet gathered up under him, and waited. ·

Meantime, Baloo and Bagheera were furious with rage and grief. Bagheera climbed as he had never climbed before, but the thin branches broke beneath his weight, and he slipped down, his claws full of **bark**③.

"Why didst thou not warn the man-cub?" he roared to poor Baloo, who had set off at a clumsy trot in the hope of overtaking the monkeys. "What was the use of half **slaying**④ him with blows if thou didst not warn him?"

"Haste! O haste! We—we may catch them yet!" Baloo panted.

"At that speed! It would not tire a wounded cow. Teacher of the Law—cub-beater—a mile of that rolling to and fro would burst thee open. Sit still and think! Make a plan. This is no time for chasing. They may drop him if we follow too close."

"Arrula! Whoo! They may have dropped him already, being tired of carrying him. Who can trust the Bandar-log? Put dead bats on my head! Give me black bones to eat! Roll me into the hives of the wild bees that I may be stung to death, and bury me with the Hyaena, for I am most miserable of bears! Arulala! Wahooa! O Mowgli, Mowgli! Why did I not warn thee against the Monkey-Folk instead of breaking thy head? Now perhaps I may have knocked the day's lesson out of his mind, and he will be alone in the jungle without the Master Words."

Baloo clasped his paws over his ears and rolled to and fro **moaning**⑤.

我的踪——迹！"

最后几个字是他尖叫着喊出来的，因为他被甩到了空中。兰恩点了点头，往高处飞去，直到变得跟一颗微尘差不多小。他悬在那儿，用望远镜一般的双眼观察随着毛格利的护卫们席卷而过不断晃动的树梢。

他轻笑着说道："他们从来都走不远。他们从来都半途而废。邦达－罗格总是贪图新鲜。我要是还有点眼力的话，我敢说他们这回给自己找了个大麻烦，因为巴鲁可不是什么小毛头，巴格伊尔拉呢，据我所知，杀的可不止山羊啊。"

他拍打着翅膀，蜷起双脚，耐心地等待着。

同一时间，巴鲁和巴格伊尔拉满腔怒火，悲痛不已。巴格伊尔拉爬到从没到过的高度，但是他的体重把细枝给压断了，他滑了下来，满爪都是树皮。

他对可怜的巴鲁咆哮："你为什么不警告人崽？你不警告他，光是把他打个半死有什么用？"巴鲁笨拙地小跑着想要赶上猴子们，他上气不接下气地说："快点！快点！我们——我们也许还能赶上他们！"

"就你那速度！就是受伤的母牛都能跑得再快点。法则大师——打幼崽的家伙——再像那样滚来滚去地跑个一英里你就该爆炸了。坐下来好好想想！拿个方案出来。现在不是一味傻追的时候。要是我们跟得太紧了，他们可能会把他扔下来的。"

"啊呜啦！呼——！他们有可能觉得带着他太累，已经把他丢下了。谁能信任邦达－罗格呀？还不如把死蝙蝠放在我头上呢！或者给我啃发黑的骨头！要不就把我赶进野蜂窝里让我被蜇死，再把我跟土狼埋一块儿得了，我算是顶顶倒霉的熊了。啊呜啦啦！噢呼啊！哦，毛格利，毛格利！我干吗不警告你小心猴民呀，反倒打破你的头？他被我揍得可能都忘掉今天学了些啥了，孤零零地一个人在丛林里却没有密语可以保护他。"

巴鲁用爪子捂住耳朵，滚来滚去地呻吟着。

"At least he gave me all the Words correctly a little time ago," said Bagheera impatiently. "Baloo, thou hast neither memory nor respect. What would the jungle think if I, the Black Panther, curled myself up like Ikki the Porcupine, and howled?"

"What do I care what the jungle thinks? He may be dead by now."

"Unless and until they drop him from the branches in sport, or kill him out of **idleness**①, I have no fear for the man-cub. He is wise and well taught, and above all he has the eyes that make the Jungle-People afraid. But (and it is a great evil) he is in the power of the Bandar-log, and they, because they live in trees, have no fear of any of our people." Bagheera licked one forepaw **thoughtfully**②.

"Fool that I am! Oh, fat, brown, root-digging fool that I am," said Baloo, **uncoiling**③ himself with a jerk, "it is true what Hathi the Wild Elephant says: 'To each his own fear'; and they, the Bandar-log, fear Kaa the Rock Snake. He can climb as well as they can. He steals the young monkeys in the night. The whisper of his name makes their **wicked**④ tails cold. Let us go to Kaa."

"What will he do for us? He is not of our tribe, being footless—and with most evil eyes," said Bagheera.

"He is very old and very cunning. Above all, he is always hungry," said Baloo hopefully. "Promise him many goats."

"He sleeps for a full month after he has once eaten. He may be asleep now, and even were he awake what if he would rather kill his own goats?" Bagheera, who did not know much about Kaa, was naturally **suspicious**⑤.

"Then in that case, thou and I together, old hunter, might make him see reason." Here Baloo **rubbed** his faded brown shoulder **against**⑥ the Panther, and they went off to look for Kaa the Rock Python.

They found him stretched out on a warm ledge in the afternoon sun, admiring his beautiful new coat, for he had been in retirement for the last ten days changing his skin, and now he was very splendid—darting his big blunt-nosed head along the ground, and twisting the thirty feet of his body into

巴格伊尔拉不耐烦地说："好歹刚才他还给我把那些口诀都正确地背出来了嘛。巴鲁，你不长记性也不懂得自重。要是我黑豹也像豪猪伊吉那样缩成一团发出惨叫，丛林里的动物会怎么想呢？"

"我管丛林里的动物怎么想呢？他现在可能都死了。"

"除非他们闹着玩儿把他从树上扔下来，或者出于无聊把他给弄死了，要不然我一点都不担心人嘛。他人聪明，学得又好，而且关键的是他有一双能让丛林动物恐惧的眼睛。但是（很糟糕的是）眼下他在邦达－罗格的手里，他们因为住在树上所以丝毫不惧怕我们这些族群。"巴格伊尔拉满怀心事地舔着一只前爪。

巴鲁说："哎呀，我真是个傻瓜呀！哦，我这个大黑胖子，挖草根吃的傻子哟。"他突然一下直起身来说："野象哈提说得没错，'一物降一物'。邦达－罗格他们害怕岩蟒卡，因为卡能像他们一样攀爬，还会在夜里偷走小猴子。光是提起卡的名字就足以吓得他们脊梁骨发寒。咱们去找卡吧。"

巴格伊尔拉说："可是他能为我们做什么呢？他又不是我们这一族的，他没有脚，却有着顶顶邪恶的眼睛。"

巴鲁满怀信心地说："他的确老奸巨滑。但是，最重要的是，他总是很饿。咱们可以许诺给他很多山羊。"

巴格伊尔拉不太了解卡，自然有点怀疑。"他一吃饱就会睡上整整一个月。他现在可能就正睡着呢。就算他醒了，要是他宁愿自己捕杀山羊，那又怎么办呢？"

"要是那样的话，你，老猎手，就和我一起跟他讲讲道理呗。"巴鲁用他那褪色的棕色肩膀蹭蹭黑豹，他们就一起出发去找岩蟒卡了。

他们找到卡时，他正躺在一处温暖的山脊上享受午后的阳光，一边欣赏自己漂亮的新衣——那是他十天来刚刚换好的新皮——现在他看上去真是容光焕发。他沿

① idleness ['aidlnəs] *n.* 懒惰

② thoughtfully ['θɔtfəli] *ad.* 沉思地

③ uncoil [ˌʌn'kɔil] *v.* 展开

④ wicked ['wikid] *a.* 令人讨厌的

⑤ suspicious [sə'spiʃəs] *a.* 表示怀疑的

⑥ rub against 与……相摩擦

fantastic knots and curves, and licking his lips as he thought of his dinner to come.

"He has not eaten," said Baloo, with a grunt of relief, as soon as he saw the beautifully **mottled**① brown and yellow jacket. "Be careful, Bagheera! He is always a little blind after he has changed his skin, and very quick to **strike**②."

Kaa was not a poison snake—in fact he rather despised the poison snakes as cowards—but his strength lay in his **hug**③, and when he had once lapped his huge **coils**④ round anybody there was no more to be said. "Good hunting!" cried Baloo, sitting up on his haunches. Like all snakes of his **breed**⑤ Kaa was rather deaf, and did not hear the call at first. Then he curled up ready for any accident, his head lowered.

"Good hunting for us all," he answered. "Oho, Baloo, what dost thou do here? Good hunting, Bagheera. One of us at least needs food. Is there any news of game **afoot**⑥? A **doe**⑦ now, or even a young buck? I am as empty as a dried well."

"We are hunting," said Baloo carelessly. He knew that you must not hurry Kaa. He is too big.

"Give me permission to come with you," said Kaa. "A blow more or less is nothing to thee, Bagheera or Baloo, but I—I have to wait and wait for days in a wood-path and climb half a night on the mere chance of a young ape. Psshaw! The branches are not what they were when I was young. Rotten twigs and dry boughs are they all."

"Maybe thy great weight has something to do with the matter," said Baloo.

"I am a fair length—a fair length," said Kaa with a little pride. "But for all that, it is the fault of this new-grown **timber**⑧. I came very near to falling on my last hunt—very near indeed—and the noise of my slipping, for my tail was not tight wrapped around the tree, waked the Bandar-log, and they called me most evil names."

着地面上下点头，那足足有三十英尺长的身体扭成各种令人惊奇的角度，打着结，一边还舔着嘴唇，琢磨着接下来该吃些什么。

一看见岩蟒那镶嵌着棕黄斑点的美丽外衣，巴鲁就松了一口气，嘟囔着说："他还没吃呢。小心点，巴格伊尔拉！他每次刚换完皮都看不太清东西，而且出手很快。"

① mottled ['mɔtld] *a.* 有花纹的

② strike [straik] *v.* 击，打，敲击

③ hug [hʌg] *n.* 紧抱

④ coil [kɔil] *n.*（绳等的）卷，盘

⑤ breed [bri:d] *n.* 种类，类别，类型

卡不是毒蛇，实际上他很看不起那些毒蛇，觉得他们都是些胆小鬼。他的厉害之处在于他那有力的"拥抱"，一旦被他庞大的身躯缠上了，就没什么好说的了。巴鲁坐起来，对他喊道："祝你打猎顺利！"就像其他的岩蟒一样，卡的听力不好，所以一开始他并没有听见巴鲁的叫声，后来他蜷起身子以备不测，然后低下头来，回答说："愿我们大家都打猎顺利。哦呵，巴鲁，什么风把你给吹来了？祝你打猎顺利，巴格伊尔拉。咱们当中至少有个人饿了。你们知道哪儿有猎物在活动吗？一头母鹿，或者甚至一头年轻的公鹿？我的肚子现在就跟枯井一样空空如也"。

⑥ afoot [ə'fut] *ad.* 在进行中

⑦ doe [dəu] *n.*【动物】雌鹿

巴鲁假装漫不经心地说道："我们正在打猎呢。"他知道对待卡可不能心急，岩蟒的个头太大了。

卡说："那请允许我跟你们一起吧。对你们，巴格伊尔拉或者巴鲁来说，多打一点少打一点算不了什么，可是我——我得在林间小道上等上好几天，再爬半个晚上才可能逮到一只小猿猴。呸，现在的树枝也跟我年轻时那会儿不一样，小的嘛都烂了，大点的呢也都是干枯的。"

巴鲁说："也许这跟您现在可观的体重有点儿关系。"

⑧ timber ['timbə] *n.* 森林

卡稍稍带点骄傲地说道："我的体长很标准，正正好。但是说来说去，主要还是怪这些新长出来的树不好。我上次捕猎就差点儿摔下来了——就差那么一点点——而且当时因为我的尾巴没有牢牢地缠在树上，所以我滑下去的响声把邦达－罗格都惊醒了，他们把我骂了个狗血淋头。"

"Footless, yellow earth-worm," said Bagheera under his whiskers, as though he were trying to remember something.

"Sssss! Have they ever called me that?" said Kaa.

"Something of that kind it was that they shouted to us last moon, but we never noticed them. They will say anything—even that thou hast lost all thy teeth, and wilt not face anything bigger than a kid, because (they are indeed shameless, these Bandar-log)—because thou art afraid of the he-goat's horns," Bagheera went on sweetly.

Now a snake, especially a **wary**① old **python**② like Kaa, very seldom shows that he is angry, but Baloo and Bagheera could see the big swallowing muscles on either side of Kaa's throat ripple and **bulge**③.

"The Bandar-log have shifted their grounds," he said quietly. "When I came up into the sun today I heard them whooping among the tree-tops."

"It—it is the Bandar-log that we follow now," said Baloo, but the words stuck in his throat, for that was the first time in his memory that one of the Jungle-People had owned to being interested in the doings of the monkeys.

"Beyond doubt then it is no small thing that takes two such hunters—leaders in their own jungle I am certain—on the trail of the Bandar-log," Kaa replied **courteously**④, as he **swelled**⑤ with curiosity.

"Indeed," Baloo began, "I am no more than the old and sometimes very foolish Teacher of the Law to the Seeonee wolf-cubs, and Bagheera here—"

"Is Bagheera," said the Black Panther, and his jaws shut with a snap, for he did not believe in being humble. "The trouble is this, Kaa. Those nut-stealers and pickers of palm leaves have stolen away our man-cub of whom thou hast perhaps heard."

"I heard some news from Ikki (his **quills**⑥ make him **presumptuous**⑦) of a man-thing that was entered into a wolf pack, but I did not believe. Ikki is full of stories half heard and very badly told."

"But it is true. He is such a man-cub as never was," said Baloo. "The best and wisest and boldest of man-cubs—my own pupil, who shall make

巴格伊尔拉好像想起了什么，从胡须底下冒出来几个词："没脚的黄蚯蚓。"

"嘶！他们是这么骂我的吗？"卡问道。

巴格伊尔拉温柔地接着说："跟这差不多吧，上个月他们还朝我们俩乱嚷嚷来着，但是我们没搭理他们。他们可是什么都说得出口——好比说你牙齿都掉光了，或者你不敢面对任何比小孩儿大点儿的对手，因为（这些邦达-罗格真的是恬不知耻）——因为你害怕公羊的角。"

本来呢，一条蛇，尤其是像卡这样机警的老蟒蛇，是极少流露出怒火的，但是巴鲁和巴格伊尔拉都看见卡的咽喉两边巨大的吞咽肌波动着又鼓起来。

卡轻轻地说："邦达-罗格刚搬了家。今早我起来的时候，听见他们在树梢大声叫唤呢。"

"那就是——就是我们正在追的一群邦达-罗格。"巴鲁说，但是这句话就好像卡在他喉咙里一样，因为在他记忆里这还是第一次有丛林动物承认自己关注了猴子的举动。

"毫无疑问，能够让您二位如此伟大的猎手、丛林的领袖来追踪邦达-罗格的肯定不是什么小事。"卡礼貌地回答道，好奇得不得了。

巴鲁开始说："实际上，我不过是个有时脑子进了水的老头子，只配给西翁尼的狼崽子们教教丛林法则，而巴格伊尔拉呢——"

"就是巴格伊尔拉。"黑豹一声断喝，因为他才不相信谦逊是美德。"事情是这样的，卡。那些偷坚果、捡棕叶的家伙们偷走了我们的人崽，你也许听说过他。"

"我从伊吉——他那身尖刺让他有点太自我膨胀了——那儿听说有个人类的小孩儿被狼群给接纳了，当时我还不相信呢。伊吉满肚子都是些道听途说、瞎扯八道的故事。"

巴鲁说："可这是真的呀，从来没有像他那样聪明的人娃娃呢。他可是所有人崽儿当中最优秀、最聪明也

① wary ['wɛəri] *a.* 谨慎的，小心的

② python ['paiθən] *n.* 大蟒，巨蛇

③ bulge [bʌldʒ] *n.* 膨胀，肿胀

④ courteously ['kəːtiəsli] *ad.* 有礼貌地

⑤ swell [swel] *v.* 使情绪高涨

⑥ quill [kwil] *n.*（豪猪、刺猬等的）刚毛

⑦ presumptuous [pri'zʌmptjuəs] *a.* 自以为是的

the name of Baloo famous through all the jungles; and besides, I—we—love him, Kaa."

"Ts! Ts!" said Kaa, weaving his head to and fro. "I also have known what love is. There are tales I could tell that—"

"That need a clear night when we are all well fed to praise properly," said Bagheera quickly. "Our man-cub is in the hands of the Bandar-log now, and we know that of all the Jungle-People they fear Kaa alone."

"They fear me alone. They have good reason," said Kaa. "Chattering, foolish, **vain**①—vain, foolish, and chattering, are the monkeys. But a man-thing in their hands is in no good luck. They grow tired of the nuts they pick, and throw them down. They carry a branch half a day, meaning to do great things with it, and then they snap it in two. That man-thing is not to be envied. They called me also—'yellow fish' was it not?"

"Worm—worm—earth-worm," said Bagheera, "as well as other things which I cannot now say for shame."

"We must remind them to speak well of their master. Aaa-ssp! We must help their **wandering**② memories. Now, whither went they with the cub?"

"The jungle alone knows. Toward the sunset, I believe," said Baloo. "We had thought that thou wouldst know, Kaa."

"I? How? I take them when they come in my way, but I do not hunt the Bandar-log, or frogs—or green **scum**③ on a water-hole, for that matter."

"Up, Up! Up, Up! Hillo! Illo! Illo, look up, Baloo of the Seeonee Wolf Pack!"

Baloo looked up to see where the voice came from, and there was Rann the Kite, sweeping down with the sun shining on the upturned **flanges**④ of his wings. It was near Rann's bedtime, but he had ranged all over the jungle looking for the Bear and had missed him in the thick **foliage**⑤.

"What is it?" said Baloo.

最勇敢的，又是我的学生，将来准能让我巴鲁的名字响遍丛林；而且，我——我们——都爱他，卡。"

卡把头摇来摆去，一边说道："呲！呲！我也知道什么是爱。我也有好些故事——"

巴格伊尔拉赶紧说："可以等到一个天气好的晚上，等咱们都吃饱喝足了，再来好好捧个场。现在我们的人娃娃落在猴族的手里了，我们还知道在所有丛林动物中只有卡让他们害怕。"

① vain [vein] *a.* 自负的

卡说："他们是只怕我，那是理所当然的。这些猴子，嘴碎、愚蠢、虚荣——虚荣、愚蠢、嘴碎。但是一个人类落在他们手里可是要遭殃的。他们自己摘的坚果一不想吃了就会扔下来。他们可以扛着根树枝扛上半天，本来是想拿它干点什么大事，但是最后却把它咔嚓掰断了。那个人娃娃在他们那儿可讨不了好去。他们还管我叫什么'黄鱼'来着，是吗？"

巴格伊尔拉说："黄虫——虫——蚯蚓，还有些别的话，我都不好意思说。"

② wandering ['wɔndəriŋ] *a.*（精神）恍惚的

"那我们得提醒一下他们不应该说主人的坏话。啊嘶！我们必须帮他们长点记性。他们带着人崽往哪个方向去了？"

巴鲁说："只有丛林才知道。不过我相信是朝日落的方向去了。我们原以为你会知道呢，卡。"

③ scum [skʌm] *n.*（死水潭或污染水源中的）浮藻

"我？怎么会呢？我只在他们靠近的时候才抓他们来吃，我可不会去追那些猴子，或者青蛙——或者水坑上漂的绿渣滓，它们对我来说都差不多。"

"往上，往上！往上，往上！哈罗！嗨！嗨，往上看啊，西翁尼狼族的巴鲁！"

④ flange [flændʒ] *n.* 边缘

巴鲁抬头寻找那个声音的来处，看见了鸢鹰兰恩正往下快速掠过，阳光在他翘起的翅尖闪烁。现在快到兰恩回巢的时间了，但是他一直在整个丛林上空来回寻找棕熊，可惜棕熊被茂密的枝叶挡住了。

⑤ foliage ['fəuliidʒ] *n.*（一株植物或树的）全部叶子

巴鲁说："怎么了？"

"I have seen Mowgli among the Bandar-log. He bade me tell you. I watched. The Bandar-log have taken him beyond the river to the monkey city—to the Cold Lairs. They may stay there for a night, or ten nights, or an hour. I have told the bats to watch through the dark time. That is my message. Good hunting, all you below!"

"Full gorge and a deep sleep to you, Rann," cried Bagheera. "I will remember thee in my next kill, and put aside the head for thee alone, O best of kites!"

"It is nothing. It is nothing. The boy held the Master Word. I could have done no less," and Rann circled up again to his roost.

"He has not forgotten to use his tongue," said Baloo with a chuckle of pride. "To think of one so young remembering the Master Word for the birds too while he was being pulled across trees!"

"It was most firmly driven into him," said Bagheera. "But I am proud of him, and now we must go to the Cold Lairs."

They all knew where that place was, but few of the Jungle People ever went there, because what they called the Cold Lairs was an old deserted city, lost and buried in the jungle, and beasts seldom use a place that men have once used. The wild **boar**① will, but the hunting tribes do not. Besides, the monkeys lived there as much as they could be said to live anywhere, and no self-respecting animal would come within **eyeshot**② of it except in times of drought, when the half-ruined tanks and **reservoirs**③ held a little water.

"It is half a night's journey—at full speed," said Bagheera, and Baloo looked very serious. "I will go as fast as I can," he said anxiously.

"We dare not wait for thee. Follow, Baloo. We must go on the quick-foot—Kaa and I."

"Feet or no feet, I can keep **abreast**④ of all thy four," said Kaa shortly. Baloo made one effort to hurry, but had to sit down panting, and so they left him to come on later, while Bagheera hurried forward, at the quick panther-

"我看到毛格利了，他在猴族那。他让我通知你。我看见了，猴族把他带到河对面的猴城——冷巢去了。他们也许会在那儿待一个晚上，或者十个晚上，或者一个钟头。我已经跟蝙蝠说好了让他们夜里好好盯着。这就是我要带的话。下面所有人，祝你们狩猎愉快！"

巴格伊尔拉叫道："愿你吃得饱，睡得好，兰恩。我会在下次狩猎时记得单独给你留个猎物的头，你是最棒的鸢鹰！"

"这不算什么，真不算什么。那个孩子的丛林密语说得真好。我只是做了我应该做的。"兰恩再次盘旋上升准备回巢了。

巴鲁骄傲地笑着说道："他没有忘记用他的舌头。想想看这么小的孩子就能记住鸟类的密语，而且还是在被拖着穿过树林的时候。"

巴格伊尔拉说："那都是因为你对他严加管教。不过我也为他感到骄傲，现在咱们必须赶到冷巢去。"

他们都知道冷巢在哪儿，但是丛林动物几乎从不踏足于此。这个被他们叫作冷巢的地方是一个老旧、废弃的人类城市，尽管早就湮没在丛林中，然而野兽们很少会使用人类曾经居住过的地方。野猪会去，但是游猎的族群从不去。除了野猪，只有猴群常常到此一游，反正他们也是四海为家、散漫惯了的。其他自尊自重的动物根本连靠都不会靠近一步，除非是在旱季，因为那里破损的水槽和蓄水池还会残留些许水源。

巴格伊尔拉说："到那儿去需要半个晚上的时间，前提是我们必须全速前进。"巴鲁神色非常沉重，他紧张地回答道："我会尽快的。"

"我们可不敢停下来等你。你跟在后面吧，巴鲁。我和卡必须撒开丫子跑了。"

卡没好气地说："有没有脚，我都能追上你那四条腿。"巴鲁尝试着快跑了一阵，可是最终不得不坐下来喘气，他们只好先走一步，让巴鲁慢慢赶上来。巴格伊

① boar [bɔː] n.【动物】成年公猪

② eyeshot ['aiʃɔt] n. 视野，视界

③ reservoir ['rezəvwɑː] n. 蓄水池

④ abreast [ə'brest] a. 与……齐头并列

canter. Kaa said nothing, but, strive as Bagheera might, the huge Rock-python held level with him. When they came to a hill stream, Bagheera gained, because he bounded across while Kaa swam, his head and two feet of his neck clearing the water, but on level ground Kaa made up the distance.

"By the Broken Lock that freed me," said Bagheera, when twilight had fallen, "thou art no slow goer!"

"I am hungry," said Kaa. "Besides, they called me **speckled**① frog."

"Worm — earth-worm, and yellow to boot."

"All one. Let us go on," and Kaa seemed to pour himself along the ground, finding the shortest road with his steady eyes, and keeping to it.

In the Cold Lairs the Monkey-People were not thinking of Mowgli's friends at all. They had brought the boy to the Lost City, and were very much pleased with themselves for the time. Mowgli had never seen an Indian city before, and though this was almost a **heap**② of ruins it seemed very wonderful and splendid. Some king had built it long ago on a little hill. You could still trace the stone **causeways**③ that led up to the ruined gates where the last **splinters**④ of wood hung to the worn, rusted **hinges**⑤. Trees had grown into and out of the walls; the **battlements**⑥ were tumbled down and decayed, and wild creepers hung out of the windows of the towers on the walls in bushy hanging clumps.

A great roofless palace crowned the hill, and the marble of the courtyards and the fountains was split, and stained with red and green, and the very cobblestones in the courtyard where the king's elephants used to live had been thrust up and apart by grasses and young trees. From the palace you could see the rows and rows of roofless houses that made up the city looking like empty honeycombs filled with blackness; the shapeless block of stone that had been an idol in the square where four roads met; the pits and **dimples**⑦ at street corners where the public wells once stood, and the shattered domes of temples with wild figs sprouting on their sides. The monkeys called the place their city, and pretended to despise the Jungle-People because they lived in the forest. And yet they never knew what the buildings were made for nor how to use them. They

尔拉小跑着往前赶，卡虽然什么也没说，但是不管黑豹跑得多快，巨大的岩蟒也始终没有落下半步。当他们经过一条溪涧时，巴格伊尔拉终于占了先，因为他只需纵身一跃就跳过了小溪，而卡还得游过去，用自己的头和两英尺长的颈部去破开水面。但是一到了平地上卡就赶上来了。

夜幕落下时，巴格伊尔拉说："凭那把解放了我的破锁起誓，你可真是一点也不慢啊！"

卡回答道："我饿了。再说他们不是管我叫斑点蛙吗？"

"虫——蚯蚓，而且是黄色的。"

"都差不多。走吧。"卡如流水一般贴地而行，用他那双目光坚毅的双眼找到捷径，然后沿着这条路走下去，毫不偏离。

此时在冷巢里的猴民丝毫没有想到毛格利的朋友们会来。他们把小男孩带到这个失落城，眼下正得意扬扬地举行庆祝呢。毛格利从来没见过印度城市，所以，虽然现在这里已是一堆废墟，但在他看来依然非常壮观宏伟。很久以前有个国王在一个小山丘上建造了这座城市。如今你依然可以看到巨石堆砌的坡道一直通向残破的大门，老旧、生锈的合页上还残留着一些木头碎片。树木已经伸出了城墙，城垛都已坍塌毁坏，茂密的野藤从城楼的窗户中垂吊下来，蔓生开去。

山顶上矗立着一座宏伟的无顶宫殿。庭院和喷泉里的大理石都已开裂，染上了斑斑驳驳的红色和绿色，国王的象群以前就住在铺满鹅卵石的庭院，这里的地面也被野草和树苗顶开、掀翻了。从宫殿望出去，你能看到城里一排排的无顶房屋，好像黑洞洞的蜂巢；连接四条道路的广场上仁立着曾经的神像，如今已经面目全非；街角的公共水井现在也已经变成坑洞和水洼；寺庙的穹顶早已坍塌，两边长出了野生的无花果树。猴民管这片地方叫他们的城市，并且声称他们看不起丛林动物，因为丛林动物住在密林里。但是猴子

① speckled ['spekld] a. 有斑点的

② heap [hiːp] n. 堆，堆积

③ causeway ['kɔːzwei] n. （穿过洼地的）堤道

④ splinter ['splintə] n. （木、石、骨等的）碎片

⑤ hinge [hindʒ] n. 铰链

⑥ battlement ['bætlmənt] n. 城垛

⑦ dimple ['dimpl] n. （任何类似的）浅凹，小凹

would sit in circles on the hall of the king's council chamber, and scratch for fleas and pretend to be men; or they would run in and out of the roofless houses and collect pieces of plaster and old bricks in a corner, and forget where they had hidden them, and fight and cry in scuffling crowds, and then break off to play up and down the **terraces**① of the king's garden, where they would shake the rose trees and the oranges in sport to see the fruit and flowers fall. They explored all the passages and dark tunnels in the palace and the hundreds of little dark rooms, but they never remembered what they had seen and what they had not; and so drifted about in ones and twos or crowds telling each other that they were doing as men did. They drank at the tanks and made the water all muddy, and then they fought over it, and then they would all rush together in **mobs**② and shout: "There is no one in the jungle so wise and good and clever and strong and gentle as the Bandar-log." Then all would begin again till they grew tired of the city and went back to the tree-tops, hoping the Jungle-People would notice them.

Mowgli, who had been trained under the Law of the Jungle, did not like or understand this kind of life. The monkeys dragged him into the Cold Lairs late in the afternoon, and instead of going to sleep, as Mowgli would have done after a long journey, they joined hands and danced about and sang their foolish songs. One of the monkeys made a speech and told his companions that Mowgli's **capture**③ marked a new thing in the history of the Bandar-log, for Mowgli was going to show them how to weave sticks and **canes**④ together as a protection against rain and cold. Mowgli picked up some creepers and began to work them in and out, and the monkeys tried to imitate; but in a very few minutes they lost interest and began to pull their friends' tails or jump up and down on all fours, **coughing**⑤.

"I wish to eat," said Mowgli. "I am a stranger in this part of the jungle. Bring me food, or give me leave to hunt here."

Twenty or thirty monkeys bounded away to bring him nuts and wild **pawpaws**⑥. But they fell to fighting on the road, and it was too much trouble

① terrace ['terəs] n.（房屋前面的）露台；阳台

从来也不清楚这些建筑都是用来干什么的，该怎么使用。他们只会围成圈坐在王宫的议会厅里，翻找身上的虱子，假装自己是人；或者在没有屋顶的房子里跑进跑出，寻找角落里的灰泥块和旧砖头，虽然那些都是他们自己藏起来然后又忘记了的；又或者成群结队地喧嚷打闹，然后又突然散开跑到国王的花园里，在台阶上上蹿下跳，摇晃玫瑰花树和橘子树，只为了看花果掉下来好玩儿。他们去过王宫里所有的走廊和幽深的隧道以及数百个黑暗的小房间，但是他们从来都记不住自己见过些什么，只是三三两两或者三五成群地晃

② mob [mɔb] n.（牛、马、羊的）群

来晃去，告诉彼此他们的行为和人类一样。他们在水槽边喝水，把水搅得一片浑浊，接着又互相争抢，然后又成群横冲直撞，嘴里嚷嚷着："丛林里谁也没有我们猴民这样智慧、善良、聪明、强壮又温柔。"接下来他们又会重复之前干过的那些把戏，直到玩腻了，再重新回到树顶上去，希望丛林动物会注意到他们。

毛格利接受过丛林法则的训练，因此不喜欢也不理解猴民的这种生活。猴子们把他拽进冷巢时已经快到晚上了。要是毛格利的话，像这样经过一番长途跋涉，肯定会先去睡一觉。然而猴子们却不，他们手拉着手，跳来跳去，还唱着他们那些愚蠢的歌。有只猴子甚至发表了一番讲话，告诉同伴们他们逮住毛格利标志着猴族历史上的一个新事件，因为毛格利将会向他们演示如何将

③ capture ['kæptʃə] n. 捕获，俘获

④ cane [kein] n.【植物学】长而有节的茎

树枝和藤条编织起来遮风挡雨。毛格利捡起一些爬藤，动手编起来，猴子们试着模仿他的动作。但是很快他们就失去了兴趣，开始拉扯同伴的尾巴，或者一边叫唤，一边手脚并用上蹿下跳。

⑤ cough [kɔf] v. 发出嗓音

毛格利说："我想吃东西。我对这片丛林不熟。给我拿些食物来，或者放开我，让我在这儿打猎。"

二三十只猴子蹦蹦跳跳地跑开去给他找坚果和野木瓜。但是他们在路上就打了起来，打完了又觉得要把剩

⑥ pawpaw ['pɔːpɔː] n. 木瓜

to go back with what was left of the fruit. Mowgli was sore and angry as well as hungry, and he roamed through the empty city giving the Strangers' Hunting Call from time to time, but no one answered him, and Mowgli felt that he had reached a very bad place indeed. "All that Baloo has said about the Bandar-log is true," he thought to himself. "They have no Law, no Hunting Call, and no leaders—nothing but foolish words and little picking **thievish**① hands. So if I am starved or killed here, it will be all my own fault. But I must try to return to my own jungle. Baloo will surely beat me, but that is better than chasing silly rose leaves with the Bandar-log."

No sooner had he walked to the city wall than the monkeys pulled him back, telling him that he did not know how happy he was, and **pinching**② him to make him grateful. He set his teeth and said nothing, but went with the shouting monkeys to a terrace above the red sandstone reservoirs that were half-full of rain water. There was a ruined summer-house of white **marble**③ in the center of the terrace, built for queens dead a hundred years ago. The domed roof had half fallen in and blocked up the underground passage from the palace by which the queens used to enter. But the walls were made of screens of marble tracery—beautiful milk-white **fretwork**④, set with **agates**⑤ and **cornelians**⑥ and jasper and lapis lazuli, and as the moon came up behind the hill it shone through the open work, casting shadows on the ground like black velvet embroidery. Sore, sleepy, and hungry as he was, Mowgli could not help laughing when the Bandar-log began, twenty at a time, to tell him how great and wise and strong and gentle they were, and how foolish he was to wish to leave them. "We are great. We are free. We are wonderful. We are the most wonderful people in all the jungle! We all say so, and so it must be true," they shouted. "Now as you are a new listener and can carry our words back to the Jungle-People so that they may notice us in future, we will tell you all about our most excellent selves." Mowgli made no objection, and the monkeys gathered by hundreds and hundreds on the terrace to listen to their own speakers singing the praises of the Bandar-log, and whenever a speaker stopped for want of breath they would all

① thievish ['θiːviʃ] a. 有偷窃习惯的

② pinch [pintʃ] v. 捏

③ marble ['mɑːbl] n. 大理石，大理岩

④ fretwork ['fretwɜːk] n.【建筑工程】回纹细工，万字细工

⑤ agate ['ægət] n. 玛瑙
⑥ cornelian [kɔːˈniːljən] n.【矿物】光玉髓，肉红玉髓

下的果实残渣带回去又太麻烦了。所以毛格利又饿又气，还浑身酸痛。他在空城里游荡，不时发出陌生人的打猎号子，但是没有人应答他。毛格利不由得觉得自己来到了一个糟糕透顶的地方。他心里想着："巴鲁说的关于猴民的话一点没错。他们没有法则，没有打猎号子，也没有首领——只会说傻兮兮的话，干偷偷摸摸的勾当。所以要是我在这儿被饿死了或者弄死了，那都是我自个儿的错。但是我必须想办法回到我自己的丛林里去。巴鲁肯定会揍我一顿，但是那也比跟猴民一起追玫瑰花的叶子强。"

毛格利刚靠近城墙，猴子们就把他拉了回来，跟他说他压根儿不明白自己现在多幸福，然后使劲儿掐他逼他感恩。他咬紧牙关一言不发，只是跟着那些大呼小叫的猴子们登上一个平台，底下红色沙石砌成的水塘里还装着一半儿的雨水。平台的中央有一栋白色大理石的凉亭，是给一百多年前香消玉殒的王后们修建的，现在已经荒废了。凉亭的穹顶有一半塌了，堵住了通向王宫的地下通道，以前王后们就从那里进出。那一扇扇用乳白色大理石做成的花饰窗格雕刻精美绝伦，上面镶嵌着玛瑙、红玉髓、碧玉和青金石。当月亮从山后升起来时，月光从窗格中透过来，投在地上的影子好像黑色的天鹅绒刺绣一般。当二十来只猴子同时跟毛格利吹嘘猴族有多么伟大、聪慧、强壮和温柔，指责他离开他们的举动又是多么愚蠢时，虽然已经又饿又困、浑身酸痛，毛格利还是忍不住笑了起来。猴子们嚷嚷着说："我们是伟大的，我们是自由的。我们可棒了，我们是丛林里最棒的！我们都这么说，所以这肯定是真的。现在你是一个新的听众，你能把我们的话传给丛林族群，好让他们今后能关注我们，所以我们会一五一十地告诉你我们有多么卓越。"毛格利并没有表示拒绝，所以成百上千的猴子开始聚拢到平台上，倾听他们的演说家如何称颂猴族。每当一位发言人停下来喘口气时，他们就会齐声大喊："说

shout together: "This is true; we all say so." Mowgli nodded and blinked, and said "Yes" when they asked him a question, and his head spun with the noise. "Tabaqui the Jackal must have bitten all these people," he said to himself, "and now they have madness. Certainly this is dewanee, the madness. Do they never go to sleep? Now there is a cloud coming to cover that moon. If it were only a big enough cloud I might try to run away in the darkness. But I am tired."

That same cloud was being watched by two good friends in the ruined ditch below the city wall, for Bagheera and Kaa, knowing well how dangerous the Monkey-People were in large numbers, did not wish to run any risks. The monkeys never fight unless they are a hundred to one, and few in the jungle care for those odds.

"I will go to the west wall," Kaa whispered, "and come down swiftly with the slope of the ground in my favor. They will not throw themselves upon my back in their hundreds, but—"

"I know it," said Bagheera. "Would that Baloo were here, but we must do what we can. When that cloud covers the moon I shall go to the terrace. They hold some sort of council there over the boy."

"Good hunting," said Kaa **grimly**[①], and **glided**[②] away to the west wall. That happened to be the least ruined of any, and the big snake was delayed **awhile**[③] before he could find a way up the stones. The cloud hid the moon, and as Mowgli wondered what would come next he heard Bagheera's light feet on the terrace. The Black Panther had raced up the slope almost without a sound and was striking—he knew better than to waste time in biting—right and left among the monkeys, who were seated round Mowgli in circles fifty and sixty deep. There was a howl of **fright**[④] and rage, and then as Bagheera tripped on the rolling kicking bodies beneath him, a monkey shouted: "There is only one here! Kill him! Kill." A **scuffling**[⑤] mass of monkeys, biting, scratching, tearing, and pulling, closed over Bagheera, while five or six laid hold of Mowgli, dragged

得没错，我们都这么说！"当他们问毛格利的意见时，他就点点头、眨眨眼，说"是的"。猴群发出的嘈杂声让他头昏脑涨。他想："他们肯定都被豺狗子塔巴奇咬过，所以他们都发疯了。他们肯定是害了疯癫症。他们难道从不睡觉吗？现在月亮快被一块云遮住了。要是这片云够大，我就试试看能不能趁黑逃走。唉，但是我好累呀。"

同一时间，两个好朋友也在看着那片云，他们正是躲在城墙底下废弃沟渠里的巴格伊尔拉和卡，因为他们深知大群的猴民有多危险，所以他们一点也不想以身犯险。一般来说，只有在己方人多，比如一百比一的情况下，猴子才会跟敌人打起来，而一旦遇到这种局面几乎不会有哪个丛林动物愿意跟他们斗。

卡低声说道："我会到西墙那儿去，顺着斜坡快快地滑下去，这对我有利。他们倒是不会一窝蜂地扑到我身上来，不过要是——"

巴格伊尔拉说："我知道，要是巴鲁在这儿就更好了，但是我们必须尽力一搏。等那片云遮住月亮，我就到平台那儿去。他们好像正在那里开个什么会讨论关于男孩儿的事情。"

卡神色严肃地说："祝你好运。"然后他就朝西墙爬过去了。那面墙恰好是保存最完好的，没什么破损的地方，所以大蛇颇花了些时间才爬上石墙。月亮被云遮住了，正当毛格利猜想接下来会发生什么的时候，他听到了巴格伊尔拉落在平台上的轻巧的足音。黑豹几乎是悄无声息地冲上了山坡，立刻就在猴群中左冲右突地开始猛攻，他没有用嘴咬，因为那太费时间了。当时猴子们正一圈圈地围着毛格利坐着，从最外圈到男孩儿大概隔着五六十只猴子那么多。只听猴群迸发出充满恐惧和愤怒的尖叫，然后巴格伊尔拉被一堆打着滚、胡乱踢腾的猴子绊倒了，接着一只猴子就嚷起来："只有他一个，杀死他！杀呀！"于是一大群猴子立马扑到巴格伊尔拉身上去了，他们又是抓又是咬，又是拉又是扯。另一边

① grimly ['grimli] *ad.* 严肃地

② glide [glaid] *v.* 悄悄地过去

③ awhile [ə'wail] *ad.* 一小会儿

④ slope [sləup] *n.* 斜坡，坡地

⑤ fright [frait] *n.*（突然而极端的）恐惧

him up the wall of the summerhouse and pushed him through the hole of the broken dome. A man-trained boy would have been badly bruised, for the fall was a good fifteen feet, but Mowgli fell as Baloo had taught him to fall, and landed on his feet.

"Stay there," shouted the monkeys, "till we have killed thy friends, and later we will play with thee—if the Poison-People leave thee alive."

"We be of one blood, ye and I," said Mowgli, quickly giving the Snake's Call. He could hear rustling and hissing in the rubbish all round him and gave the Call a second time, to make sure.

"Even ssso! Down hoods all!" said half a dozen low voices (every ruin in India becomes sooner or later a **dwelling**① place of snakes, and the old summerhouse was alive with **cobras**②). "Stand still, Little Brother, for thy feet may do us harm."

Mowgli stood as quietly as he could, peering through the open work and listening to the furious **din**③ of the fight round the Black Panther—the yells and chatterings and scufflings, and Bagheera's deep, hoarse cough as he backed and **bucked**④ and twisted and plunged under the heaps of his enemies. For the first time since he was born, Bagheera was fighting for his life.

"Baloo must be at hand; Bagheera would not have come alone," Mowgli thought. And then he called aloud: "To the tank, Bagheera. Roll to the water tanks. Roll and plunge! Get to the water!"

Bagheera heard, and the cry that told him Mowgli was safe gave him new courage. He worked his way **desperately**⑤, inch by inch, straight for the reservoirs, halting in silence. Then from the ruined wall nearest the jungle rose up the rumbling war-shout of Baloo. The old Bear had done his best, but he could not come before. "Bagheera," he shouted, "I am here. I climb! I haste! Ahuwora! The stones slip under my feet! Wait my coming, O most infamous Bandar-log!" He panted up the terrace only to disappear to the head in a wave of monkeys, but he threw himself squarely on his haunches, and, spreading out his

呢，大概五六只猴子抓住了毛格利，把他拖到凉亭的墙上去，又逼着他钻过那个破穹顶上的洞跳下去。屋顶离地足足有十五英尺高，要是换了一个人类养大的孩子一准儿会摔伤了，但是毛格利按着巴鲁教他的方法跳下去，落地的时候双脚着地，所以并没受什么伤。

猴子们对他喊道："待在那儿，等我们杀掉你的朋友，再来找你玩儿——要是有毒一族还没咬死你的话。"

毛格利一听就发出了蛇族的丛林密语："你和我，我们拥有共同的血缘。"他听见从四周的垃圾里传来窸窸窣窣和嘶嘶吐信的声音，于是为了保险又说了一遍密语。

"这样啊！大家都把兜帽收起来吧！"五六个声音一起低低地说道（印度的每一处废墟最终都会成为蛇类聚居的场所，这座破旧的凉亭自然也不例外，到处都是眼镜蛇）。"小兄弟，你可站稳了别动，你有可能踩到我们。"

毛格利尽量悄无声息地站着，从窗格里往外偷看，竖耳听着黑豹周围一片混战的喧闹声——猴子们在尖叫、咒骂、扭打，黑豹发出低沉、喑哑的叫声，同时后退一步，弓起背，猛地转身冲向他那成堆的敌人。这真是黑豹生平第一次为了活命竭力而战。

毛格利心想："巴鲁肯定就在旁边；巴格伊尔拉不会一个人来的。"他大声叫起来："巴格伊尔拉，到池子那儿去。滚到水池边上，滚啊，然后跳下去！到水里去！"

巴格伊尔拉听见了，知道毛格利现在还是安全的，让他又有了勇气。他奋力拼搏，一点一点直朝着水池一路杀过去，然后停了下来。就在此时，从最靠近丛林的断壁那里传来了巴鲁雷鸣般的战吼。老棕熊已经尽了全力奔跑，这才赶到。他大喊道："巴格伊尔拉，我来了。我爬啊，我赶啊，啊呼哇啦！我脚下的石头尽打滑！等着我，哦，你们这些最最无耻的猴民！"他气喘吁吁刚爬上平台就被一大波猴子涌上来压住，只剩头露在外面，但是他干脆一屁股坐下来，伸开前爪一把搂住尽可

① dwelling ['dweliŋ] *n.* 住处
② cobra ['kəubrə] *n.*【动物】眼镜蛇

③ din [din] *n.* 喧嚣，噪声
④ buck [bʌk] *v.* 用头（或角）顶撞

⑤ desperately ['despərətli] *ad.* 铤而走险地，不顾一切地

forepaws, hugged as many as he could hold, and then began to hit with a regular bat-bat-bat, like the flipping strokes of a paddle wheel. A crash and a splash told Mowgli that Bagheera had fought his way to the tank where the monkeys could not follow. The Panther lay gasping for breath, his head just out of the water, while the monkeys stood three deep on the red steps, dancing up and down with rage, ready to spring upon him from all sides if he came out to help Baloo. It was then that Bagheera lifted up his dripping chin, and in despair gave the Snake's Call for protection—"We be of one blood, ye and I"—for he believed that Kaa had turned tail at the last minute. Even Baloo, half **smothered**① under the monkeys on the edge of the terrace, could not help chuckling as he heard the Black Panther asking for help.

Kaa had only just worked his way over the west wall, landing with a **wrench**② that dislodged a coping stone into the ditch. He had no intention of losing any advantage of the ground, and coiled and uncoiled himself once or twice, to be sure that every foot of his long body was in working order. All that while the fight with Baloo went on, and the monkeys yelled in the tank round Bagheera, and Mang the Bat, flying to and fro, carried the news of the great battle over the jungle, till even Hathi the Wild Elephant **trumpeted**③, and, far away, scattered bands of the Monkey-Folk woke and came leaping along the tree-roads to help their **comrades**④ in the Cold Lairs, and the noise of the fight roused all the day birds for miles round. Then Kaa came straight, quickly, and anxious to kill. The fighting strength of a python is in the driving blow of his head backed by all the strength and weight of his body. If you can imagine a **lance**⑤, or a battering ram, or a hammer weighing nearly half a ton driven by a cool, quiet mind living in the handle of it, you can roughly imagine what Kaa was like when he fought. A python four or five feet long can knock a man down if he hits him fairly in the chest, and Kaa was thirty feet long, as you know. His first stroke was delivered into the heart of the crowd round Baloo. It was sent home with shut mouth in silence, and there was no need of a second. The monkeys scattered with cries of—"Kaa! It is Kaa! Run! Run!"

能多的猴子，然后就像快速翻转的桨轮一样开始啪啪啪地拍击那些猴子。接着毛格利听到砰的一声，然后又是哗啦一声，他知道巴格伊尔拉已经跳到水池里，那些猴子追不上了。黑豹躺着呼哧呼哧直喘气，只把头露出水面。猴子在红色的台阶上站了有两三排那么多，全都气得上蹿下跳，一旦他要从水里出来去帮巴鲁，他们就准备一窝蜂地从四面扑到他身上去。直到此刻巴格伊尔拉才抬起滴水的下巴，绝望地喊出了蛇类寻求庇护的丛林密语：“我和你，我们拥有共同的血缘。”因为他以为卡在这最后关头已经掉头逃跑了。就连巴鲁——虽然他自己在平台边上快被猴群给压死了——听到黑豹祈求帮助时，也禁不住轻笑起来。

　　卡呢，刚刚才越过西墙，一扭身子落到地上，连带把一块压顶石掀翻了滚落到地沟里。他不想放弃在地面上的丝毫优势，把身子盘起来又松开，以确保自己长长的身体每一节都还能正常工作。就在他做这番准备的同时，巴鲁还在奋勇战斗，猴子们正在水池里围着巴格伊尔拉叫嚣，蝙蝠芒恩也在来回穿梭着把这场大战的消息传回丛林，就连野象哈提也发出了怒吼。而在更遥远的地方，其他的猴群也醒来并沿着树顶的小路跳跃着赶来帮助他们冷巢的同伴。大战的喧闹声还惊醒了方圆几英里以内所有的栖鸟。紧接着，卡就飞速直奔过去，急着大开杀戒。蟒蛇的战斗力就在头部的猛击，靠的是全身的力气和重量。如果你能想象出一只几乎半吨重的标枪或者攻城槌，再或者锤子，被把手里的一颗冷静的大脑操纵着去敲击，你就差不多能明白卡进攻的时候是什么样子。一条四五英尺长的蟒蛇只要对准胸口，就能够一下击倒一个男子，而你知道，卡可是有三十英尺长呢。他的第一下攻击直劈围着巴鲁的猴群中心，连嘴都没张，悄无声息就起到了效果，根本用不着来第二下，猴子们就四散而逃，叫着：“卡！是卡来了！跑啊，跑啊！”

① smother ['smʌðə] v. 使窒息

② wrench [rentʃ] n. 猛扭

③ trumpet ['trʌmpit] v.（大象等）吼叫

④ comrade ['kɔmrid] n. 同伴，伙伴

⑤ lance [lɑːns] n. 长矛

Generations of monkeys had been scared into good behavior by the stories their elders told them of Kaa, the night thief, who could slip along the branches as quietly as moss grows, and steal away the strongest monkey that ever lived; of old Kaa, who could make himself look so like a dead branch or a rotten stump that the wisest were deceived, till the branch caught them. Kaa was everything that the monkeys feared in the jungle, for none of them knew the limits of his power, none of them could look him in the face, and none had ever come alive out of his hug. And so they ran, stammering with terror, to the walls and the roofs of the houses, and Baloo drew a deep breath of relief. His fur was much thicker than Bagheera's, but he had suffered **sorely**① in the fight. Then Kaa opened his mouth for the first time and spoke one long hissing word, and the far-away monkeys, hurrying to the defense of the Cold Lairs, stayed where they were, **cowering**②, till the loaded branches bent and crackled under them. The monkeys on the walls and the empty houses stopped their cries, and in the stillness that fell upon the city Mowgli heard Bagheera shaking his wet sides as he came up from the tank. Then the **clamor**③ broke out again. The monkeys leaped higher up the walls. They clung around the necks of the big stone **idols**④ and shrieked as they skipped along the battlements, while Mowgli, dancing in the summerhouse, put his eye to the screenwork and hooted owl-fashion between his front teeth, to show his **derision**⑤ and contempt.

"Get the man-cub out of that trap; I can do no more," Bagheera gasped. "Let us take the man-cub and go. They may attack again."

"They will not move till I order them. Stay you sssso!" Kaa hissed, and the city was silent once more. "I could not come before, Brother, but I think I heard thee call"—this was to Bagheera.

"I—I may have cried out in the battle," Bagheera answered. "Baloo, art thou hurt?

"I am not sure that they did not pull me into a hundred little bearlings," said Baloo, gravely shaking one leg after the other. "Wow! I am sore. Kaa, we owe thee, I think, our lives—Bagheera and I."

一代又一代的猴民都曾用卡的故事来吓唬小辈守规矩。夜贼卡能顺着树枝滑行，如同青苔生长一般不发出一丁点声响，偷走最强壮的猴子；老蛇卡能够伪装成枯枝或者朽木，等着猴子出现，就连最聪明的猴子也会上当。卡是丛林里最让猴子害怕的东西，没有哪只猴子清楚他究竟有多大威力，没有哪只猴子敢于直视他的脸，也没有哪只猴子能从他的怀抱中逃生。所以他们吓得话都说不清了，纷纷逃到城墙和屋顶上。巴鲁这才深深地松了一口气。虽然他的皮毛比巴格伊尔拉的要厚实许多，但是他也被打得够呛。这时卡才第一次张开嘴，发着嘶嘶的声音，说了一个长长的单词，于是从远处赶来冷巢帮忙的猴子都停下不动了，蜷起身子直到身下的树枝承不住他们的重量被压弯了噼啪作响，城墙和空屋顶上的猴子也都停止了叫喊。就在笼罩全城的一片死寂中，毛格利听到巴格伊尔拉从水池里跳出来，抖落身上的水。然后喧哗声再次响起，猴子们跳到城墙的更高处，或者紧紧地搂着大石像的颈部，或是尖叫着沿着城垛奔跑。毛格利也在凉亭里手舞足蹈，眼睛贴在窗格上往外看，还从门牙里发出猫头鹰般的叫声，以表示对猴子的嘲笑和蔑视。

巴格伊尔拉气喘吁吁地说："把人崽儿从那个陷阱里弄出来吧；我是啥也干不了了。咱们赶紧带上人崽走。他们也许还会发动进攻。"

"我不下命令的话，他们不会动的。你们，就这么待着！"卡嘶嘶地说，全城又静了下来。"之前我没法赶过来，兄弟，可是我想我听到你的呼叫了。"这是对巴格伊尔拉说的。

巴格伊尔拉回答说："我，我在打架时可能是喊了一嗓子。巴鲁，你受伤了没？"

巴鲁说："我不知道他们是不是把我给扯成了一百只小小熊，"他板着脸抖抖一只腿，又抖抖另一只。"嗷！我疼死了。卡，我想我们——我和巴格伊尔拉——欠你两条命。"

① sorely ['sɔ:li] *ad.* 疼痛地,剧痛地

② cower ['kauə] *v.* 蜷缩

③ clamor ['klæmə] *n.* 大的叫喊声；嘈杂声

④ idol ['aidəl] *n.* 雕像

⑤ derision [di'riʒən] *n.* 嘲笑

"No matter. Where is the manling?"

"Here, in a trap. I cannot climb out," cried Mowgli. The curve of the broken dome was above his head.

"Take him away. He dances like Mao the Peacock. He will crush our young," said the cobras inside.

"Hah!" said Kaa with a chuckle, "he has friends everywhere, this manling. Stand back, manling. And hide you, O Poison People. I break down the wall."

Kaa looked carefully till he found a discolored crack in the marble tracery showing a weak spot, made two or three light **taps**[①] with his head to get the distance, and then lifting up six feet of his body clear of the ground, sent home half a dozen full-power smashing blows, nose-first. The screen-work broke and fell away in a cloud of dust and rubbish, and Mowgli leaped through the opening and flung himself between Baloo and Bagheera—an arm around each big neck.

"Art thou hurt?" said Baloo, hugging him softly.

"I am sore, hungry, and not a little bruised. But, oh, they have handled ye **grievously**[②], my Brothers! Ye bleed."

"Others also," said Bagheera, licking his lips and looking at the monkey-dead on the terrace and round the tank.

"It is nothing, it is nothing, if thou art safe, oh, my pride of all little frogs!" **whimpered**[③] Baloo.

"Of that we shall judge later," said Bagheera, in a dry voice that Mowgli did not at all like. "But here is Kaa to whom we owe the battle and thou owest thy life. Thank him according to our customs, Mowgli."

Mowgli turned and saw the great Python's head swaying a foot above his own.

"So this is the manling," said Kaa. "Very soft is his skin, and he is not unlike the Bandar-log. Have a care, manling, that I do not mistake thee for a monkey some twilight when I have newly changed my coat."

"We be one blood, thou and I," Mowgli answered. "I take my life from thee tonight. My kill shall be thy kill if ever thou art hungry, O Kaa."

"这没什么。人崽儿在哪儿呢？"

毛格利喊道："这儿呢，陷阱里。我爬不出来。"他的头上是塌陷的穹顶那弯曲的拱部。

屋里的眼镜蛇说："把他带走吧。他跟孔雀摩尔一样乱蹦乱跳的。他会踩死我们的孩子的。"

卡咯咯笑着说："哈！这个人孩儿，他可是到处都有朋友。往后站，小孩儿。噢，有毒一族，你们也藏好自己。我要把墙推倒。"

① tap [tæp] n. 轻敲声

卡仔细查看，发现大理石窗格上有一处裂缝已经变色了，说明这里容易击破，于是他用头轻轻地点了两三次，掌握好距离，然后就把头竖起来，离地六英尺高，鼻子朝前用尽全力对准那处狠狠砸了几下。窗格被击碎了，尘土飞扬，只剩一堆垃圾。毛格利从裂口处一跃而出，扑到巴鲁和巴格伊尔拉之间，两只胳膊分别搂着一只粗壮的脖颈。

巴鲁温柔地拥抱着他，问道："你受伤了吗？"

② grievously ['gri:vəsli] ad. 令人悲伤地

"我浑身疼，又饿，身上到处是瘀青。哦，可是我的兄弟们，你们可被猴子折腾坏啦！你们都流血啦！"

"他们也没好到哪儿去。"巴格伊尔拉说着舔了舔嘴唇，看了一眼平台上和水池四周死去的猴子。

③ whimper ['wimpə] v. 呜咽着说

巴鲁呜咽着说："没事儿，没事儿，只要你安全就好，哦，所有小青蛙里最让我骄傲的宝贝儿啊！"

"这事儿咱们晚点再说，"巴格伊尔拉说这话时声音干巴巴的，毛格利一点也不喜欢。"先来见见卡吧，我们能打赢多亏了他，你的命也是他救的。毛格利，按照咱们的规矩好好向他表示感谢。"

毛格利转过身去，看见巨蟒的头在他自己头上一英尺高的地方晃动。

卡说："看来这就是人崽儿了。他的皮肤可真软啊，他长得跟猴民倒是有点像。人崽，你可要当心啊，别碰上我换了新衣的哪个黄昏，让我把你当成只猴子啦。"

毛格利回答说："你和我，我们拥有共同的血缘。

"All thanks, Little Brother," said Kaa, though his eyes twinkled. "And what may so bold a hunter kill? I ask that I may follow when next he goes abroad."

"I kill nothing,—I am too little,—but I drive goats toward such as can use them. When thou art empty come to me and see if I speak the truth. I have some skill in these [he held out his hands], and if ever thou art in a trap, I may pay the debt which I owe to thee, to Bagheera, and to Baloo, here. Good hunting to ye all, my masters."

"Well said," **growled**[1] Baloo, for Mowgli had returned thanks very **prettily**[2]. The Python dropped his head lightly for a minute on Mowgli's shoulder. "A brave heart and a courteous tongue," said he. "They shall carry thee far through the jungle, manling. But now go hence quickly with thy friends. Go and sleep, for the moon sets, and what follows it is not well that thou shouldst see."

The moon was sinking behind the hills and the lines of trembling monkeys **huddled**[3] together on the walls and battlements looked like ragged shaky fringes of things. Baloo went down to the tank for a drink and Bagheera began to put his fur in order, as Kaa glided out into the center of the terrace and brought his jaws together with a ringing snap that drew all the monkeys' eyes upon him.

"The moon sets," he said. "Is there yet light enough to see?"

From the walls came a moan like the wind in the tree-tops—"We see, O Kaa."

"Good. Begins now the dance—the Dance of the Hunger of Kaa. Sit still and watch."

He turned twice or **thrice**[4] in a big circle, weaving his head from right to left. Then he began making **loops**[5] and figures of eight with his body, and soft, **oozy**[6] **triangles**[7] that melted into squares and five-sided figures, and coiled mounds, never resting, never hurrying, and never stopping his low

今晚我的命是你给的。哦，卡，今后一旦你饿了，那我杀的猎物就归你。"

"小兄弟，太感谢你了，"卡说，但是他的目光闪烁了一下，"不过，这么勇敢的猎手会杀死什么样的猎物呢？我问问，下次他外出打猎时才好跟着去呢。"

"我什么也不杀——我太小了——但是谁用得上山羊，我就会把羊赶到谁那儿去。等你肚子瘪了，你可以来找我看看我说的是不是实话。我这些地方（他伸出双手）还是有点用处的，一旦你哪天掉进陷阱了，我就可以偿还今天跟你、巴格伊尔拉，还有巴鲁欠下的债。祝你们打猎顺利，我的师傅们。"

"说得好！"巴鲁低低地吼①了一声，毛格利的这番致谢非常得体。蟒蛇把头低下来，在毛格利的肩头轻轻地靠了一会儿，然后说："你内心勇敢，言语谦恭②，它们会帮助你在丛林里大展宏图的，人孩儿。但是现在赶紧和你的朋友离开吧。回去睡一觉，月亮已经落山了，接下来的可不是什么你该看的事儿啦。"

月亮确实正往山坡后头沉下去，城墙和城垛上猴群正在瑟瑟发抖挤作一团③，月光勾勒出他们的侧影，好像什么东西破破烂烂的颤动的毛边。巴鲁走到水池边上喝了口水，巴格伊尔拉开始打理自己的毛皮，而卡呢，慢慢地滑行到平台的中央，把上下颌嘭的一声合上，那声音带着回响，引来了所有猴子的目光。

他说："月亮落了，你们还看得见吗？"

如一阵风掠过树梢，一声呻吟从城墙上传来："哦，卡，我们看得见。"

"那好。现在开始跳舞了——卡的饥饿之舞。坐着别动，好好地看。"

他沿着一个大圈转了两三④次，头也从右边摆到左边。然后他开始把身子扭成环形和数字八的形状，还有软绵绵的、歪歪扭扭的三角⑦形，又慢慢变成方形和五边形，抑或是盘⑤起来的小山丘，整个过程持续不断、不疾

① growl [graul] v. 嗥叫，狂吠
② prettily ['pritili] ad. 有礼貌地
③ huddle ['hʌdl] v. 挤作一团
④ thrice [θrais] ad. 三次，三回
⑤ loop [lu:p] n. 圈
⑥ oozy ['u:zi] a. 潮湿的，湿淋淋的
⑦ triangle ['traiæŋgl] n. 三角形物体

humming song. It grew darker and darker, till at last the dragging, shifting coils disappeared, but they could hear the rustle of the scales.

Baloo and Bagheera stood still as stone, growling in their throats, their neck hair bristling, and Mowgli watched and wondered.

"Bandar-log," said the voice of Kaa at last, "can ye stir foot or hand without my order? Speak!"

"Without thy order we cannot **stir**① foot or hand, O Kaa!"

"Good! Come all one pace nearer to me."

The lines of the monkeys swayed forward helplessly, and Baloo and Bagheera took one stiff step forward with them.

"Nearer!" hissed Kaa, and they all moved again.

Mowgli laid his hands on Baloo and Bagheera to get them away, and the two great beasts started as though they had been waked from a dream.

"Keep thy hand on my shoulder," Bagheera whispered. "Keep it there, or I must go back—must go back to Kaa. Aah!"

"It is only old Kaa making circles on the dust," said Mowgli. "Let us go." And the three slipped off through a gap in the walls to the jungle.

"Whoof!" said Baloo, when he stood under the still trees again. "Never more will I make an ally of Kaa," and he shook himself all over.

"He knows more than we," said Bagheera, trembling. "In a little time, had I stayed, I should have walked down his throat."

"Many will walk by that road before the moon rises again," said Baloo. "He will have good hunting—after his own fashion."

"But what was the meaning of it all?" said Mowgli, who did not know anything of a python's powers of **fascination**②. "I saw no more than a big snake making foolish circles till the dark came. And his nose was all sore. Ho! Ho!"

不徐，而且始终伴随着低低的哼唱。天色越来越暗，直到那徐徐拖曳、颤动、缠绕的身影终于看不见了，但是他们仍能听到蛇鳞发出的沙沙声。

巴鲁和巴格伊尔拉像石像一般静立着，只有喉咙里发出低低的咆哮，颈子上的鬃毛都竖了起来。毛格利在一旁仔细地看着，心里纳闷不已。

终于，卡的声音响起："猴民啊，没有我的命令，你们的手脚能动吗？说话！"

"哦，卡，没有您的命令，我们绝不敢动一下手或脚。"

"好！全都向我靠近一步。"

绝望中，猴子们的身影摇摇晃晃地往前移动，巴鲁和巴格伊尔拉也跟着他们往前迈了僵硬的一步。

卡发出嘶嘶的声音，命令："再近点！"他们又都动了一下。

毛格利把手放在巴鲁和巴格伊尔拉身上好把他们拉回来，两头巨兽这才吃了一惊，恍如刚从梦中惊醒一般。

巴格伊尔拉悄悄地说："把你的手一直放在我肩头上，别拿开，不然我肯定又会回那边去——回卡那边去了。啊！"

毛格利说："那不过是老卡在尘土上画圈圈嘛。咱们走吧。"于是他们仨偷偷地从城墙上的一个破口溜出去，往丛林那边去了。

等到他们又站在静立的大树下时，巴鲁长出了一口气："呼——，我可再也不要跟卡联手了。"他浑身上下打了个冷战。

巴格伊尔拉也颤抖着说："他比我们更清楚。刚才我要是待在那儿，再过那么一小会儿，我肯定就会自己走进他喉咙里去。"

巴鲁说："月亮升起之前，会有很多猎物走上那条路的。他会满载而归——以他特有的方式。"

然而毛格利并不明白蟒蛇迷惑猎物的威力在哪儿，他问道："可是那到底是什么意思呢？我只看见一条大蛇在那儿傻乎乎地画圈子，一直画到天黑。他的鼻子肯定都画疼了，呵呵！"

① stir [stə:] v. 移动

② fascination [fæsi'neiʃən] n. 迷惑，蛊惑

"Mowgli," said Bagheera angrily, "his nose was sore **on thy account**[①], as my ears and sides and paws, and Baloo's neck and shoulders are bitten on thy account. **Neither** Baloo **nor**[②] Bagheera will be able to hunt with pleasure for many days."

"It is nothing," said Baloo; "we have the man-cub again."

"True, but he has cost us heavily in time which might have been spent in good hunting, in wounds, in hair—I am half plucked along my back—and last of all, in honor. For, remember, Mowgli, I, who am the Black Panther, was forced to call upon Kaa for protection, and Baloo and I were both made stupid as little birds by the Hunger Dance. All this, man-cub, came of thy playing with the Bandar-log."

"True, it is true," said Mowgli **sorrowfully**[③]. "I am an **evil**[④] man-cub, and my stomach is sad in me."

"Mf! What says the Law of the Jungle, Baloo?"

Baloo did not wish to bring Mowgli into any more trouble, but he could not **tamper**[⑤] with the Law, so he **mumbled**[⑥]: "Sorrow never stays **punishment**[⑦]. But remember, Bagheera, he is very little."

"I will remember. But he has done **mischief**[⑧], and **blows**[⑨] must be dealt now. Mowgli, hast thou anything to say?"

"Nothing. I did wrong. Baloo and thou are wounded. It is just."

Bagheera gave him half a dozen love-taps from a panther's point of view (they would hardly have waked one of his own cubs), but for a seven-year-old boy they amounted to as severe a beating as you could wish to avoid. When it was all over Mowgli sneezed, and picked himself up without a word.

"Now," said Bagheera, "jump on my back, Little Brother, and we will go home."

One of the beauties of Jungle Law is that punishment settles all **scores**[⑩]. There is no nagging afterward.

Mowgli laid his head down on Bagheera's back and slept so deeply that he never waked when he was put down in the home-cave.

① on one's account 为了某人

② neither...nor... 既不是……也不是……

③ sorrowfully ['sɔrəufəli] *ad.* 悲哀地
④ evil ['iːvəl] *a.* 坏的

⑤ tamper ['tæmpə] *v.* 篡改
⑥ mumble ['mʌmbl] *v.* 含糊地说
⑦ punishment ['pʌniʃmənt] *n.* 罚，惩罚，处罚
⑧ mischief ['mistʃif] *n.* 恶作剧，捣蛋，胡闹
⑨ blow [bləu] *n.* 擤（鼻子）

⑩ score [skɔː] *n.*（该报的）仇恨

巴格伊尔拉生气地说："毛格利，他的鼻子疼可都是因为你啊，就像我的耳朵、双肋和爪子，还有巴鲁的脖子和肩膀也是因为你才被咬伤的。接下来有好多天巴鲁和巴格伊尔拉都没法高高兴兴地打猎了。"

巴鲁说："这没什么，我们总算把人崽带回来了。"

"话是没错，但是他毕竟害我们损失惨重，浪费了宝贵的狩猎时间，还让我们受了这么多伤，丢了这么多毛发——我背上一半的毛都被拔掉了——更不用说还让我们丢了脸。毛格利，你要记住，我，伟大的黑豹，可是因为你才不得不向卡祈求庇护，巴鲁和我还都被他的饥饿之舞给弄得神魂颠倒，跟两只笨鸟似的。所有这一切，人崽，都是因为你跟猴民厮混才惹出来的。"

毛格利伤心地说："没错，是的，我是个坏崽子，我很难过。"

"嗯！巴鲁，丛林法则怎么说的来着？"

巴鲁并不想让毛格利再受罪了，但是他又不敢践踏法则，所以他只好吞吞吐吐地说："再难过也不能逃脱惩罚。但是巴格伊尔拉，要记住他还很小呢。"

"我会记着的。但是他犯了错，所以现在必须挨打。毛格利，你还有什么要说的吗？"

"没有。我做了错事。巴鲁和你都受了伤。这很公平。"

巴格伊尔拉打了他几下。要按豹子的眼光来看，这几下不过是爱抚罢了（力道如此轻柔，恐怕连他自己的一只豹崽儿都拍不醒），但对一个七岁大的男孩来说，那可算得上一场谁都避之不及的痛打。结束以后，毛格利打了个喷嚏，默默地爬了起来。

巴格伊尔拉说："好了，现在跳到我背上来吧，小兄弟，咱们回家了。"

丛林法则的一个好处就是惩罚完了就完了，之后不会再有什么唠叨。

毛格利把头放在巴格伊尔拉的背上，沉沉地睡去，直到被带回洞穴的家里也没有醒来。

Road-Song of the Bandar-Log

*Here we go in a flung **festoon**①,*
*Half-way up to the **jealous**② moon!*
*Don't you envy our **pranceful**③ **bands**④?*
Don't you wish you had extra hands?
Wouldn't you like if your tails were—so—
*Curved in the shape of a Cupid's **bow**⑤?*
  Now you're angry, but—never mind,
  Brother, thy tail hangs down behind!

Here we sit in a branchy row,
Thinking of beautiful things we know;
Dreaming of deeds that we mean to do,
All complete, in a minute or two—
Something noble and wise and good,
Done by merely wishing we could.
  We've forgotten, but—never mind,
  Brother, thy tail hangs down behind!

All the talk we ever have heard

猴民的路歌

① festoon [fesˈtuːn] n. （两端挂着中间下垂的）花彩
② jealous [ˈdʒeləs] a. 妒忌的
③ pranceful [ˈprɑːnsful] a. 雀跃的，昂首阔步的
④ band [bænd] n. 一伙人；一群动物
⑤ bow [bəu] n. 弓

我们穿过一个低垂的花环，
纵身跃向那嫉妒的月亮！
你不羡慕我们欢愉的队伍？
你不希望能多长一双手？
如果尾巴弯成丘比特之弓，
难道你不会喜笑颜开？
现在你生气啦，不过——没关系，
兄弟，你的尾巴吊在身后！

我们坐着排成行，就像树枝一个样，
思忖着我们知道的美好事物；
幻想着我们要实现的英雄伟业，
只要一两分钟，就可以全部完成——
这事业崇高、明智，又美好，
只要想想就能成，
我们忘记啦，不过——没关系，
兄弟，你的尾巴吊在身后！

我们听到所有的语言，

Uttered by bat or beast or bird—
*Hide or **fin**① or scale or feather—*
***Jabber**② it quickly and all together!*
Excellent! Wonderful! Once again!
Now we are talking just like men!
   Let's pretend we are ... never mind,
   Brother, thy tail hangs down behind!
   This is the way of the Monkey-kind.

*Then join our leaping lines that **scumfish**③ through the pines,*
That rocket by where, light and high, the wild grape swings.
By the rubbish in our wake, and the noble noise we make,
*Be sure, be sure, we're going to do some **splendid**④ things!*

① fin [fin] *v.* 潜泳，在水下
游泳
② jabber ['dʒæbə] *v.* 急促
地说出

③ scumfish ['skʌmfiʃ] *v.* 使
窒息

④ splendid ['splendid] *a.* 辉
煌的，显赫的

蝙蝠、野兽或飞鸟的交谈——
兽皮、鱼鳍、鳞片，还是羽毛——
一起叽叽喳喳说得快！
好极！妙极！再来一遍！
现在我们说话就像人！
咱们装成人的模样……没关系，
兄弟，你的尾巴吊在身后！
这就是猴民的活法。

加入我们吧！跳跃着把松林搜遍，
直冲到野葡萄藤轻轻摇曳的高处，势如火箭，
凭我们丢弃的垃圾，凭我们发出的高尚的声响，
我们的事业一定，一定会无比辉煌！

"Tiger! Tiger!"

What of the hunting, hunter bold?
  Brother, the watch was long and cold.
What of the quarry ye went to kill?
  Brother, he crops in the jungle still.
Where is the power that made your pride?
  *Brother, it **ebbs**[1] from my **flank**[2] and side.*
*Where is the **haste**[3] that ye hurry by?*
  Brother, I go to my lair—to die.

Now we must go back to the first tale. When Mowgli left the wolf's cave after the fight with the Pack at the Council Rock, he went down to the plowed lands where the villagers lived, but he would not stop there because it was too near to the jungle, and he knew that he had made at least one bad enemy at the Council. So he hurried on, keeping to the rough road that ran down the valley, and followed it at a steady jog-trot for nearly twenty miles, till he came to a country that he did not know. The valley opened out into a great **plain**[4] dotted over with rocks and cut up by **ravines**[5]. At one end stood a little village, and at the other the thick jungle came down in a sweep to the grazing-grounds, and stopped there as though it had been cut off with a **hoe**[6]. All over the plain,

"虎！虎！"

勇敢的猎手，打猎可顺利？

兄弟，等候猎物漫长而寒冷。

你去猎杀的猎物怎样了？

兄弟，他还在丛林里找食吃。

那曾经让你自豪的力量呢？

兄弟，它已从我的身体两侧流走。

那你现在如此慌张是为了什么？

兄弟，我要回我的窝去——等死。

现在让我们回到第一个故事。在议会岩与狼群大闹一场之后，毛格利离开了狼穴，去了村民居住的耕地，但是他并没有待在那儿，因为那里离丛林还是太近了，他也清楚自己在狼族议会里招惹了不止一个仇人。所以他继续赶路，沿着峡谷里那条崎岖小路，保持匀速快步走了大概二十英里远，来到了一片陌生的乡村。在这里，山谷豁然开朗，眼前一片宽广的平原，其间不乏大石和沟壑。平原的一头有一处小小的村落，另一头，浓密的丛林沿着山坡绵延到牧场时戛然而止，边缘齐整得像用锄头修过一样。整个平原上，到处是耕牛和水牛在吃草，

① ebb [eb] *v.* 变弱，减弱

② flank [flæŋk] *n.*（人或动物的）胁（部）

③ haste [heist] *n.* 快，急速，迅速

④ plain [plein] *n.* 平地，平原，旷野

⑤ ravine [rə'viːn] *n.* 沟壑

⑥ hoe [həu] *n.* 锄

cattle and **buffaloes**① were grazing, and when the little boys in charge of the herds saw Mowgli they shouted and ran away, and the yellow **pariah**② dogs that hang about every Indian village barked. Mowgli walked on, for he was feeling hungry, and when he came to the village gate he saw the big thorn-bush that was drawn up before the gate at twilight, pushed to one side.

"Umph!" he said, for he had come across more than one such barricade in his night rambles after things to eat. "So men are afraid of the People of the Jungle here also." He sat down by the gate, and when a man came out he stood up, opened his mouth, and pointed down it to show that he wanted food. The man stared, and ran back up the one street of the village shouting for the **priest**③, who was a big, fat man dressed in white, with a red and yellow mark on his forehead. The priest came to the gate, and with him at least a hundred people, who stared and talked and shouted and pointed at Mowgli.

"They have no manners, these Men Folk," said Mowgli to himself. "Only the gray ape would behave as they do." So he **threw back**④ his long hair and **frowned**⑤ at the crowd.

"What is there to be afraid of?" said the priest. "Look at the marks on his arms and legs. They are the bites of wolves. He is but a wolf-child run away from the jungle."

Of course, in playing together, the cubs had often nipped Mowgli harder than they intended, and there were white scars all over his arms and legs. But he would have been the last person in the world to call these bites, for he knew what real biting meant.

"Arre! Arre!" said two or three women together. "To be bitten by wolves, poor child! He is a handsome boy. He has eyes like red fire. By my honor, Messua, he is not unlike thy boy that was taken by the tiger."

"Let me look," said a woman with heavy copper rings on her wrists and ankles, and she peered at Mowgli under the palm of her hand. "Indeed he is not. He is thinner, but he has the very look of my boy."

① buffalo ['bʌfələu] n.【动物】水牛；野牛
② pariah ['pæriə] n. 印度南部最下层的民众；被社会遗弃的人

放牛的小孩们看见毛格利时大叫着跑开了，印度村落里随处可见的黄色流浪狗也大声狂吠。毛格利没有停下脚步，他觉得很饿。走到村口时，他发现一堆巨大的荆棘丛，这玩意儿每到黄昏时会被拉起来挡住门口，现在被推到了一边。

"啊哈！看来这里的人也害怕丛林动物啊。"他说，这样的路障以前他夜里出来找食物时看见过不止一次。他在门边坐了下来，等到一个人出来，他站起来，张开嘴，朝里面指指示意自己想要点儿吃的。那个男人盯着他，然后跑回村里那唯一的一条街上喊来了祭司。

③ priest [pri:st] n. 僧侣

祭司是个胖胖的大个子，穿着一身白衣，额头上点了个红色和黄色的印记。祭司来到村口，后面还跟着至少一百来个人，他们都盯着毛格利看，七嘴八舌，指指点点。

毛格利自言自语："这些人类可真是没有礼貌。只有灰猿才像他们这样干呢。"于是他把长发往后一甩，皱着眉看着这些人。

④ throw back 使（头、肩等）向后，向后扬
⑤ frown [fraun] v.（不悦、深思时）皱眉

祭司说："有什么好害怕的？看看他胳膊和腿上的印子，那都是被狼咬伤的。他只不过是个从森林里逃出来的狼孩儿罢了。"

当然啦，狼崽们和毛格利嬉闹时经常会咬着玩儿，但是他们往往控制不好力道，所以毛格利的四肢上到处都是白色的疤痕。但是不管别人怎么说，他才不会认为这些印迹是咬伤呢，因为他知道真的被咬了会是什么样子。

两三个妇女齐声叫了起来："哎呀，哎呀！被狼咬了，可怜的孩子！他长得可真好看呢。他的眼睛就像通红的火一样。梅斯娃，我敢发誓，他真有点像你家那个被老虎叼走的男娃娃呢。"

"让我看看。"一个女人说道，她的手腕和脚踝上都戴着沉甸甸的铜环。她手搭凉棚，仔细地看了看毛格利，说："他才不是呢。他瘦一些，不过他的样子倒是跟我儿子一模一样。"

The priest was a clever man, and he knew that Messua was wife to the richest villager in the place. So he looked up at the sky for a minute and said solemnly: "What the jungle has taken the jungle has restored. Take the boy into thy house, my sister, and forget not to honor the priest who sees so far into the lives of men."

"By the Bull that bought me," said Mowgli to himself, "but all this talking is like another looking-over by the Pack! Well, if I am a man, a man I must become."

The crowd parted as the woman **beckoned**① Mowgli to her **hut**②, where there was a red lacquered **bedstead**③, a great earthen grain chest with funny raised patterns on it, half a dozen copper cooking pots, an image of a Hindu god in a little **alcove**④, and on the wall a real looking glass, such as they sell at the country fairs.

She gave him a long drink of milk and some bread, and then she laid her hand on his head and looked into his eyes; for she thought perhaps that he might be her real son come back from the jungle where the tiger had taken him. So she said, "Nathoo, O Nathoo!" Mowgli did not show that he knew the name. "Dost thou not remember the day when I gave thee thy new shoes?" She touched his foot, and it was almost as hard as horn. "No," she said sorrowfully, "those feet have never worn shoes, but thou art very like my Nathoo, and thou shalt be my son."

Mowgli was uneasy, because he had never been under a roof before. But as he looked at the **thatch**⑤, he saw that he could tear it out any time if he wanted to get away, and that the window had no fastenings. "What is the good of a man," he said to himself at last, "if he does not understand man's talk? Now I am as silly and dumb as a man would be with us in the jungle. I must speak their talk."

It was not for fun that he had learned while he was with the wolves to imitate the challenge of bucks in the jungle and the grunt of the little wild pig. So, as soon as Messua pronounced a word Mowgli would imitate it almost perfectly, and before dark he had learned the names of many things in the hut.

祭司是个聪明人，他知道梅斯娃的丈夫是当地最富有的村民。所以他抬头看看天，然后郑重其事地说："丛林夺走的，又被丛林归还了。我的姊妹，把这孩子带回家吧。还有，别忘了向祭司表达敬意，他可是能看透凡人的生命呢。"

毛格利自言自语道："以赎我的那头公牛起誓，听着这些人的话就像是被狼群再审查一次！好吧，要是我真的是人，那就让我变成一个人吧。"

人群散开了，那个女人招呼毛格利去她的茅屋。屋里有一个红漆床架，一个装粮食的硕大的陶柜，上面有些稀奇古怪的凸起的花纹，五六只铜锅，一个小小的壁龛里摆着一个印度教的神像，墙上还挂了一面真正的镜子，和市集上卖的那些一样。

她给毛格利倒了好些牛奶，又让他吃了点面包。她把手放在毛格利头上，盯着他的眼睛看了又看，觉得真有可能是儿子回来了，当年那个被老虎带到丛林里去的儿子。于是她说："纳都，哦，纳都！"毛格利对这个名字没什么反应。"你不记得了吗？那天我给了你一双新鞋？"她摸摸他的脚，硬得跟牛角似的。她难过地说："唉，这双脚是从来没有穿过鞋的。但是你真的很像我的纳都，你就当我的儿子吧。"

毛格利有些不安，因为他从来没有在屋顶下待过。但是他看看茅草屋顶，知道自己如果想逃的话，随时可以把它扯开，而且窗户也没有加闩。最后他对自己说："要是连人话都听不懂，当人有什么用？现在我就像个在丛林里遇到我们的人一样，又蠢又呆。我必须学会他们的语言。"

毛格利跟狼群在一起时，不是为了好玩才去学习模仿丛林里雄鹿发起挑战的声音和小野猪的哼哼声。所以现在梅斯娃每说一个字，毛格利就会差不多一模一样地模仿出来，天黑以前他就已经学会说茅屋里很多东西的名称了。

① beckon ['bekən] v.（以招手、点头）表示招呼
② hut [hʌt] n.（简陋的）小屋
③ bedstead ['bedsted] n. 床架
④ alcove ['ælkəuv] n. 壁龛

⑤ thatch [θætʃ] n.（用茅草或稻草等盖的）茅屋顶

There was a difficulty at bedtime, because Mowgli would not sleep under anything that looked so like a panther trap as that hut, and when they shut the door he went through the window. "Give him his will," said Messua's husband. "Remember he can never till now have slept on a bed. If he is indeed sent in the place of our son he will not run away."

So Mowgli stretched himself in some long, clean grass at the edge of the field, but before he had closed his eyes a soft gray nose poked him under the chin.

"Phew!" said Gray Brother (he was the eldest of Mother Wolf's cubs). "This is a poor **reward**[1] for following thee twenty miles. Thou smellest of wood smoke and cattle—altogether like a man already. Wake, Little Brother; I bring news."

"Are all well in the jungle?" said Mowgli, hugging him.

"All except the wolves that were burned with the Red Flower. Now, listen. Shere Khan has gone away to hunt far off till his coat grows again, for he is badly **singed**[2]. When he returns he swears that he will lay thy bones in the Waingunga."

"There are two words to that. I also have made a little promise. But news is always good. I am tired to-night,—very tired with new things, Gray Brother,—but bring me the news always."

"Thou wilt not forget that thou art a wolf? Men will not make thee forget?" said Gray Brother **anxiously**[3].

"Never. I will always remember that I love thee and all in our cave. But also I will always remember that I have been **cast**[4] out of the Pack."

"And that thou mayest be cast out of another pack. Men are only men, Little Brother, and their talk is like the talk of **frogs**[5] in a pond. When I come down here again, I will wait for thee in the bamboos at the edge of the grazing-ground."

For three months after that night Mowgli hardly ever left the village gate, he was so busy learning the ways and customs of men. First he had to wear a cloth round him, which annoyed him horribly; and then he had to learn about money,

　　睡觉的时候出了点麻烦，毛格利怎么也不肯睡在茅屋里，因为它看上去太像个关豹子的笼子了。大人一关上门他就从窗户爬了出去。梅斯娃的丈夫说："随他去吧，要知道他到现在还没在一张床上睡过呢。如果他真的是被送来代替我们儿子的话，他不会逃走的。"

　　于是毛格利就在田边上一些干净的草地上伸展四肢躺下来。可是还没等他合上眼呢，一个柔软的灰鼻头就碰了碰他的下巴。

　　灰哥（他是狼妈妈最大的孩子）说："呵！跟着你跑了二十英里，就给我这么点报酬。你身上一股子烧木头和耕牛的味道——差不多就跟人的气味一样啦。小兄弟，醒醒，我有消息给你。"

　　"大家在丛林里都好吗？"毛格利说着，抱了抱他。

　　"都好，除了那些被红花烧伤的狼。好了，你听着，希尔汗的毛被燎得可厉害了，所以他已经跑到老远的地方去猎食啦，不到他的毛长好他是不会回来的。但是他回来时发誓要把你的骨头丢到瓦因刚加河里去。"

　　"对此我只有两个字可说。我也曾经发了一个小小的誓呀。不过有消息总是好的。今晚我累了——学这些新东西可是把我累坏了，灰哥，——不过以后你要一直给我带消息来呀。"

　　灰哥焦急地说："你不会忘了你是头狼吧？人类不会让你忘掉这一点吧？"

　　"永远也不会。我会一直记得我爱你，爱咱们洞里所有的狼。但是我也会记得我已经被赶出了狼群。"

　　"你也可能被另一个族群赶出去。人就是人，小兄弟，他们说的话就跟池塘里的青蛙叫唤一样。下次我再来这儿，我会在牧场边上的竹林里等你。"

　　那晚以后有三个月毛格利几乎一步也没离开过村口。他忙于学习人类的规矩和行为方式。首先他得在身上裹块布，这让他很是恼火；然后他还得学习用钱，虽然他压根也不明白为什么；他还要学习耕田，尽管

① reward [ri'wɔːd] n. 报答

② singe [sindʒ] v. 把……的表面烫焦

③ anxiously ['æŋkʃəsli] ad. 不安地，忧虑地

④ cast [kɑːst] v. 投，掷，扔

⑤ frog [frɒg] n.【动物】蛙

which he did not in the least understand, and about plowing, of which he did not see the use. Then the little children in the village made him very angry. Luckily, the Law of the Jungle had taught him to keep his temper, for in the jungle life and food depend on keeping your **temper**[1]; but when they made fun of him because he would not play games or fly kites, or because he **mispronounced**[2] some word, only the knowledge that it was unsportsmanlike to kill little naked cubs kept him from picking them up and breaking them in two.

He did not know his own strength in the least. In the jungle he knew he was weak compared with the beasts, but in the village people said that he was as strong as a bull.

And Mowgli had not the faintest idea of the difference that caste makes between man and man. When the **potter**[3]'s donkey slipped in the **clay**[4] pit, Mowgli hauled it out by the tail, and helped to stack the pots for their journey to the market at Khanhiwara. That was very shocking, too, for the potter is a low-caste man, and his donkey is worse. When the priest scolded him, Mowgli threatened to put him on the donkey too, and the priest told Messua's husband that Mowgli had better be set to work as soon as possible; and the village head-man told Mowgli that he would have to go out with the buffaloes next day, and herd them while they **grazed**[5]. No one was more pleased than Mowgli; and that night, because he had been appointed a servant of the village, as it were, he went off to a circle that met every evening on a **masonry**[6] platform under a great fig-tree. It was the village club, and the head-man and the watchman and the barber, who knew all the gossip of the village, and old Buldeo, the village hunter, who had a Tower musket, met and smoked. The monkeys sat and talked in the upper branches, and there was a hole under the platform where a cobra lived, and he had his little platter of milk every night because he was **sacred**[7]; and the old men sat around the tree and talked, and pulled at the big huqas (the water-pipes) till far into the night. They told wonderful tales of gods and men and ghosts; and Buldeo told even more wonderful ones of the ways of beasts in the jungle, till the eyes of the children sitting outside the circle bulged out of their heads. Most

他也不知道有什么用。村里的那些小孩也让他很生气。幸运的是，丛林法则教会他要控制自己的怒火，因为在丛林里要想有东西吃、保住性命，就必须得管住自己的脾气。尽管如此，当他们因为他不肯玩游戏或者放风筝，抑或说错了什么话就嘲笑他时，多亏他还记着杀死光溜溜的小崽子是不光彩的，要不然他就会把他们抓起来撕成两半。

① temper ['tempə] *n.* 情绪
② mispronounce [ˌmisprə'nauns] *v.* 发错音，读错音

　　他根本不清楚自己的力气究竟有多大。在丛林里，他知道自己和野兽比起来是弱小的，但是在村子里，人们说他跟公牛一样强壮。

③ potter ['pɔtə] *n.* 陶工
④ clay [klei] *n.* （制砖瓦、陶瓷制品的）黏土，陶土

　　毛格利也一点都不明白种姓制度使得人和人之间存在多大的差别。陶匠的驴子滑倒在黏土坑里时，毛格利抓住驴子尾巴把它拉了出来，又帮着重新码好陶罐，以便运到康尼瓦拉的集市上去卖。这事引起了轰动，因为陶匠来自一个低等种姓，至于他的驴子嘛，那就更糟糕啦。后来祭司责骂了毛格利，男孩威胁说要把祭司也放到驴背上去。祭司就跟梅斯娃的丈夫说最好让毛格利尽快开始工作。村长告诉毛格利他第二天就必须跟水牛一

⑤ graze [greiz] *v.* （牲畜）啃食

起出去，负责放牧牛群。没有人能比毛格利更感到开心了。既然他已经成了村子的一名公仆——如果可以这么说的话——当天晚上毛格利就去参加了一个集会，这样的集会每天晚上都举行，地点就在一棵大无花果树下的砖石台上。在这个乡村俱乐部里，村长和守更人，还有整个村子的闲话都无所不知的理发师，再加上有一支陶尔式火枪的猎人老布尔迪奥，几个人聚在一起抽烟。在那棵无花果树上层的树枝间坐着些猴子，他们也在聊天；石台下有个洞，里面住着一条眼镜蛇，每天晚上他都能得着一小碟牛奶，因为他是条神蛇；老人们则围坐在树下，一边聊天，一边吸着大大的水烟枪，直到夜深。他们讲了好些有关神啊、人啊，还有鬼怪的离奇故事，布尔迪奥讲的关于丛林野兽的那些故事则更加离奇，听得坐在老人圈外的那些孩子们眼珠子都要掉出来了。大

⑥ masonry ['meisənri] *n.* 石造（或砖砌）建筑

⑦ sacred ['seikrid] *a.* 受尊敬的，受崇敬的

of the tales were about animals, for the jungle was always at their door. The deer and the wild pig grubbed up their crops, and now and again the tiger carried off a man at twilight, within sight of the village gates.

Mowgli, who naturally knew something about what they were talking of, had to cover his face not to show that he was laughing, while Buldeo, the Tower musket across his knees, climbed on from one wonderful story to another, and Mowgli's shoulders shook.

Buldeo was explaining how the tiger that had carried away Messua's son was a **ghost**①-tiger, and his body was inhabited by the ghost of a wicked, old money-lender, who had died some years ago. "And I know that this is true," he said, "because Purun Dass always limped from the blow that he got in a riot when his account books were burned, and the tiger that I speak of he limps, too, for the tracks of his pads are unequal."

"True, true, that must be the truth," said the gray-beards, nodding together.

"Are all these tales such **cobwebs**② and moon talk?" said Mowgli. "That tiger limps because he was born lame, as everyone knows. To talk of the soul of a money-lender in a beast that never had the courage of a jackal is child's talk."

Buldeo was speechless with surprise for a moment, and the head-man stared.

"Oho! It is the jungle **brat**③, is it?" said Buldeo. "If thou art so wise, better bring his hide to Khanhiwara, for the Government has set a hundred **rupees**④ on his life. Better still, talk not when thy elders speak."

Mowgli rose to go. "All the evening I have lain here listening," he called back over his shoulder, "and, except once or twice, Buldeo has not said one word of truth concerning the jungle, which is at his very doors. How, then, shall I believe the tales of ghosts and gods and **goblins**⑤ which he says he has seen?"

"It is full time that boy went to herding," said the head-man, while Buldeo

多数的故事都跟动物有关，毕竟丛林就近在眼前，野鹿和野猪常来祸害他们的庄稼，老虎也时不时地在傍晚跑来拖走一个人，这一切站在村口就能看得见。

对于他们说的这些，毛格利自然明白内情，他不得不捂住脸，免得被人看见他在笑。布尔迪奥把陶尔式火枪横放在膝盖上，慢吞吞地从一个惊险的故事讲到另一个故事，毛格利呢，肩膀不住地抖动。

这会儿，布尔迪奥正在解释为什么拖走梅斯娃儿子的那头老虎是只鬼虎，因为它的身体里住着一个鬼魂，那是几年前死去的一个邪恶的老放贷人。他说："我知道这是真的，因为普伦·达斯以前在一次暴乱中挨了一下打，从此以后他走路就一瘸一拐的，那次暴乱还把他的账本也烧掉了。我讲的那只老虎也是瘸了一条腿，因为他留下的爪印深浅不一样。"

灰白胡子的老人们都一起点着头，说："没错，没错，肯定是真的。"

毛格利说："难道这些故事都是像这样捕风捉影、瞎扯淡的吗？那只老虎走路一瘸一拐是因为他生下来就是瘸的，大家都知道啊。他的胆子还没有豺狗的大，居然说什么他被放贷人的鬼魂附身了，真是小孩说瞎话呢。"

布尔迪奥惊呆了，好一会儿没说话，村长也瞪大了双眼。

布尔迪奥说："哦呵，你就是那个丛林来的野孩子吧，是吗？你要真是这么聪明的话，就把老虎的皮拿到康尼瓦拉去呀，政府悬赏一百卢比买它的性命呢。再说了，长辈讲话的时候你就该闭上嘴。"

毛格利站起来就走，他扭过头说道："整个晚上我都躺在这儿听着，除了一两次以外，布尔迪奥说的关于丛林的事情没有一句是真的，哪怕丛林就在他自己的家门外。那么，我又为什么要相信他说的那些鬼神和妖精的故事是真的呢，哪怕他说是他亲眼看见的？"

毛格利的粗鲁无礼把布尔迪奥气得吹胡子瞪眼，村

① ghost [gəust] *n.* 鬼

② cobweb ['kɔbweb] *n.* 蜘蛛网

③ brat [bræt] *n.* [贬语、轻蔑语或戏谑语] 乳臭小儿

④ rupee [ru:'pi:] *n.* 卢比（印度、巴基斯坦、尼泊尔、斯里兰卡、毛里求斯等国的货币单位）

⑤ goblin ['gɔblin] *n.* 【民间传说】（调皮捣蛋的）小妖精，小鬼

puffed and snorted at Mowgli's impertinence.

The custom of most Indian villages is for a few boys to take the cattle and buffaloes out to graze in the early morning, and bring them back at night. The very cattle that would **trample**① a white man to death allow themselves to be banged and bullied and shouted at by children that hardly come up to their noses. So long as the boys keep with the herds they are safe, for not even the tiger will charge a mob of cattle. But if they straggle to pick flowers or hunt **lizards**②, they are sometimes carried off. Mowgli went through the village street in the dawn, sitting on the back of Rama, the great herd bull. The slaty-blue buffaloes, with their long, backward-sweeping horns and savage eyes, rose out their byres, one by one, and followed him, and Mowgli made it very clear to the children with him that he was the master. He beat the buffaloes with a long, **polished**③ bamboo, and told Kamya, one of the boys, to graze the cattle by themselves, while he went on with the buffaloes, and to be very careful not to stray away from the herd.

An Indian grazing ground is all rocks and scrub and **tussocks**④ and little ravines, among which the herds scatter and disappear. The buffaloes generally keep to the pools and muddy places, where they lie wallowing or basking in the warm mud for hours. Mowgli drove them on to the edge of the plain where the Waingunga came out of the jungle; then he dropped from Rama's neck, trotted off to a bamboo **clump**⑤, and found Gray Brother. "Ah," said Gray Brother, "I have waited here very many days. What is the meaning of this cattle-herding work?"

"It is an order," said Mowgli. "I am a village herd for a while. What news of Shere Khan?"

"He has come back to this country, and has waited here a long time for thee. Now he has gone off again, for the game is scarce. But he means to kill thee."

"Very good," said Mowgli. "So long as he is away do thou or one of the four brothers sit on that rock, so that I can see thee as I come out of the village. When he comes back wait for me in the ravine by the dhak tree in the center of the plain. We need not walk into Shere Khan's mouth."

长说："是时候让这孩子去放牛了。"

　　绝大多数印度村庄的惯例是让几个男孩早晨把耕牛和水牛带出去吃草，晚上再把牛群带回来。说也奇怪，那些能把一个白人成年男子活活踩死的耕牛却能忍受孩童的捶打、欺侮和吼叫，尽管这些孩子可能还不到它们鼻子那儿高。而只要这些孩子始终跟牛群在一块儿，他们的安全就足以得到保障，因为即使是老虎也不敢袭击一群耕牛。但是如果他们走开，跑去摘花或者抓蜥蜴，有时就会被拖走。拂晓的时候，毛格利骑在大公牛拉玛的背上穿过村里的街道。青灰色的水牛瞪着凶狠的眼睛，长长的角向后伸着，一只接一只地从牛棚里起身，跟在毛格利的后面。毛格利让同行的小孩都明白他们都得听他的。他用一根长长的光滑竹竿抽打水牛，告诉其中一个孩子卡姆亚，让他们各自带着耕牛去吃草，但是要小心不要离开大队伍，他自己则专门负责水牛群。

　　印度的牧场上通常尽是些岩石、灌木丛、草丛和溪涧，牛群散开来，隐没其间。水牛一般待在池塘和泥沼里，他们在温暖的烂泥里打滚、晒太阳，一待就是好几个小时。毛格利把他们赶到平原边上瓦因刚加河流出丛林的地方，然后就从拉玛的脖子上跳下来，快步跑到一丛竹林那儿，找到了灰哥。灰哥说："啊，我都在这儿等了好多天了。你这放牛的活儿有啥意思啊？"

　　毛格利说："这是个任务。我要给村里当一阵子的放牛倌。希尔汗有什么消息没？"

　　"他已经回到这片地区了，而且在这里等了你好长一段时间。不过他现在又走了，因为这儿的猎物太少了。但是他可是打定主意要杀你的。"

　　毛格利说，"太好了。只要他没回来，你，或者其他四兄弟当中的一个，就坐在那块岩石上，这样我从村里出来时就能看见你们。等他回来了，你们就到平原中央的那棵鸽豆树旁的沟渠里等我。我们用不着去希尔汗跟前送死。"

---

① trample ['træmpl] v. 粗暴地对待

② lizard ['lizəd] n. 【动物】蜥蜴

③ polished ['pɔliʃt] a. 平滑的

④ tussock ['tʌsək] n. 【植物学】丛生草，草丛丘

⑤ clump [klʌmp] n. 群

Then Mowgli picked out a **shady**[1] place, and lay down and slept while the buffaloes grazed round him. Herding in India is one of the laziest things in the world. The cattle move and crunch, and lie down, and move on again, and they do not even low. They only grunt, and the buffaloes very seldom say anything, but get down into the muddy pools one after another, and work their way into the mud till only their noses and staring china-blue eyes show above the surface, and then they lie like **logs**[2]. The sun makes the rocks dance in the heat, and the herd children hear one **kite**[3] (never any more) whistling almost out of sight overhead, and they know that if they died, or a cow died, that kite would sweep down, and the next kite miles away would see him drop and follow, and the next, and the next, and almost before they were dead there would be a score of hungry kites come out of nowhere. Then they sleep and wake and sleep again, and weave little baskets of dried grass and put grasshoppers in them; or catch two praying **mantises**[4] and make them fight; or string a necklace of red and black jungle nuts; or watch a lizard basking on a rock, or a snake hunting a frog near the wallows. Then they sing long, long songs with odd native **quavers**[5] at the end of them, and the day seems longer than most people's whole lives, and perhaps they make a mud castle with mud figures of men and horses and buffaloes, and put reeds into the men's hands, and pretend that they are kings and the figures are their armies, or that they are gods to be worshiped. Then evening comes and the children call, and the buffaloes lumber up out of the sticky mud with noises like gunshots going off one after the other, and they all string across the gray plain back to the twinkling village lights.

Day after day Mowgli would lead the buffaloes out to their wallows, and day after day he would see Gray Brother's back a mile and a half away across the plain (so he knew that Shere Khan had not come back), and day after day he would lie on the grass listening to the noises round him, and dreaming of old days in the jungle. If Shere Khan had made a false step with his lame paw up in the jungles by the Waingunga, Mowgli would have heard him in those long, still mornings.

① shady ['ʃeidi] *a.* 背阴的

毛格利捡了一块阴凉地儿，躺下来睡了一觉，水牛就在他的周围吃草。在印度，放牧可算是世界上最最轻闲的活计了。耕牛走一段，咔嚓咔嚓地啃几下草，然后躺下来，过一会儿又往前走，他们甚至连叫唤都不叫唤一声。他们只是哼哼几下，水牛则几乎不发出任何声音，只会一个接一个地下到泥塘里去，全身都钻进泥里，只把鼻子和圆圆的瓷青色的眼睛露出来，然后就躺在那儿一动不动好似一根根原木。太阳晒得石头好像都在热气里跳舞，放牧的小孩们听见一只鸢鹰（永远都是一只）在头顶几乎看不见的地方发出尖啸，他们知道要是自己死了，或者一头牛死了，那只鸢鹰就会猛扑下来，而几英里外的另外一只鸢鹰看见他下落也会跟来，接着是另一只，又一只，这样还不等他们完全死去，就会有一打饥饿的鸢鹰从不知道从哪里冒出来。小孩们睡了又醒，醒了又睡。他们有的用干草编成一只只的小篮子，在里面装上蝈蝈；有的抓来两只螳螂让它们打架；有的用红色和黑色的坚果做一串项链；还有的就看蜥蜴在石头上晒太阳，或者看蛇在泥洼旁捕食青蛙。然后他们还会唱很长很长的歌谣，结尾总有一节当地特有的奇怪的颤音。这样的日子好像比大多数人的一生还要漫长。小孩们也许会用泥巴堆一个城堡，捏些泥人、泥马和泥水牛，泥人手里还会放些芦苇。孩子们假装自己是国王，而泥偶是他们的军队，或者自己是受到崇拜的神祇。夜晚终于来临，在孩子们的呼唤下，水牛拖着笨重的身躯从黏答答的烂泥里爬出来，那声音就像一下接一下的枪响，就这样，他们排成一队穿过灰蒙蒙的原野回到灯火摇曳的村子里去。

② log [lɔg] *n.* 原木
③ kite [kait] *n.*【鸟类】鸢

④ mantises ['mæntis] *n.* 螳螂

⑤ quaver ['kweivə] *n.* 颤音

一天又一天，毛格利领着水牛去他们的泥塘；一天又一天，他都会看到一英里半以外的平原上冒出灰哥的背来（这样他就知道希尔汗还没有回来）；一天又一天，他躺在草丛里聆听周围的声响，回想着丛林里的旧时光。在那些漫长而寂静的上午，只要希尔汗的瘸爪在瓦因刚加河畔的丛林里踏错哪怕一步，都会被毛格利听得一清二楚。

At last a day came when he did not see Gray Brother at the signal place, and he laughed and headed the buffaloes for the ravine by the dhâk tree, which was all covered with golden-red flowers. There sat Gray Brother, every bristle on his back lifted.

"He has hidden for a month to throw thee off thy guard. He crossed the ranges last night with Tabaqui, hot-foot on thy trail," said the Wolf, panting.

Mowgli frowned. "I am not afraid of Shere Khan, but Tabaqui is very cunning."

"Have no fear," said Gray Brother, licking his lips a little. "I met Tabaqui in the dawn. Now he is telling all his **wisdom**① to the kites, but he told me everything before I broke his back. Shere Khan's plan is to wait for thee at the village gate this evening — for thee and for no one else. He is lying up now, in the big dry ravine of the Waingunga."

"Has he eaten today, or does he hunt empty?" said Mowgli, for the answer meant life and death to him.

"He killed at **dawn**②, — a pig, — and he has drunk too. Remember, Shere Khan could never fast, even for the sake of **revenge**③."

"Oh! Fool, fool! What a cub's cub it is! Eaten and drunk too, and he thinks that I shall wait till he has slept! Now, where does he lie up? If there were but ten of us we might pull him down as he lies. These buffaloes will not charge unless they **wind**④ him, and I cannot speak their language. Can we get behind his track so that they may smell it?"

"He swam far down the Waingunga to cut that off," said Gray Brother.

"Tabaqui told him that, I know. He would never have thought of it alone." Mowgli stood with his **finger**⑤ in his mouth, thinking. "The big ravine of the Waingunga. That opens out on the plain not half a mile from here. I can take the herd round through the jungle to the head of the ravine and then sweep down — but he would slink out at the foot. We must block that end. Gray Brother, canst thou cut the herd in two for me?"

　　终于有一天他没看到灰哥出现在约好的地点，他笑了起来，领着水牛找到鸽豆树旁的溪涧，树上此刻开满了金红色的花朵。灰哥坐在那儿，背上的毛全都竖了起来。

　　狼喘着粗气对他说："他躲了一个月好让你放松警惕。昨晚他跟塔巴奇一起穿过牧场，一路跟踪着你。"

　　毛格利皱了皱眉头。"我倒是不害怕希尔汗，但是塔巴奇太狡猾了。"

　　灰哥舔舔嘴唇，说道："别怕，今早我遇到了塔巴奇，我还没打断他的背，他就把一切都告诉了我。现在他大概正在跟鸢鹰吹嘘自己有多聪明吧。希尔汗计划今天晚上在村口那儿等你——就你一个人，没有别人。现在他正躲在瓦因刚加干涸的大峡谷里。"

　　毛格利问："他今天吃过了吗？还是什么也没抓到？"这个问题的答案对他来说可是性命攸关啊。

　　"早上的时候他杀了一头猪——还喝了些水。记住，希尔汗从来都不肯禁食，哪怕是为了报仇。"

　　"哦！傻瓜，傻瓜！真是个幼崽生的幼崽！吃了东西，还喝了水，他以为我还会等到他再睡一觉吗？好吧，他在哪儿藏着呢？要是现在有十个兄弟就好了，我们就能趁他躺着把他给干掉。这些水牛除非闻到他的气味，否则不会发起冲击，我又不懂他们的语言。咱们能绕到他后面去，好让水牛闻到他的味儿吗？"

　　灰哥说："他沿着瓦因刚加河游了很长一段，把气味给截断了。"

　　"我知道是塔巴奇教他这么做的，他自己肯定想不到这一点。"毛格利把手指含在嘴里，动起了脑筋。"瓦因刚加河的大峡谷直通向平原，出口就在离这儿不到半英里的地方。我可以带着牛群穿过丛林绕到峡谷的上游去，然后从上面直冲下来，但是他也许会从另一头偷偷溜走。所以我们必须把那头堵上。灰哥，你能帮我把牛群分成两拨吗？"

① wisdom ['wizdəm] *n.* 聪颖

② dawn [dɔːn] *n.* 黎明，拂晓

③ revenge [ri'vendʒ] *n.* 报仇

④ wind [wind] *v.* 听到风声

⑤ finger ['fiŋgə] *n.* 指，手指（尤指大拇指以外的手指）

"Not I, perhaps—but I have brought a wise helper." Gray Brother trotted off and dropped into a hole. Then there lifted up a huge gray head that Mowgli knew well, and the hot air was filled with the most **desolate**① cry of all the jungle—the hunting howl of a wolf at midday.

"Akela! Akela!" said Mowgli, clapping his hands. "I might have known that thou wouldst not forget me. We have a big work in hand. Cut the herd in two, Akela. Keep the cows and **calves**② together, and the bulls and the plow buffaloes by themselves."

The two wolves ran, ladies'-chain fashion, in and out of the herd, which snorted and threw up its head, and separated into two clumps. In one, the cow-buffaloes stood with their calves in the center, and glared and pawed, ready, if a wolf would only stay still, to charge down and trample the life out of him. In the other, the bulls and the young bulls snorted and **stamped**③, but though they looked more imposing they were much less dangerous, for they had no calves to protect. No six men could have divided the herd so neatly.

"What orders!" panted Akela. "They are trying to join again."

Mowgli slipped on to Rama's back. "Drive the bulls away to the left, Akela. Gray Brother, when we are gone, hold the cows together, and drive them into the foot of the ravine."

"How far?" said Gray Brother, panting and snapping.

"Till the sides are higher than Shere Khan can jump," shouted Mowgli. "Keep them there till we come down." The bulls swept off as Akela **bayed**④, and Gray Brother stopped in front of the cows. They **charged down**⑤ on him, and he ran just before them to the foot of the ravine, as Akela drove the bulls far to the left.

"Well done! Another charge and they are fairly started. Careful, now—careful, Akela. A snap too much and the bulls will charge. Hujah! This is wilder work than driving black-buck. Didst thou think these creatures could move so swiftly?" Mowgli called.

"I have—have hunted these too in my time," gasped Akela in the dust.

① desolate ['desələt] *a.* 孤
独的，孤寂的

② calves [kɑ:vz] *n.*（calf
的复数）小牛，犊

③ stamp [stæmp] *v.*（用足）
踏，用力踩

④ bay [bei] *v.* 嗥叫
⑤ charge down 向前冲击

"我也许办不到，——不过我带了个聪明的帮手来。"
灰哥快步跑开，跳进一个洞里。从那儿冒出来一个毛格
利熟悉的灰色大脑袋，闷热的空气里立刻传来整个丛林
最为凄凉的叫声——那是一头狼在中午时分狩猎的嗥叫。

"阿凯拉，阿凯拉！"毛格利喊道，拍起了手。"我
就知道你不会忘了我。现在我们有桩大事要干。阿凯拉，
把牛群分开，让母牛和小牛在一起，让公牛和耕田的牛
在一块儿。"

两只狼像跳"小姐环"舞那样在牛群里跑进跑出，
使得牛都喷着鼻息，扬起头，分成了两群。一群是母牛，
她们把小牛围在中间，瞪着眼睛，拿蹄子刨地，准备一
旦哪只狼停下来就立马冲上去把他踩死。另外一边，成
年的公牛和小公牛鼻息咻咻，跺着脚，虽然他们看上去
更吓人，但其实并没有那么危险，因为没有小牛需要他
们保护。可以说即使是六个男人也没法像这样干净利落
地把牛群分开。

阿凯拉喘着粗气儿说："有什么命令吗！他们又要
合拢了。"

毛格利一下蹿上拉玛的背。"阿凯拉，把公牛赶到
左边去。灰哥，等我们走了，你把母牛聚在一起，赶到
峡谷低处去。"

"赶多远？"灰哥问，一边喘气，一边冲着牛大声威吓。

毛格利大声说："直到两边高得希尔汗跳不上去为止。
你把她们留在那儿，直到我们下来。"在阿凯拉的嗥叫中，
公牛狂奔而过，灰哥挡在母牛的前面，她们向着他冲过
去，但是灰哥总是跑在她们前面，引着她们直朝峡谷的
低处跑去，而阿凯拉则赶着公牛远远地往左边去了。

毛格利喊道："干得好！再来一下冲刺，她们就会
真正跑起来了。小心，现在——小心，阿凯拉。你叫得
太狠，公牛就会往前冲了。呼呀！这可比赶印度羚要费
劲多了。你以前知道这些家伙跑起来能有这么快吗？"

阿凯拉在尘土中喘着气回答说："我年轻的时候也

"Shall I turn them into the jungle?"

"Ay! Turn. Swiftly turn them! Rama is mad with rage. Oh, if I could only tell him what I need of him to-day."

The bulls were turned, to the right this time, and crashed into the standing thicket. The other herd children, watching with the cattle half a mile away, hurried to the village as fast as their legs could carry them, crying that the buffaloes had gone mad and run away.

But Mowgli's plan was simple enough. All he wanted to do was to make a big circle **uphill**① and get at the head of the ravine, and then take the bulls down it and catch Shere Khan between the bulls and the cows; for he knew that after a meal and a full drink Shere Khan would not be in any condition to fight or to clamber up the sides of the ravine. He was soothing the buffaloes now by voice, and Akela had dropped far to the rear, only whimpering once or twice to hurry the rear-guard. It was a long, long circle, for they did not wish to get too near the ravine and give Shere Khan warning. At last Mowgli rounded up the bewildered herd at the head of the ravine on a grassy patch that sloped steeply down to the ravine itself. From that height you could see across the tops of the trees down to the plain below; but what Mowgli looked at was the sides of the ravine, and he saw with a great deal of satisfaction that they ran nearly straight up and down, while the **vines**② and **creepers**③ that hung over them would give no foothold to a tiger who wanted to get out.

"Let them breathe, Akela," he said, holding up his hand. "They have not winded him yet. Let them breathe. I must tell Shere Khan who comes. We have him in the trap."

He put his hands to his mouth and shouted down the ravine—it was almost like shouting down a **tunnel**④—and the **echoes**⑤ jumped from rock to rock.

After a long time there came back the drawling, sleepy snarl of a full-fed tiger just wakened.

"Who calls?" said Shere Khan, and a splendid peacock fluttered up out of the ravine screeching.

——也猎杀过这些家伙。现在我该转弯把他们赶进丛林里去吗？"

"好，转吧，动作快点！拉玛都快气疯了。哦，要是我能告诉他我今天需要他做什么就好了。"

这回公牛被赶向了右边，一下冲进了直立的灌木丛中。其他放牛的小孩在半英里外看见了这一切，赶紧撒丫子跑回村里去，大叫着水牛发疯了、逃走了。

但是毛格利的计划其实很简单。他只是想绕一个大圈上山，跑到峡谷上游去，然后顺着河谷把公牛赶下来，将希尔汗堵在公牛群和母牛群之间，因为他知道希尔汗大吃大喝一顿以后肯定不在状态，没法再打架或者跳出深深的河沟。现在他正用声音来安抚水牛，阿凯拉已经落在后面很远的地方，只是偶尔哼哼两声催促押后的公牛往前走。他们绕了一个很大的圈子，因为不想太靠近河沟，以免惊动希尔汗。最后，在河沟顶端的一片草地上，毛格利把稀里糊涂的牛群聚拢到一块儿，这里有个很陡的斜坡，直插向下面的峡谷。站在这样的高度，就能透过树林的顶部看到下面的平原。但是毛格利现在看的不是那个，而是河沟的两边，他非常满意地发现河岸两旁几乎是直上直下的，上面还爬满了青藤，老虎想要出去的话也没法踩在这些藤蔓上面借力。

他举起一只手，说："阿凯拉，让他们喘口气吧。他们现在还没闻到老虎的气味。我得告诉希尔汗谁来了。这下他可是落到咱们的陷阱里了。"

他把手围在嘴边，朝着河沟大喊——差不多就像冲着一个地道大喊一样——一阵阵回声在岩间回荡。

过了很长时间才传来了刚被惊醒的老虎那拖长了声音、睡意蒙胧的嘶吼，他吃饱了，正在睡大觉呢。

希尔汗说："谁在嚷嚷？"一只漂亮的孔雀尖叫着从峡谷里扑腾着飞起来。

① uphill ['ʌp'hil] *n.* 上坡

② vine [vain] *n.*【植物】藤本植物
③ creeper ['kri:pə] *n.*【植物】匍匐植物

④ tunnel ['tʌnəl] *n.* 隧道，隧洞
⑤ echo ['ekəu] *n.* 回声，回音

"I, Mowgli. Cattle thief, it is time to come to the Council Rock! Down—hurry them down, Akela! Down, Rama, down!"

The herd paused for an instant at the edge of the slope, but Akela gave tongue in the full hunting-yell, and they pitched over one after the other, just as steamers shoot rapids, the sand and stones spurting up round them. Once started, there was no chance of stopping, and before they were fairly in the bed of the ravine Rama winded Shere Khan and bellowed.

"Ha! Ha!" said Mowgli, on his back. "Now thou knowest!" and the torrent of black horns, foaming **muzzles**[①], and staring eyes whirled down the ravine just as boulders go down in floodtime; the weaker buffaloes being shouldered out to the sides of the ravine where they tore through the creepers. They knew what the business was before them—the terrible charge of the buffalo herd against which no tiger can hope to stand. Shere Khan heard the **thunder**[②] of their **hoofs**[③], picked himself up, and **lumbered**[④] down the ravine, looking from side to side for some way of escape, but the walls of the ravine were straight and he had to hold on, heavy with his dinner and his drink, willing to do anything rather than fight. The herd **splashed**[⑤] through the pool he had just left, bellowing till the narrow cut rang. Mowgli heard an answering bellow from the foot of the ravine, saw Shere Khan turn (the tiger knew if the worst came to the worst it was better to meet the bulls than the cows with their calves), and then Rama tripped, stumbled, and went on again over something soft, and, with the bulls at his heels, crashed full into the other herd, while the weaker buffaloes were lifted clean off their feet by the shock of the meeting. That charge carried both herds out into the plain, goring and stamping and snorting. Mowgli watched his time, and slipped off Rama's neck, laying about him right and left with his stick.

"Quick, Akela! Break them up. Scatter them, or they will be fighting one another. Drive them away, Akela. Hai, Rama! Hai, hai, hai! my children. Softly now, softly! It is all over."

Akela and Gray Brother ran to and fro nipping the buffaloes' legs, and

"是我，毛格利。偷牛贼，你该去议会岩啦！下去——把他们都赶下去，阿凯拉！下去，拉玛，下去！"

牛群在坡顶犹豫了一瞬间，然而阿凯拉用尽全力吹响了狩猎的号角，于是他们一个接一个地跳下去，就像蒸汽轮船穿越一个个急流，牛群周围激起无数沙石。一旦他们开始奔跑，就停不住脚了。牛群还没完全冲进河床，拉玛就闻到了希尔汗的气味，大吼起来。

骑在他背上的毛格利说："哈，哈！这下你知道了！"只见众多黑黑的牛角、泛着白沫的口鼻和圆睁的牛眼汇成一股激流沿着河沟奔流而下，就像泛洪时一块块石头被洪水席卷而来。身体弱一点的水牛被挤到了河沟的两边，把藤蔓给扯破了。他们知道眼下该干什么——没有哪只老虎敢于抵抗水牛群如此凶猛的冲锋。希尔汗听见牛群响雷般的蹄声，连忙站起来，慌里慌张地沿着河谷奔跑，左右看看想要找条出路，但是河沟的两岸都是直立的陡坡，他只好继续往前跑。此刻他肚子里装满了食物和水，身子沉重，压根就不想战斗。牛群冲过他刚离开的那个水潭，溅起了水花，一边发出怒吼，整个狭窄的河谷里都是回声。河谷的尽头这时也传来一声应和的吼叫，毛格利看见希尔汗转过身来（老虎明白如果出现最糟糕的情况，同时遇上了公牛和母牛，那么对付公牛还是要比面对带着小牛的母牛容易些），接着拉玛绊了一跤，踉跄了几步，然后踏过什么软乎乎的东西继续往前跑，接踵而来的公牛群和他一起正好撞上了对面的牛群。这一下子，撞得那些弱点儿的公牛全都四蹄离地了。这场冲锋挟裹着两群牛来到了外面的平原上，大家伙儿又是踢又是踹，用角顶来顶去，使劲儿喷着鼻息。毛格利看准时机，从拉玛的脖子上滑下来，左右挥舞着他的竹竿。

"阿凯拉，快，分开他们。把他们都散开，不然他们会打起来的。阿凯拉，把他们赶走。嗨，拉玛！嗨，嗨，嗨！我的孩子们。轻点儿，轻点儿！都结束了。"

阿凯拉和灰哥来回奔跑，轻轻地咬水牛的腿，虽然

① muzzle ['mʌzl] *n.*（狗、马等的）鼻口部

② thunder ['θʌndə] *n.* 轰隆声

③ hoof [huːf] *n.*（牛、马等的）蹄

④ lumber ['lʌmbə] *v.* 迈（沉重的）步走，笨重地移动

⑤ splash [splæʃ] *v.* 溅着水（或泥浆等）行进

though the herd wheeled once to charge up the ravine again, Mowgli managed to turn Rama, and the others followed him to the wallows.

Shere Khan needed no more trampling. He was dead, and the kites were coming for him already.

"Brothers, that was a dog's death," said Mowgli, feeling for the knife he always carried in a **sheath**① round his neck now that he lived with men. "But he would never have shown fight. His hide will look well on the Council Rock. We must get to work swiftly."

A boy trained among men would never have dreamed of skinning a ten-foot tiger alone, but Mowgli knew better than anyone else how an animal's skin is fitted on, and how it can be taken off. But it was hard work, and Mowgli slashed and tore and grunted for an hour, while the wolves lolled out their tongues, or came forward and tugged as he ordered them. Presently a hand fell on his shoulder, and looking up he saw Buldeo with the Tower **musket**②. The children had told the village about the buffalo stampede, and Buldeo went out angrily, only too anxious to correct Mowgli for not taking better care of the herd. The wolves dropped out of sight as soon as they saw the man coming.

"What is this folly?" said Buldeo angrily. "To think that thou canst skin a tiger! Where did the buffaloes kill him? It is the Lame Tiger too, and there is a hundred rupees on his head. Well, well, we will overlook thy letting the herd run off, and perhaps I will give thee one of the rupees of the reward when I have taken the skin to Khanhiwara." He **fumbled**③ in his waist cloth for **flint**④ and steel, and stooped down to singe Shere Khan's whiskers. Most native hunters always singe a tiger's whiskers to prevent his ghost from haunting them.

"Hum!" said Mowgli, half to himself as he ripped back the skin of a **forepaw**⑤. "So thou wilt take the hide to Khanhiwara for the reward, and perhaps give me one rupee? Now it is in my mind that I need the skin for my own use. Heh! Old man, take away that fire!"

"What talk is this to the chief hunter of the village? Thy luck and the

牛群转了个弯想要再次冲进河谷里去，毛格利最终还是成功地让拉玛转了回来，带着其他水牛往泥塘那边去了。

希尔汗已经不需要再挨上两脚了。他已经死了。鸢鹰正冲着他飞过去。

毛格利摸摸自己的小刀（自从跟人住在一起，他就总是带着这把刀，用个套子装着挂在脖子上）说："兄弟们，这就是一条狗的死法儿。不过他本来也没个打架的样子。他的皮放在议会岩上倒是挺好看的。我们得快点动手了。"

一个人类训练出来的男孩永远也不会想到独自给一头身长十英尺的老虎剥皮，但是毛格利比谁都清楚野兽的皮是怎么长上去的，又该怎么脱下来。不过这活计一点也不轻松，毛格利又是割又是撕，吭哧吭哧地忙活了一个钟头，两只狼在一边舌头耷拉着，听见他的命令就上前帮忙扯一下。突然，一只手落在他的肩头上，毛格利抬头一看，是布尔迪奥带着他的陶尔式火枪来了。之前孩子们跟村里报告了水牛集体狂奔一事，布尔迪奥就气冲冲地跑出来，急着教训毛格利，怪他没有照看好牛群。两匹狼刚看见男人过来的身影就立马溜走了。

布尔迪奥生气地说："你在瞎鼓捣什么呢？你以为你能给老虎剥皮吗？水牛在哪儿把他弄死的？这可是瘸虎啊，他的头可值一百个卢比呢。好吧，好吧，我们倒是可以不计较你放跑了牛群，等我把虎皮拿到康尼瓦拉去换了奖赏，我也许还能给你一个卢比呢。"他从围裙里掏出来燧石与火镰，蹲下身去想要烧烧希尔汗的胡须。当地大多数的猎人都会把虎须给燎一下，以免被老虎的鬼魂纠缠。

毛格利正在撕一只前爪上的皮，他半是自言自语地说："哈！所以你打算把这皮拿去康尼瓦拉领赏，然后可能赏我一个卢比？那我的想法是，这张皮我要留着自己用。嘿，老头，把那火拿开！"

"你怎么敢这样对村里的头号猎手说话？你能杀了

① sheath [ʃiːθ] n.（匕首、刀、剑等的）鞘

② musket ['mʌskit] n. 滑膛枪（旧式步枪），火枪

③ fumble ['fʌmbl] v. 乱摸，（暗中）摸索

④ flint [flint] n. 火燧石，火石

⑤ forepaw ['fɔːpɔː] n.【动物学】前蹄，前爪

· 125 ·

stupidity of thy buffaloes have helped thee to this kill. The tiger has just fed, or he would have gone twenty miles by this time. Thou canst not even skin him properly, little beggar brat, and forsooth I, Buldeo, must be told not to singe his whiskers. Mowgli, I will not give thee one **anna**① of the reward, but only a very big beating. Leave the carcass!"

"By the Bull that bought me," said Mowgli, who was trying to get at the shoulder, "must I stay babbling to an old ape all noon? Here, Akela, this man **plagues**② me."

Buldeo, who was still stooping over Shere Khan's head, found himself **sprawling**③ on the grass, with a gray wolf standing over him, while Mowgli went on skinning as though he were alone in all India.

"Ye-es," he said, between his teeth. "Thou art altogether right, Buldeo. Thou wilt never give me one anna of the reward. There is an old war between this lame tiger and myself—a very old war, and—I have won."

To do Buldeo justice, if he had been ten years younger he would have taken his chance with Akela had he met the wolf in the woods, but a wolf who obeyed the orders of this boy who had private wars with man-eating tigers was not a common animal. It was **sorcery**④, magic of the worst kind, thought Buldeo, and he wondered whether the **amulet**⑤ round his neck would protect him. He lay as still as still, expecting every minute to see Mowgli turn into a tiger too.

"Maharaj! Great King," he said at last in a **husky**⑥ whisper.

"Yes," said Mowgli, without turning his head, chuckling a little.

"I am an old man. I did not know that thou wast anything more than a herdsboy. May I rise up and go away, or will thy servant tear me to pieces?"

"Go, and peace go with thee. Only, another time do not meddle with my game. Let him go, Akela."

Buldeo hobbled away to the village as fast as he could, looking back over his shoulder in case Mowgli should change into something terrible. When he got to the village he told a tale of magic and **enchantment**⑦ and sorcery that made the priest look very **grave**⑧.

这只老虎靠的是你的运气和那些水牛的愚蠢。要不是老虎刚吃了东西，这会儿他都能跑出去二十英里远了。讨饭吃的小兔崽子，你连皮都剥不好，竟敢对我布尔迪奥说不要烧老虎的须子？毛格利，那赏金我一个铜钱也不会给你，只会赏你一顿好打。放开老虎的尸体！"

毛格利此刻正在试着对付老虎肩膀上的皮，听了此话，他说道："凭买下我的那头公牛起誓，我干嘛非得在这儿跟只老猴子废话一中午呢？过来，阿凯拉，这个人让我烦死了。"

布尔迪奥本来正蹲在希尔汗的头那儿看呢，突然发现自己四仰八叉躺在草地上了，一头灰狼正俯视着他，毛格利还在忙着剥皮，好像全印度就他一个人似的。

毛格利从牙缝里挤出声音："是——的，布尔迪奥，您说的都对。您永远也不会给我一个铜钱的赏金。这头瘸腿老虎和我之间的过节可是由来已久——很久很久——不过现在我赢了。"

说句公道话，要是布尔迪奥再年轻十岁，要是他是在树林里碰见的阿凯拉，那他也许还有可能跟这狼斗斗看，但是这匹狼是由一个敢跟吃人的老虎算账的男孩来指挥的，可不是什么普普通通的动物。布尔迪奥心想这一定是巫术、最可怕的魔法，他都不知道他脖子上挂的护身符是否能保护他。他躺着一动都不敢动，觉得每分钟都可能看见毛格利也变成一只老虎。

最后他嗓音低哑地说："大王！伟大的国王啊。"

毛格利头都没转过来，轻轻地笑了笑说："嗯？"

"我是老头啦。我以前以为您就是个放牛娃而已。现在我能站起来走了吗？还是您的仆人要把我撕成碎片？"

"走吧，也祝你安宁。只是，下次可别再乱碰我的猎物了。让他走吧，阿凯拉。"

布尔迪奥以最快的速度跌跌撞撞地朝着村子跑去，不时回头看看毛格利是不是变成了什么可怕的东西。当他回到村里，他讲了一个魔法、施咒和巫术的故事，祭

---

① anna ['ænə] *n.* 安那（旧时印度、巴基斯坦、缅甸的旧辅币单位，等于1卢比的1／16）

② plague [pleig] *v.* 使苦恼

③ sprawl [sprɔːl] *v.* 四肢伸开地躺着（或坐着）

④ sorcery ['sɔːsəri] *n.* 妖术，巫术，魔法

⑤ amulet ['æmjulit] *n.* 护（身）符，驱邪符

⑥ husky ['hʌski] *a.*（嗓音）有些沙哑的，喉咙发干的，嘶哑的

⑦ enchantment [in'tʃɑːntmənt] *n.* 妖术，魔法，法术

⑧ grave [greiv] *a.* 庄严肃穆的，庄重的

Mowgli went on with his work, but it was nearly twilight before he and the wolves had drawn the great gay skin clear of the body.

"Now we must hide this and take the buffaloes home! Help me to herd them, Akela."

The herd rounded up in the misty twilight, and when they got near the village Mowgli saw lights, and heard the conches and bells in the temple blowing and banging. Half the village seemed to be waiting for him by the gate. "That is because I have killed Shere Khan," he said to himself. But a shower of stones whistled about his ears, and the villagers shouted: "Sorcerer! Wolf's brat! Jungle demon! Go away! Get hence quickly or the priest will turn thee into a wolf again. Shoot, Buldeo, shoot!"

The old Tower musket went off with a bang, and a young buffalo **bellowed**[①] in pain.

"More sorcery!" shouted the villagers. "He can turn bullets. Buldeo, that was thy buffalo."

"Now what is this?" said Mowgli, bewildered, as the stones flew thicker.

"They are not unlike the Pack, these brothers of thine," said Akela, sitting down composedly. "It is in my head that, if bullets mean anything, they would cast thee out."

"Wolf! Wolf's cub! Go away!" shouted the priest, waving a **sprig**[②] of the sacred **tulsi**[③] plant.

"Again? Last time it was because I was a man. This time it is because I am a wolf. Let us go, Akela."

A woman—it was Messua—ran across to the herd, and cried: "Oh, my son, my son! They say thou art a sorcerer who can turn himself into a beast at will. I do not believe, but go away or they will kill thee. Buldeo says thou art a wizard, but I know thou hast avenged Nathoo's death."

"Come back, Messua!" shouted the crowd. "Come back, or we will stone thee."

司听完神色非常严肃。

毛格利继续干他的活，直到快天黑了，他和两只狼才把那张漂亮硕大的毛皮给完全剥下来。

"现在咱们得把这个藏起来，然后把水牛赶回家。阿凯拉，帮我赶牛吧。"

在薄雾笼罩的傍晚，牛群被聚拢来，当他们靠近村子时，毛格利看到了灯光，听见寺庙里吹起了螺号，敲起了钟。一半的村民好像都在村口等着他。他心想："这肯定是因为我杀死了希尔汗。"可是急雨般的石头从他耳边呼啸而过，村民们大叫着："巫师！狼崽子！丛林魔鬼！滚开！快滚，要不然祭司就会把你重新变成一头狼。布尔迪奥，开枪，开枪啊！"

只听老陶尔火枪嘭地一响，一头年轻的水牛发出了痛苦的嘶吼。

村民们喊道："又是巫术！他能把子弹弄偏。布尔迪奥，那是你家的水牛啊。"

更多的石头向他飞来，毛格利被弄得莫名其妙，问："这是怎么回事？"

阿凯拉沉着地坐下来，说："你的这些兄弟，他们跟狼群倒是没什么两样。我觉得如果这些子弹有什么意义的话，那表示他们想要把你赶走。"

祭司挥舞着一根圣罗勒的枝条，喊着："狼！狼崽！滚！"

"又要赶我？上次是因为我是人。这次又因为我是狼。阿凯拉，咱们走吧。"

一个女人——那是梅斯娃——跑到牛群边上来，哭着说："哦，我的儿子，我的儿子！他们说你是个巫师，会随意变成任何一头野兽。我不相信他们。不过你还是走吧，不然他们会杀了你的。布尔迪奥说你是个魔法师，但是我知道你不过是为纳都报仇罢了。"

人群喊道："回来，梅斯娃！回来！不然我们就扔石头砸你了。"

① bellow ['beləu] v.（公牛、母牛、雄象等）吼叫

② sprig [sprig] n. 小枝
③ tulsi ['tʌlsi] n. 罗勒属植物

Mowgli laughed a little short ugly laugh, for a stone had hit him in the mouth. "Run back, Messua. This is one of the foolish tales they tell under the big tree at dusk. I have at least paid for thy son's life. Farewell; and run quickly, for I shall send the herd in more swiftly than their brickbats. I am no wizard, Messua. Farewell!"

"Now, once more, Akela," he cried. "Bring the herd in."

The buffaloes were anxious enough to get to the village. They hardly needed Akela's yell, but charged through the gate like a **whirlwind**①, scattering the crowd right and left.

"**Keep count**②!" shouted Mowgli scornfully. "It may be that I have stolen one of them. Keep count, for I will do your herding no more. Fare you well, children of men, and thank Messua that I do not come in with my wolves and hunt you up and down your street."

He turned on his heel and walked away with the Lone Wolf, and as he looked up at the stars he felt happy. "No more sleeping in traps for me, Akela. Let us get Shere Khan's skin and go away. No, we will not hurt the village, for Messua was kind to me."

When the moon rose over the plain, making it look all milky, the horrified villagers saw Mowgli, with two wolves at his heels and a **bundle**③ on his head, trotting across at the steady wolf's trot that eats up the long miles like fire. Then they banged the temple bells and blew the conches louder than ever. And Messua cried, and Buldeo **embroidered**④ the story of his **adventures**⑤ in the jungle, till he ended by saying that Akela stood up on his hind legs and talked like a man.

The moon was just going down when Mowgli and the two wolves came to the hill of the Council Rock, and they stopped at Mother Wolf's cave.

"They have cast me out from the Man-Pack, Mother," shouted Mowgli, "but I come with the hide of Shere Khan to keep my word."

Mother Wolf walked stiffly from the cave with the cubs behind her, and her eyes glowed as she saw the skin.

"I told him on that day, when he crammed his head and shoulders into this

毛格利短促地苦笑了一下，一块石头砸到他的嘴了。"跑回去吧，梅斯娃。他们跟你说的不过就是他们傍晚在大树下讲的那些蠢故事而已。好在我至少替你儿子报了仇。再见啦，快点跑吧，我会把牛群赶进去的，保证比他们的碎砖头还快。梅斯娃，我不是什么魔法师。永别了！"

他叫道："现在，阿凯拉，再来一次。把牛群赶进来。"

水牛等不及要回到村里去。几乎不用阿凯拉吼叫，他们就像旋风一般冲进村口，把人群冲得左突右散。

毛格利轻蔑地喊道："好好数数！说不定我偷了一只牛呢。数清楚了，我可再也不会为你们放牛了。人类的孩子们，永别啦，你们该感谢梅斯娃，要不是因为她，我会带着我的狼冲进来，追得你们沿街逃窜。"

他转过身，和独狼一起走开了。当他抬头看着星星时，他觉得心底很快活。"阿凯拉，这下我不用再在笼子里睡觉了。咱们去拿上希尔汗的皮，走吧。不，咱们不要去伤害那些村民，因为梅斯娃对我很好。"

月亮高高挂在上空，平原抹上了一层乳白色，惊恐万分的村民看见毛格利头上顶着个包袱，脚边跟着两头狼，像狼一样稳步小跑，如同吞噬一切的火焰一般，很快就不见了踪影。村民们敲响了寺庙的钟，吹起了螺号，声音比过去任何时候都要大。梅斯娃哭了，布尔迪奥则又添油加醋地讲起他在丛林里的冒险经历，结尾是阿凯拉用后腿立起来，像人一样说话。

月亮刚开始下沉，毛格利和两只狼就回到了议会岩的山下，他们在狼妈妈的洞穴前停了下来。

毛格利喊道："母亲，他们把我从人族里赶出来了。但是我遵守我的诺言，带来了希尔汗的皮。"

狼妈妈步伐僵硬地从洞里走出来，身后跟着狼崽，当她看见虎皮时，眼睛都亮了。

"小青蛙，那天他为了要你的命，把头和肩膀硬挤进这个洞里来的时候，我就警告过他——我跟他说猎人

① whirlwind ['wə:lwind] *n.*【气象学】旋风

② keep count 保持联系

③ bundle ['bʌndl] *n.* 捆（或包、扎）在一起的东西

④ embroider [im'brɔidə] *v.* 对（某事、叙述等）添枝加叶，渲染

⑤ adventure [əd'ventʃə] *n.* 冒险

cave, hunting for thy life, Little Frog—I told him that the hunter would be the hunted. It is well done."

"Little Brother, it is well done," said a deep voice in the thicket. "We were lonely in the jungle without thee," and Bagheera came running to Mowgli's bare feet. They clambered up the Council Rock together, and Mowgli spread the skin out on the flat stone where Akela used to sit, and pegged it down with four slivers of bamboo, and Akela lay down upon it, and called the old call to the Council, "Look—look well, O Wolves," exactly as he had called when Mowgli was first brought there.

Ever since Akela had been **deposed**①, the Pack had been without a leader, hunting and fighting at their own pleasure. But they answered the call from habit; and some of them were lame from the traps they had fallen into, and some **limped**② from shot wounds, and some were **mangy**③ from eating bad food, and many were missing. But they came to the Council Rock, all that were left of them, and saw Shere Khan's striped hide on the rock, and the huge claws dangling at the end of the empty dangling feet. It was then that Mowgli made up a song that came up into his throat all by itself, and he shouted it aloud, leaping up and down on the rattling skin, and beating time with his heels till he had no more breath left, while Gray Brother and Akela **howled**④ between the **verses**⑤.

"Look well, O Wolves. Have I kept my word?" said Mowgli. And the wolves bayed "Yes," and one tattered wolf howled:

"Lead us again, O Akela. Lead us again, O Man-cub, for we be sick of this lawlessness, and we would be the Free People once more."

"Nay," purred Bagheera, "that may not be. When ye are full-fed, the madness may come upon you again. Not for nothing are ye called the Free People. Ye fought for freedom, and it is yours. Eat it, O Wolves."

"Man-Pack and Wolf-Pack have cast me out," said Mowgli. "Now I will hunt alone in the jungle."

也会变成猎物的。干得好！"

灌木丛里传来一个低沉的声音："小兄弟，干得漂亮。丛林里没有你，我们都觉得很孤单。"巴格伊尔拉跑过来，靠近毛格利赤裸的双脚。他们一起费劲地爬上议会岩，毛格利把虎皮铺在阿凯拉以前坐的大平石上，还用四根竹片把它钉起来，阿凯拉在上面躺下来，再次发出召开议会的呼号"看啊，好好看啊，所有的狼"，就跟当初毛格利第一次被带到这里，他呼唤大家过来一模一样。

自从阿凯拉被赶下王位，狼群就一直没有领袖，不管猎食还是打架都是各顾各的。但是现在他们遵从习惯，回应了独狼的呼唤。有些狼因为掉进过陷阱变成了残废，有些因为受了枪伤也一瘸一拐，还有些因为吃了腐烂的食物长了皮癣，而更多的狼则消失了。但是狼群还是来到了议会岩，能来的狼全都到了。他们都看见岩石上铺着希尔汗布满条纹的毛皮，四只巨大的虎爪在空荡荡的四条腿末端耷拉着。就在这时，毛格利编了一首歌，这首歌完全是自动从他嗓子里钻出来的。他放声高歌，在沙沙作响的虎皮上蹦蹦跳跳，用脚跟打着拍子，直到最后一点力气都没有了才停下来。灰哥和阿凯拉也在一旁趁着他演唱的间隙吼上两声。

毛格利说："哦，群狼，好好看啊。我有没有信守诺言？"

群狼高呼："有！"一只身上的毛都烂糟糟的狼吼道："哦，阿凯拉，重新领导我们吧。哦，人崽，重新领导我们吧，我们受够了这种混乱，让我们再次成为自由民吧。"

巴格伊尔拉低声说："不，那可不行。等你们填饱了肚子，你们疯病又该发作了。你们想当自由民可不是白当的。过去你们为赢得自由而战斗过，所以现在自由归你们所有了。哦，群狼，你们就该自食其果。"

毛格利说："人族和狼族都曾驱赶我，现在我要独自在丛林里狩猎。"

① depose [di'pəuz] v. 把……（尤指从高职位）免职

② limp [limp] v. 一瘸一拐地走

③ mangy ['meindʒi] a. 患病的

④ howl [haul] v.（狼、犬等）嗥叫

⑤ verse [vəːs] n. 诗句

"And we will hunt with thee," said the four cubs.

So Mowgli went away and hunted with the four cubs in the jungle from that day on. But he was not always alone, because, years afterward, he became a man and married.

But that is a story for grown-ups.

四个狼崽说："那我们都跟着你打猎。"

于是毛格利离开了。从此以后，他就跟四头狼崽一起在丛林里打猎。但是他也并不是一直孤身一人，因为多年以后，他长大成人，结了婚。

不过，那就是另外一个讲给大人听的故事了。

Mowgli's Song

THAT HE SANG AT THE COUNCIL ROCK WHEN HE
DANCED ON SHERE KHAN'S HIDE

*The Song of Mowgli—I, Mowgli, am singing. Let the jungle listen to the
things I have done.*

*Shere Khan said he would kill—would kill! At the gates in the twilight he
would kill Mowgli, the Frog!*

*He ate and he drank. Drink deep, Shere Khan, for when wilt thou drink
again? Sleep and dream of the kill.*

*I am alone on the grazing-grounds. Gray Brother, come to me! Come to me,
Lone Wolf, for there is big game **afoot**[1]!*

*Bring up the great **bull**[2] buffaloes, the blue-skinned herd bulls with the
angry eyes. Drive them **to and fro**[3] as I order.*

Sleepest thou still, Shere Khan? Wake, oh, wake! Here come I, and the bulls

毛格利之歌

这就是在议会岩那儿毛格利踩着希尔汗的皮跳舞时唱的那首歌。

毛格利的歌——我，毛格利，在唱歌。让整个丛林都听听我做过的事情。

希尔汗声称他要杀人——他要杀！就在村口，就在黄昏的时候，他要杀了青蛙毛格利！

他吃了，又喝了。多喝点，希尔汗，你下次喝该是啥时候？睡吧，梦见你的杀戮。

我自个儿在牧场上。灰哥，到我这儿来！独狼，到我这儿来！这里马上会有大猎物！

把大公水牛带过来，那些蓝皮肤的、眼神凶悍的大公牛。听我的命令把他们赶来赶去。

希尔汗，你还在睡吗？醒醒，哦，醒醒！我来啦，

① afoot [ə'fut] *ad.* 正在进行的

② bull [bul] *n.* 公牛

③ to and fro 来回地

are behind.

Rama, the King of the Buffaloes, **stamped**[1] with his foot. Waters of the Waingunga, **whither**[2] went Shere Khan?

He is not Ikki to dig **holes**[3], nor Mao, the Peacock, that he should fly. He is not Mang the Bat, to hang in the branches. Little bamboos that **creak**[4] together, tell me where he ran?

Ow! He is there. Ahoo! He is there. Under the feet of Rama lies the Lame One! Up, Shere Khan!

Up and kill! Here is meat; break the necks of the bulls!

Hsh! He is asleep. We will not wake him, for his strength is very great. The kites have come down to see it. The black ants have come up to know it. There is a great assembly in his honor.

Alala! I have no cloth to wrap me. The kites will see that I am naked. I am ashamed to meet all these people.

Lend me thy coat, Shere Khan. Lend me thy gay striped coat that I may go to the Council Rock.

By the Bull that bought me I made a **promise**[5]—a little promise. Only thy coat is lacking before I keep my word.

With the knife—with the knife that men use—with the knife of the hunter, I will stoop down for my gift.

公牛在后面。

水牛之王，拉玛，跺着脚。瓦因刚加河的河水啊，希尔汗到哪儿去了？

他又不是豪猪伊吉会打洞，也不是孔雀摩尔会飞走。更不是蝙蝠芒恩会上树。一起嘎吱嘎吱响的小竹苗啊，告诉我，他跑到哪里去了？

噢！他在那儿。啊哈！他在那儿。瘸腿的那位就躺在拉玛的脚下！起来，希尔汗！

起来，杀啊！肉来啦，咬断公牛的脖子啊！

嘘！他睡着了。我们不要吵醒他，他的力气无比大。鸢鹰飞下来看到了。黑蚂蚁爬上来发现了。这么庞大的聚会，都是为着向他致敬。

阿拉啦！我没有布可以裹在身上。鸢鹰会发现我浑身赤裸。我没脸去见这么多人。

希尔汗，把你的衣服借给我。把你这身漂亮的条纹大衣借给我吧，好让我穿着去议会岩啊。

凭赎买我的那头公牛起誓，我许下了一个诺言——一个小小的诺言。我要说话算话，就缺你的大衣啦。

有了这把刀，人类使用的刀，猎人用的刀，我将蹲下身收割我的礼物。

① stamp [stæmp] v. 跺脚
② whither ['wiðə] ad. 到哪里
③ hole [həul] n. 洞，孔
④ creak [kri:k] v. 嘎吱嘎吱作响
⑤ promise ['prɔmis] n. 允诺

Waters of the Waingunga, Shere Khan gives me his coat for the love that he bears me.Pull, Gray Brother! Pull, Akela! Heavy is the hide of Shere Khan.

*The Man Pack are angry. They throw stones and talk child's talk. My mouth is **bleeding**[①]. Let me run away.*

*Through the night, through the hot night, run **swiftly**[②] with me, my brothers. We will leave the lights of the village and go to the low moon.*

*Waters of the Waingunga, the Man-Pack have **cast me out**[③]. I did them no harm, but they were afraid of me. Why?*

*Wolf Pack, ye have cast me out too. The jungle is **shut**[④] to me and the village gates are shut. Why?*

As Mang flies between the beasts and birds, so fly I between the village and the jungle. Why?

I dance on the hide of Shere Khan, but my heart is very heavy. My mouth is cut and wounded with the stones from the village, but my heart is very light, because I have come back to the jungle. Why?

These two things fight together in me as the snakes fight in the spring. The water comes out of my eyes; yet I laugh while it falls. Why?

I am two Mowglis, but the hide of Shere Khan is under my feet.

瓦因刚加河的水啊，出于对我的爱，希尔汗把他的大衣给了我。扯啊，灰哥！拉啊，阿凯拉！希尔汗的皮真沉啊。

人群生气啦。他们扔石头，说些孩子气的话。我的嘴流血了。让我跑吧。

我的兄弟们，穿过黑夜，穿过这闷热的黑夜，和我一起快快地跑吧。我们将离开村里的灯火，跑到低沉的月亮那儿去。

瓦因刚加河的水啊，人族把我赶出来啦。我可没有害他们，他们却害怕我。这是为什么？

狼群啊，你们也曾经驱逐我。丛林向我关上了大门，村庄也向我关上了大门。这是为什么？

就像芒恩徘徊于兽类和鸟类之间，我也徘徊于村庄和丛林之间。这是为什么？

我在希尔汗的皮上跳舞，可是我的心无比沉重。我的嘴被村民的石头砸伤了，破了一条口子，我的心却很轻松，因为我又回到了丛林。这又是为什么？

这两件事在我心里打架，就像蛇在春天互相缠斗。我的眼睛里流出水来啦，掉下来的时候我却笑了。到底是为什么？

我成了两个毛格利，但是到底希尔汗的皮被我踩在了脚下。

① bleeding ['bliːdiŋ] *a.* 出血的，流血的

② swiftly ['swiftli] *ad.* 很快地

③ cast out 驱逐，赶出

④ shut [ʃʌt] *a.* 关上的，关闭的

All the jungle knows that I have killed Shere Khan. Look—look well, O Wolves!

Ahae! My heart is **heavy**[1] with the things that I do not understand.

整个丛林都知道我杀了希尔汗。看——好好看啊，群狼！

啊嘿！这些事我都不明白，我的心啊无比沉重。

① heavy ['hevi] *a.* 负担过重的

The White Seal

Oh! hush thee, my baby, the night is behind us,
    And black are the waters that **sparkled**[1] so green.
The moon, o'er the **combers**[2], looks downward to find us
    At rest in the **hollows**[3] that rustle between.
Where billow meets billow, then soft be thy pillow,
    Ah, weary wee flipperling, curl at thy ease!
The storm shall not wake thee, nor shark overtake thee,
    Asleep in the arms of the slow-swinging seas!

Seal Lullaby

All these things happened several years ago at a place called Novastoshnah, or North East Point, on the Island of St. Paul, away and away in the Bering Sea. Limmershin, the Winter Wren, told me the tale when he was blown on to the rigging of a steamer going to Japan, and I took him down into my **cabin**[4] and warmed and fed him for a couple of days till he was fit to fly back to St. Paul's again. Limmershin is a very **quaint**[5] little bird, but he knows how to tell the truth.

Nobody comes to Novastoshnah except on business, and the only people who have regular business there are the seals. They come in the summer months by

白海豹

① sparkle ['spɑ:kl] v. 闪耀
② comber ['kəumə] n. ［美国英语］滚浪，碎浪，拍岸浪
③ hollow ['hɒləu] n. 山谷，溪谷

哦，宝贝儿，别出声，夜晚就在我们身后，
白天碧绿闪烁的海水现在一片漆黑。
在翻滚的波浪之上，月亮往下眺望，
发现我们在沙沙作响的浪窝间安睡。
巨浪一个连着一个，愿你的枕头软软和和。
疲倦的小宝贝啊，舒舒服服地蜷起来。
暴风雨吵不醒你，鲨鱼也赶不上你，
愿你就在大海慢慢摇晃的手臂间沉沉睡去。

——海豹的催眠曲

所有这一切都发生在几年前一个叫作诺瓦斯托西纳的地方。那个地方也叫作东北角，就在圣保罗岛上，在很远很远的白令海那儿。这个故事是一只叫利莫欣的冬鹬鹩告诉我的，当时他被吹到了往日本开的一艘轮船的帆索上。我把他救下来，带到我的舱房里，让他暖暖和和、吃饱喝足地待了好几天，直到他恢复健康能够飞回圣保罗岛去。利莫欣是一只非常奇怪的小鸟，但是他知道如何讲实话。

④ cabin ['kæbin] n. （轮船上的）船舱
⑤ quaint [kweint] a. 奇怪的，特殊的，不一般的

诺瓦斯托西纳没有游客，唯一常去的访客也就是海豹。在夏季的那几个月里成千上万的海豹离开寒冷灰白

hundreds and hundreds of thousands out of the cold gray sea. For Novastoshnah Beach has the finest accommodation for **seals**① of any place in all the world.

Sea Catch knew that, and every spring would swim from whatever place he happened to be in—would swim like a torpedo-boat straight for Novastoshnah and spend a month fighting with his companions for a good place on the rocks, as close to the sea as possible. Sea Catch was fifteen years old, a huge gray fur seal with almost a **mane**② on his shoulders, and long, wicked dog teeth. When he heaved himself up on his front flippers he stood more than four feet clear of the ground, and his weight, if anyone had been bold enough to weigh him, was nearly seven hundred pounds. He was scarred all over with the marks of **savage**③ fights, but he was always ready for just one fight more. He would put his head on one side, as though he were afraid to look his enemy in the face; then he would shoot it out like lightning, and when the big teeth were firmly fixed on the other seal's neck, the other seal might get away if he could, but Sea Catch would not help him.

Yet Sea Catch never chased a beaten seal, for that was against the Rules of the Beach. He only wanted room by the sea for his **nursery**④. But as there were forty or fifty thousand other seals hunting for the same thing each spring, the whistling, bellowing, roaring, and blowing on the beach was something frightful.

From a little hill called Hutchinson's Hill, you could look over three and a half miles of ground covered with fighting seals; and the **surf**⑤ was dotted all over with the heads of seals hurrying to land and begin their share of the fighting. They fought in the breakers, they fought in the sand, and they fought on the smooth-worn **basalt**⑥ rocks of the nurseries, for they were just as stupid and unaccommodating as men. Their wives never came to the island until late in May or early in June, for they did not care to be torn to pieces; and the young two-, three-, and four-year-old seals who had not begun housekeeping went inland about half a mile through the ranks of the fighters and played about on the sand **dunes**⑦ in droves and **legions**⑧, and rubbed off every single green thing that grew. They were called the holluschickie—the bachelors—and there were perhaps two or three hundred thousand of them at Novastoshnah alone.

① seal [si:l] *n.*【动物】海
豹

② mane [mein] *n.*（马、狮
的）鬃毛

③ savage ['sævidʒ] *a.* 野蛮
的

④ nursery ['nəːsəri] *n.* 保育
室

⑤ surf [səːf] *n.* 拍岸的大浪

⑥ basalt ['bæsɔːlt] *n.*【地质
学】玄武岩

⑦ dune [djuːn] *n.*（在沙漠
近湖地区由风吹积形成
的）沙丘

⑧ legion ['liːdʒən] *n.* 大量

的海水来到这里，因为对于他们来说，诺瓦斯托西纳的
海滩是全世界最舒服的休憩场所。

这一点海卡奇很清楚，所以每年春天无论在哪儿，
他都会像一只鱼雷艇一样直奔诺瓦斯托西纳而来，在这
儿待上一个月，每天都跟同伴争抢岩石上的一个好位
置，越靠近大海越好。海卡奇是一头十五岁的灰毛海豹，
身材高大，肩上几乎像披了个毛领子，嘴里还有长长的、
看上去很凶狠的犬牙。当他用前肢把身子立起来时，离
地能有四英尺多高。他的体重——如果有人敢把他抱起
来——差不多有好几百磅。他全身上下都是一次次恶战
留下的疤痕，但是他从不害怕再战一场。他会把头一偏，
好像不敢直视敌人，然后如同闪电一般直射出去，把他
的巨牙牢牢地钉在另一只海豹的颈上，这时对手也许能
想办法脱身，但是海卡奇可不会伸出援手。

不过，海卡奇从来不会去追赶被他打败的海豹，因
为那就违反了海滩法则。他只想在海边找块地方养孩子。
可是这也是四五万只海豹每年春天都想干的事情，所以
可以想见海滩上此起彼伏的口哨、怒吼和呼啸声交织在
一起是多么可怕的场景。

站在哈钦森山岗上往下俯瞰，可以看到绵延三英里
半的地面上全是在争斗的海豹，海里也是密密麻麻的脑
袋，更多的海豹正随波而来，急于加入这场争斗。他们
有的在浪里搏斗，有的在沙滩上，还有的在已经被磨得
很光滑的玄武岩育儿床上，因为他们就跟男人一样愚
蠢，不肯妥协。他们的妻子要到五月底或者六月初才会
来到岛上，因为害怕被撕成碎片。那些两到四岁的年轻
公海豹因为还没到繁殖期，他们会穿过这一排排的斗士
往半英里外的内陆去。这些年轻公海豹成群结队地在沙
丘上嬉戏，把每一丁点绿色植物都给蹭掉。这些"单身
汉"光是在诺瓦斯托西纳这个地方恐怕就有二三十万只
左右。

Sea Catch had just finished his forty-fifth fight one spring when Matkah, his soft, sleek, gentle-eyed wife, came up out of the sea, and he caught her by the scruff① of the neck and dumped her down on his reservation②, saying gruffly: "Late as usual. Where have you been?"

It was not the fashion for Sea Catch to eat anything during the four months he stayed on the beaches, and so his temper was generally bad. Matkah knew better than to answer back. She looked round and cooed③: "How thoughtful of you. You've taken the old place again."

"I should think I had," said Sea Catch. "Look at me!"

He was scratched and bleeding in twenty places; one eye was almost out, and his sides were torn to ribbons.

"Oh, you men, you men!" Matkah said, fanning herself with her hind flipper. "Why can't you be sensible and settle your places quietly? You look as though you had been fighting with the Killer Whale."

"I haven't been doing anything but fight since the middle of May. The beach is disgracefully crowded this season. I've met at least a hundred seals from Lukannon Beach, house hunting. Why can't people stay where they belong?"

"I've often thought we should be much happier if we hauled out at Otter Island instead of this crowded place," said Matkah.

"Bah! Only the holluschickie go to Otter Island. If we went there they would say we were afraid. We must preserve appearances, my dear."

Sea Catch sunk his head proudly between his fat shoulders and pretended to go to sleep for a few minutes, but all the time he was keeping a sharp lookout for a fight. Now that all the seals and their wives were on the land, you could hear their clamor miles out to sea above the loudest gales. At the lowest counting there were over a million seals on the beach—old seals, mother seals, tiny babies, and holluschickie, fighting, scuffling, bleating, crawling, and playing together—going down to the sea and coming up from it in gangs and regiments④, lying over every foot of ground as far as the eye could reach, and

① scruff [skrʌf] *n.* 颈背，后脖子

② reservation [ˌrezə'veiʃən] *n.* 专用地

③ coo [kuː] *v.* 脉脉含情地说话，温声细语

有一年春天，海卡奇刚结束第四十五场战斗，这时他那身体柔软、皮肤光滑、目光温柔的妻子玛特卡从海里爬了出来。海卡奇咬住她的颈背，把她扔到自己占好的地盘上，粗声粗气地说："又迟到了，跟平时一样。你到底去哪儿了？"

按照惯例，海卡奇停留在海滩上的这四个月里是不吃任何东西的，所以他的脾气总是不太好。玛特卡知道这种时候最好不要回嘴。她看看四周，温柔地嘟哝："你真是体贴，又抢到了咱们的老地方。"

海卡奇说："没错。你看看我。"

他身上有二十来处抓伤，都淌着血，一只眼睛几乎瞎了，两肋也被扯得稀烂。

"哦，你们男人，你们男人啊！"玛特卡一边说，一边用后鳍肢给自己扇扇。她说："你们难道就不能冷静点儿，安安静静地分好地盘吗？你这副模样就像刚跟杀人鲸打了一架似的。"

"从五月中开始，我除了打架就没干过别的。这一季的海滩挤得真是不像话。我都看见至少一百只鹿坎农海滩那边过来的家伙了，他们也来找房子。大家怎么就不能待在自己该待的地方呢？"

玛特卡说："我倒是常常觉得咱们不如去奥特岛，肯定要比待在这里挨挤快活多了呢。"

"呸！只有单身汉才去奥特岛呢。要是我们去那儿，他们肯定会说我们是胆小鬼。亲爱的，咱们可丢不起这个脸。"

海卡奇骄傲地耸起肥厚的双肩，把头缩进去，假装打了一会儿盹，其实他一直在小心提防可能的敌人。现在所有的公海豹和他们的妻子都已经登陆了，他们的喧闹声压过了最大的海风，连几英里外的海上都能听到。哪怕从最保守的估计来看，海滩上也有超过一百万只海豹，包括老海豹、母海豹、幼崽和年轻的公海豹，他们在一块争抢、扭打、叫唤、爬行和嬉闹，成群结队地从

④ regiment ['redʒimənt] *n.* 大量，大批，大群

skirmishing about in **brigades**① through the fog. It is nearly always foggy at Novastoshnah, except when the sun comes out and makes everything look all pearly and rainbow-colored for a little while.

Kotick, Matkah's baby, was born in the middle of that confusion, and he was all head and shoulders, with pale, watery blue eyes, as tiny seals must be, but there was something about his coat that made his mother look at him very closely.

"Sea Catch," she said, at last, "our baby's going to be white!"

"Empty clam-shells and dry seaweed!" **snorted**② Sea Catch. "There never has been such a thing in the world as a white seal."

"I can't help that," said Matkah; "there's going to be now." And she sang the low, crooning seal song that all the mother seals sing to their babies:

> *You mustn't swim till you're six weeks old,*
> *Or your head will be sunk by your heels;*
> *And summer gales and Killer Whales*
> *Are bad for baby seals.*

> *Are bad for baby seals, dear rat,*
> *As bad as bad can be;*
> *But splash and grow strong,*
> *And you can't be wrong.*
> *Child of the Open Sea!*

Of course the little fellow did not understand the words at first. He **paddled**③ and scrambled about by his mother's side, and learned to **scuffle**④ out of the way when his father was fighting with another seal, and the two rolled and roared up and down the slippery rocks. Matkah used to go to sea to get things to eat, and the baby was fed only once in two days, but then he ate all he could and **throve**⑤ upon it.

① brigade [briˈgeid] n. 队，队列

海里进进出出，遮住了肉眼可及的每英尺地面，一群一群海豹在大雾里打来打去。诺瓦斯托西纳总是雾气弥漫，只有太阳出来那会儿，一切才看上去珠光闪烁，五颜六色。

玛特卡的孩子，柯迪克，就在这一片混乱中降生了。他小小的个子，只看得见头和肩膀，淡蓝色的眼睛总是水汪汪的，但是他的毛皮似乎有点不对劲，他妈妈仔细地看了又看。

② snort [snɔːt] v. 用鼻子哼着说（或表示）

她说："海卡奇，咱们的孩子会是白色的。"

海卡奇嗤笑了一声，说："空贝壳和干海草！世界上压根儿就没有什么白海豹。"

玛特卡说："这我可管不了。今后就会有啦。"她开始唱起所有母海豹都会唱给宝宝听的一首歌，歌声低沉，充满了温情。

要到六周大你才能游泳啊，
不然你就会头重脚轻沉下去。
夏天的大风和杀人鲸
都是要害你的大坏蛋啊。

我亲爱的小耗子，他们都是大坏蛋，
坏到家的大坏蛋。
好好扑腾，长得壮壮的
你就不会有事，
你是大海的孩子哟！

③ paddle [ˈpædl] v. （像小孩子）摇摇晃晃地走
④ scuffle [ˈskʌfl] v. 拖着脚走路
⑤ thrive [θraiv] v. 茁壮成长

小宝贝一开始当然不明白这歌词是什么意思。他只是在妈妈身边拍水，爬来爬去，学会了一看见爸爸和别人打架就连滚带爬地躲到一边儿去，看着那两只大海豹在滑溜溜的岩石上冲着对方怒吼，上下翻滚。玛特卡去海里找吃的，刚开始两天才喂他一次，但是后来他食量大增，发育得很快。

The first thing he did was to **crawl**① inland, and there he met tens of thousands of babies of his own age, and they played together like puppies, went to sleep on the clean sand, and played again. The old people in the nurseries took no notice of them, and the holluschickie kept to their own grounds, and the babies had a beautiful playtime.

When Matkah came back from her deep-sea fishing she would go straight to their playground and call as a sheep calls for a lamb, and wait until she heard Kotick bleat. Then she would take the straightest of straight lines in his direction, striking out with her fore flippers and knocking the youngsters head over heels right and left. There were always a few hundred mothers hunting for their children through the playgrounds, and the babies were kept lively. But, as Matkah told Kotick, "So long as you don't lie in muddy water and get **mange**②, or rub the hard sand into a cut or scratch, and so long as you never go swimming when there is a heavy sea, nothing will hurt you here."

Little seals can no more swim than little children, but they are unhappy till they learn. The first time that Kotick went down to the sea a wave carried him out beyond his depth, and his big head sank and his little hind flippers flew up exactly as his mother had told him in the song, and if the next wave had not thrown him back again he would have drowned.

After that, he learned to lie in a beach pool and let the wash of the waves just cover him and lift him up while he paddled, but he always kept his eye open for big waves that might hurt. He was two weeks learning to use his **flippers**③; and all that while he **floundered**④ in and out of the water, and coughed and grunted and crawled up the beach and took catnaps on the sand, and went back again, until at last he found that he truly belonged to the water.

Then you can imagine the times that he had with his companions, ducking under the rollers; or coming in on top of a comber and landing with a swash and a splutter as the big wave went whirling far up the beach; or standing up on his tail and scratching his head as the old people did; or playing "I'm the King of the Castle" on slippery, weedy rocks that just stuck out of the wash. Now and

① crawl [krɔːl] v. 爬行

他接下来干的第一件事就是往岛上离海更远的地方爬，在那儿他遇见了成千上万只跟他同龄的幼崽。他们就像小狗崽一样在一起玩耍，在干净的沙地上睡觉，醒来又接着玩儿。育儿区的老家伙们并不关注他们，单身汉也都待在自己的地盘上，所以这些幼崽玩得非常开心。

玛特卡从深海捕鱼回来就径直跑到幼崽的游乐场去，像母羊呼唤羊羔一样发出叫唤，等到听见柯迪克的叫声，她就挑最近的路朝他直奔过去，两只前肢左右挥舞，一路把别的小海豹撞得四脚朝天。同一时间总是有好几百只母海豹在游乐场里来回搜寻自己的孩子，幼崽们也就被弄得鸡飞狗跳。但是，正如玛特卡告诉柯迪克的那样，"只要你不躺到泥水里害得自己长癣，或者把硬硬的沙子蹭到伤口里，只要你不在大海发怒时去游泳，你在这儿就不会有事。"

② mange [meindʒ] n.【兽病理学】兽疥癣

海豹幼崽并不比人类的婴儿游得更好，但是他们不学会游泳就不高兴。柯迪克第一次下海时，一个大浪把他卷出去了，他那大大的脑袋沉下去，两只小小的后鳍一下子甩过头顶，就跟妈妈在那首儿歌里唱的一模一样。要不是后面一个大浪又把他给扔了回来，他一准儿被淹死了。

从那以后，他学会了躺在沙滩的小浅坑里练习打水，让潮水将将没过自己好浮起来，但他总是特别小心注意躲过那些可能伤害他的大浪。他花了两周的时间学习使用自己的鳍肢，一直在水里扑腾来扑腾去，有时呛着水了抱怨两声，爬到沙滩上打个小盹儿，然后又爬回去，直到他终于学会了和水融为一体。

③ flipper ['flipə] n.（海豹、鲸等的）鳍状肢，鳍足，前肢

④ flounder ['flaundə] v.（在水、泥泞或深雪中）挣扎，肢体乱动

这之后你可以想象他和小伙伴们玩得有多么起劲，他们有时躲在巨浪底下，有时骑上一个拍岸浪，然后趁着巨浪呼啸着卷上海滩时，从浪尖上哗啦一声冲下来跳上岸，或者模仿大人的样子用尾巴把身子撑起来，挠挠脑袋，或是摆出一副"城堡之主"的架势站在满是海藻、

then he would see a thin **fin**①, like a big shark's fin, drifting along close to shore, and he knew that that was the Killer Whale, the Grampus, who eats young seals when he can get them; and Kotick would head for the beach like an arrow, and the fin would jig off slowly, as if it were looking for nothing at all.

Late in October the seals began to leave St. Paul's for the deep sea, by families and tribes, and there was no more fighting over the nurseries, and the holluschickie played anywhere they liked. "Next year," said Matkah to Kotick, "you will be a holluschickie; but this year you must learn how to catch fish."

They set out together across the Pacific, and Matkah showed Kotick how to sleep on his back with his flippers tucked down by his side and his little nose just out of the water. No cradle is so comfortable as the long, rocking swell of the Pacific. When Kotick felt his skin **tingle**② all over, Matkah told him he was learning the "feel of the water," and that tingly, prickly feelings meant bad weather coming, and he must swim hard and get away.

"In a little time," she said, "you'll know where to swim to, but just now we'll follow Sea Pig, the Porpoise, for he is very wise." A school of porpoises were **ducking**③ and tearing through the water, and little Kotick followed them as fast as he could. "How do you know where to go to?" he panted. The leader of the school rolled his white eye and ducked under. "My tail tingles, youngster," he said. "That means there's a **gale**④ behind me. Come along! When you're south of the Sticky Water [he meant the Equator] and your tail tingles, that means there's a gale in front of you and you must head north. Come along! The water feels bad here."

This was one of very many things that Kotick learned, and he was always learning. Matkah taught him to follow the **cod**⑤ and the **halibut**⑥ along the under-sea banks and wrench the rockling out of his hole among the weeds; how to skirt the wrecks lying a hundred **fathoms**⑦ below water and **dart**⑧ like a rifle bullet in at one **porthole**⑨ and out at another as the fishes ran; how to dance on the top of the waves when the lightning was racing all over the sky, and wave his flipper politely to the stumpy-tailed Albatross and the Man-of-war Hawk as

① fin [fin] *n.* 鳍

② tingle ['tiŋgl] *v.* 有刺痛感

③ duck [dʌk] *v.*（突然把整个身子或头）潜入水中

④ gale [geil] *n.*【气象学】8 级风，大风

⑤ cod [kɔd] *n.*【鱼类】鳕鱼

⑥ halibut ['hælibət] *n.*【鱼类】比目鱼

⑦ fathom ['fæðəm] *n.* 拓，英寻（英制水深单位，合 6 英尺或 1.6288 米，主要用于航行或采矿的度量单位）

⑧ dart [dɑːt] *v.* 投射，急投

⑨ porthole ['pɔːthəul] *n.*（船侧采光、通风的）舷窗

滑不溜秋的礁石上，脚底下就是汹涌拍岸的怒涛。偶尔他会看见一片薄薄的鱼鳍，好像一头巨鲨的背鳍那样，沿着岸边逡巡，他知道那就是虎鲸格兰普斯，那家伙一有机会就吃掉小海豹。这时柯迪克就会像箭一般射回岸边，那个鱼鳍呢，则会慢悠悠地摇晃着离开，似乎本来就是在闲逛一样。

十月末，海豹们开始拖家带口、成群结队地离开圣保罗岛前往深海，再也没有人争夺育儿地了，单身汉们想在哪儿玩就在哪儿玩。玛特卡对柯迪克说："明年，你就成了单身汉啦，可是今年你得先学会怎么捕鱼。"

他们一起出发横穿太平洋。玛特卡给柯迪克示范怎么仰泳，如何把鳍肢收拢在身体两侧，只把小鼻子露出水面。世上没有任何摇篮能比得上太平洋那长长的、起伏的波浪。柯迪克觉得全身的皮肤都有种刺痛的感觉，玛特卡告诉他这就叫"水感"，这种刺刺的、痒痒的感觉表示坏天气要来了，他必须使劲儿游争取避开。

她说："不久你就会知道该朝哪儿游了，但是现在咱们可以先跟着鼠海豚'海猪'，他可聪明了。"一群鼠海豚正在避开风浪，奋力游动，小柯迪克使尽全力跟着他们往前游。他喘着气问："你们怎么知道该去哪儿呢？"这群鼠海豚的头领转转白色的眼珠子，一下扎进水里，他说："小家伙，我的尾巴有刺刺的感觉，那说明有大风在我后面。跟上来吧！等你到了粘水——他是指赤道——南边，如果你的尾巴刺痛，那就表示前面有大风，那你就得朝北边游。快跟上，这里的水感觉可不好。"

这是柯迪克学到的第一件事，后来他又学会了很多其他的东西，他一直都在学习。玛特卡教他在浅海的海床上跟踪鳕鱼和大比目鱼，教他怎么把海泥鳅从海草间的巢穴里给揪出来；还教他绕着水底下一百英寻深处的沉船搜寻小鱼，教他怎么像来复枪子弹一样从一个舷窗射进去再从另一个窗口蹿出来；又教他在道道闪电划破长空时怎么在浪尖上跳舞，教他在尾巴粗短的信天翁

they went down the wind; how to jump three or four feet clear of the water like a dolphin, flippers close to the side and tail curved; to leave the flying fish alone because they are all **bony**[1]; to take the shoulder-piece out of a cod at full speed ten fathoms deep, and never to stop and look at a boat or a ship, but particularly a row-boat. At the end of six months what Kotick did not know about deep-sea fishing was not worth the knowing. And all that time he never set flipper on dry ground.

One day, however, as he was lying half asleep in the warm water somewhere off the Island of Juan Fernandez, he felt **faint**[2] and lazy all over, just as human people do when the spring is in their legs, and he remembered the good firm beaches of Novastoshnah seven thousand miles away, the games his companions played, the smell of the seaweed, the seal roar, and the fighting. That very minute he turned north, swimming steadily, and as he went on he met scores of his mates, all bound for the same place, and they said: "Greeting, Kotick! This year we are all holluschickie, and we can dance the Fire-dance in the breakers off Lukannon and play on the new grass. But where did you get that coat?"

Kotick's fur was almost pure white now, and though he felt very proud of it, he only said, "Swim quickly! My bones are aching for the land." And so they all came to the beaches where they had been born, and heard the old seals, their fathers, fighting in the rolling mist.

That night Kotick danced the Fire-dance with the yearling seals. The sea is full of fire on summer nights all the way down from Novastoshnah to Lukannon, and each seal leaves a **wake**[3] like burning oil behind him and a flaming flash when he jumps, and the waves break in great phosphorescent **streaks**[4] and swirls. Then they went inland to the holluschickie grounds and rolled up and down in the new wild wheat and told stories of what they had done while they had been at sea. They talked about the Pacific as boys would talk about a wood that they had been nutting in, and if anyone had understood them he could have gone away and made such a **chart**[5] of that ocean as never was. The three- and

① bony ['bəuni] *a.* 多骨的，
带骨的

② faint [feint] *a.* 虚弱的，
无力的

③ wake [weik] *n.* 痕迹，踪
迹

④ streak [stri:k] *n.* 条纹，斑
纹

⑤ chart [tʃɑ:t] *n.* 地图

和军舰鸟顺风而下时怎么用前肢跟他们彬彬有礼地打招呼；也教他像海豚一样跃出水面三四英尺高，怎么把前肢贴紧身躯、把尾巴蜷起来；教他别碰飞鱼，因为他们全身都是刺，又教他在十英寻深的水下如何咬下全速飞奔的鳕鱼的肩膀；还教他永远也不要停下来张望船只，尤其是划艇。六个月结束时，柯迪克对深海捕鱼的门道已经掌握得差不多了，而且在那么长的时间里他的鳍肢连一次也没碰过干燥的地面。

可是有一天，在胡安费南德兹岛附近的某个地方，当他正在温暖的水里泡着半睡半醒的时候，他觉得昏昏沉沉，浑身乏力，就跟人类春困时腿脚无力一样。这时，他想起了七千英里外诺瓦斯托西纳那十分坚实的沙滩，想起了他和伙伴们玩的那些游戏，海藻的味道，海豹的怒吼，还有那些打斗的场面。就在那一瞬间，他转身向北持续不断地游去，一路上遇到几十个同伴，他们也都是去往同一个目的地，他们对他说："柯迪克，你好啊！今年我们都是单身汉啦，我们可以在鹿坎农的大浪里跳火焰舞，还可以在新草上玩儿啦。你是从哪儿找来这身大衣的？"

柯迪克的毛皮现在几乎是纯白色的，虽然他很为之骄傲，但他只是说："快点游吧！我想上岸想得骨头都疼啦。"于是他们都来到了自己出生的海滩，听见老海豹，也就是他们的父辈们，在腾腾的雾气中搏斗。

那天晚上柯迪克和一岁大的海豹们跳起了火焰舞。每到夏季的夜晚，从诺瓦斯托西纳到鹿坎农的海面都是火光。每个海豹的身后都拖着一道燃烧的油一般的印迹，而当他们腾空跃起时，又会划出一道耀眼的火光。所有的波浪都碎裂成巨大的闪着磷光的条纹和旋涡。这些海豹来到岛上单身汉们的保留地，在新长出的野麦田里滚来滚去，分享他们在海上的故事。他们谈起太平洋就跟男孩们谈起从小捡坚果的树林一样，似乎要是有人能听懂他们的心声，他们就会跑到那片大洋里大展手脚，画出一幅前人从未画过的海图。那些三四岁的单身汉则从

four-year-old holluschickie romped down from Hutchinson's Hill crying: "Out of the way, youngsters! The sea is deep and you don't know all that's in it yet. Wait till you've rounded the Horn. Hi, you yearling, where did you get that white coat?"

"I didn't get it," said Kotick. "It grew." And just as he was going to roll the speaker over, a couple of black-haired men with flat red faces came from behind a sand dune, and Kotick, who had never seen a man before, coughed and lowered his head. The holluschickie just bundled off a few yards and sat staring stupidly. The men were no less than Kerick Booterin, the chief of the seal-hunters on the island, and Patalamon, his son. They came from the little village not half a mile from the sea nurseries, and they were deciding what seals they would drive up to the killing **pens**① —for the seals were driven just like sheep—to be turned into seal-skin jackets later on.

"Ho!" said Patalamon. "Look! There's a white seal!"

Kerick Booterin turned nearly white under his oil and smoke, for he was an **Aleut**②, and Aleuts are not clean people. Then he began to mutter a prayer. "Don't touch him, Patalamon. There has never been a white seal since—since I was born. Perhaps it is old Zaharrof's ghost. He was lost last year in the big gale."

"I'm not going near him," said Patalamon. "He's unlucky. Do you really think he is old Zaharrof come back? I owe him for some **gulls**③' eggs."

"Don't look at him," said Kerick. "Head off that drove of four-year-olds. The men ought to **skin**④ two hundred to-day, but it's the beginning of the season and they are new to the work. A hundred will do. Quick!"

Patalamon rattled a pair of seal's shoulder bones in front of a herd of holluschickie and they stopped dead, puffing and blowing. Then he stepped near and the seals began to move, and Kerick headed them inland, and they never tried to get back to their companions. Hundreds and hundreds of thousands of seals watched them being driven, but they went on playing just the same. Kotick was the only one who asked questions, and none of his companions could tell

哈钦森岗上轻快地跃下，一边喊着："让开，小家伙们！大海深着呢，你们还不清楚里面都有些啥。等到你们绕过合恩角再说吧。嗨，你这个一岁大的小毛头，你从哪儿搞到那件白大衣的？"

柯迪克说："这不是我搞来的，它自己长出来的。"他正要过去把对方撞翻时，两个头发漆黑、面部扁平通红的男人从沙丘背后冒出来。这是柯迪克第一次遇见人类，所以他咳嗽了一声，低下了头。而那个单身汉呢，也急忙往后退了好几码，坐在那儿傻乎乎地盯着人家看。来的这俩人正是岛上专门猎捕海豹的人类头领科瑞克布特林和他的儿子帕塔拉蒙。他们的村子距离海豹的育儿场不到半英里远，现在俩人正在商量要把哪些海豹赶到上面的屠宰圈里去——因为海豹跟羊一样都是可以被成群驱赶的——后面才好做成海豹皮夹克。

帕塔拉蒙说："呵！看哪，有只白海豹！"

科瑞克布特林满是油烟的脸几乎变得煞白，他是个阿留申人，阿留申人都不太爱干净。他开始低声祈祷起来。他说："帕塔拉蒙，别碰他。从来——从我出生以来——就没有过白海豹。也许这是老扎哈洛夫的鬼魂。去年他被大风刮走了。"

帕塔拉蒙说："我不会靠近他的。他看上去不吉利。你真的觉得他是老扎哈洛夫回来了？我还欠他几个海鸥蛋呢。"

科瑞克说："别看他。你去拦住那群四岁大的海豹。咱们的人今天应该剥出两百张海豹皮来，可是眼下狩猎季刚开始，他们手还有点生。一百只就可以了。快去！"

帕塔拉蒙对着一群单身汉把海豹的一对肩骨敲得咯咯响，这些海豹立马全都停了下来，呼哧呼哧地喘着粗气。他一靠近，海豹们就开始挪动，就这样他把他们往内陆赶去，而这些海豹压根也没试着回到同伴身边去。好几万头海豹就这样眼睁睁地看着他们被赶走，但是他们也还是照常嬉戏。柯迪克是唯一提出疑问的，但是他

him anything, except that the men always drove seals in that way for six weeks or two months of every year.

"I am going to follow," he said, and his eyes nearly **popped out**① of his head as he shuffled along in the wake of the herd.

"The white seal is coming after us," cried Patalamon. "That's the first time a seal has ever come to the killing-grounds alone."

"Hsh! Don't look behind you," said Kerick. "It is Zaharrof's ghost! I must speak to the priest about this."

The distance to the killing-grounds was only half a mile, but it took an hour to cover, because if the seals went too fast Kerick knew that they would get heated and then their fur would come off in **patches**② when they were skinned. So they went on very slowly, past Sea Lion's Neck, past Webster House, till they came to the Salt House just beyond the sight of the seals on the beach. Kotick followed, panting and wondering. He thought that he was at the world's end, but the roar of the seal nurseries behind him sounded as loud as the roar of a train in a tunnel. Then Kerick sat down on the moss and pulled out a heavy **pewter**③ watch and let the drove cool off for thirty minutes, and Kotick could hear the fog-dew dripping off the brim of his cap. Then ten or twelve men, each with an iron-bound **club**④ three or four feet long, came up, and Kerick pointed out one or two of the drove that were bitten by their companions or too hot, and the men kicked those aside with their heavy boots made of the skin of a **walrus**⑤'s throat, and then Kerick said, "Let go!" and then the men clubbed the seals on the head as fast as they could.

Ten minutes later little Kotick did not recognize his friends any more, for their skins were ripped off from the nose to the hind flippers, whipped off and thrown down on the ground in a pile. That was enough for Kotick. He turned and **galloped**⑥ (a seal can gallop very swiftly for a short time) back to the sea; his little new mustache bristling with horror. At Sea Lion's Neck, where the great sea lions sit on the edge of the surf, he flung himself flipper-overhead into the cool water and rocked there, gasping miserably. "What's here?" said a sea

的伙伴也没有谁能告诉他任何答案，他们只知道人类一直都以这样的方式驱赶海豹，每年总有一个半月或者两个月的时间是这样。

柯迪克说："我要跟上去看看。"他拖着后鳍一扭一扭地跟在海豹群的后面，好奇得连眼珠子都快瞪出来了。

帕塔拉蒙叫道："那头白海豹在追我们。这还是头一回有海豹独自跑到屠宰场来呢。"

科瑞克说："嘘！别往后看。那是扎哈洛夫的鬼魂！我得跟祭司说说这事儿。"

他们离屠宰场就半英里远，但是路上却花了一个钟头。因为科瑞克知道要是海豹走得太急了，就会发热，然后等到剥皮时，他们的毛就会成块儿地掉下来。所以他们走得很慢很慢，过了"海狮脖"，又过了韦伯斯特之家，最后来到盐屋，才刚刚离开海滩上那些海豹的视线。柯迪克一直跟着他们，一边喘气一边好奇。他以为自己来到了世界的尽头，可是从身后海豹育儿场传来的吼叫声还跟穿过隧道的火车鸣笛一样响亮。他看见科瑞克在苔藓上坐下来，掏出一只沉甸甸的白镴怀表，让海豹群歇了三十分钟，他都能听见雾气凝结成的露珠从科瑞克的帽檐上滴下来的声音。接着只见十来个男人走了过来，每个人手里都拎着一根包着铁皮、有三四英尺长的大棒。科瑞克给他们指出来一两只海豹，不是身上有咬伤的，就是走得太热的，这些男人就用他们那海象前脖子皮做成的厚靴子把这几只海豹踢到一边去。然后科瑞克说："动手！"男人们就以最快的速度用棒子敲击海豹的脑袋。

十分钟过后，柯迪克就再也认不出他的朋友们了，他们的皮从鼻子撕开一直到后鳍肢，然后扯下来扔到地上堆成了一堆。柯迪克再也受不了了。他转身飞奔（海豹在短时间内可以快速地奔跑）跑回大海，他那小小的新长出来的胡须吓得都竖了起来。到了"海狮脖"，那儿有好些巨大的海狮坐在浪边上，他头朝下一个猛子扎进凉水里，来回晃悠，痛苦地倒抽气。一头海狮粗声粗气

① pop out（眼睛）突出

② patch [pætʃ] *n.* 补丁

③ pewter ['pju:tə] *n.* 青灰色

④ club [klʌb] *n.*【造船】辅助帆杆

⑤ walrus ['wɔ:lrəs] *n.*【动物】海象

⑥ gallop ['gæləp] *v.*（马等）飞跑，疾驰

lion gruffly, for as a rule the sea lions **keep themselves to themselves**①.

"Scoochnie! Ochen scoochnie!" ("I'm lonesome, very lonesome!") said Kotick. "They're killing all the holluschickie on all the beaches!"

The Sea Lion turned his head **inshore**②. "Nonsense!" he said. "Your friends are making as much noise as ever. You must have seen old Kerick polishing off a **drove**③. He's done that for thirty years."

"It's horrible," said Kotick, backing water as a wave went over him, and steadying himself with a screw stroke of his flippers that brought him all standing within three inches of a jagged edge of rock.

"Well done for a yearling!" said the Sea Lion, who could appreciate good swimming. "I suppose it is rather awful from your way of looking at it, but if you seals will come here year after year, of course the men get to know of it, and unless you can find an island where no men ever come you will always be driven."

"Isn't there any such island?" began Kotick.

"I've followed the poltoos [the halibut] for twenty years, and I can't say I've found it yet. But look here—you seem to have a fondness for talking to your betters—suppose you go to Walrus Islet and talk to Sea Vitch. He may know something. Don't **flounce**④ off like that. It's a six-mile swim, and if I were you I should haul out and **take a nap**⑤ first, little one."

Kotick thought that that was good advice, so he swam round to his own beach, hauled out, and slept for half an hour, twitching all over, as seals will. Then he headed straight for Walrus Islet, a little low sheet of rocky island almost due northeast from Novastoshnah, all ledges and rock and gulls' nests, where the walrus herded by themselves.

He landed close to old Sea Vitch—the big, ugly, bloated, pimpled, fat-necked, long-tusked walrus of the North **Pacific**⑥, who has no manners except when he is asleep—as he was then, with his hind flippers half in and half out of the surf.

"Wake up!" barked Kotick, for the gulls were making a great noise.

① keep oneself to oneself
不与人来往

② inshore [,in'ʃɔ:] *a.* 沿海
的

③ drove [drəuv] *n.*（成群
移动的）一批相似物

④ flounce [flauns] *v.*（带着
愤怒、不耐烦或傲慢的
动作）猝然离去

⑤ take a nap 小睡一下

⑥ Pacific [pə'sifik] *n.* 太平
洋

地问："怎么啦？"因为一般来说，海狮都不喜欢管闲事。

柯迪克回答说："死库琪尼，欧肯死库琪尼（我很孤
单，孤单极了）！他们在屠杀所有海滩上的所有单身汉。"

海狮转过头朝岸上看去，说道："瞎说！你的朋友
们就跟平时一样闹哄哄的。你肯定是看见老科瑞克干掉
了一群海豹。他都干了三十年了。"

柯迪克说："太可怕了。"一个浪打过来，他往后拍
水，两只后蹼一个旋踢把整个身子立起来，在离一块嶙
峋的岩石只有三英寸的地方稳住了。

海狮佩服他的泳技，说："一个一岁大的毛毛头能
游成这样，真了不起！我想从你的眼光来看，这件事是
挺可怕的，但是你们海豹年年都到这儿来，人类当然也
就知道了，除非你们能找到一个没人去的岛，要不然你
们总是会被赶杀的。"

柯迪克问："难道说没有这样的岛吗？"

"我跟着大比目鱼都跟了二十年了，可以说还没找
到过呢。但是听着——既然你好像挺喜欢跟人请教，那
我就说说——你可以去海象小岛，跟海维奇聊聊。他也
许知道点什么。别这样像打了鸡血似的。你得游六英里
呢，我要是你，小家伙，我就先靠岸，打个小盹儿再说。"

柯迪克觉得这是好主意，于是他掉头游回自己的海
滩，上了岸，睡了半个小时，睡的时候就跟所有海豹一
样浑身颤动。然后他就直奔海象小岛而去，那是个低矮
的岩石密布的小岛，差不多就在诺瓦斯托西纳的正东北
方向，岛上全是暗礁、岩石和海鸥的鸟巢，那里正是海
象的地盘。

他在靠近老海维奇的地方上了岸。海维奇是一头北太
平洋长牙海象，又大又丑，身子臃肿，满是疙瘩，脖子肥
肥的，除了睡觉以外其他时间都举止粗俗。眼下他就正在
睡觉，两只后蹼一半儿耷拉在岸上，一半儿伸到水里。

"醒一醒！"柯迪克大声叫着，因为海鸥的声音太
响了。

"Hah! Ho! Hmph! What's that?" said Sea Vitch, and he struck the next walrus a blow with his **tusks**[1] and waked him up, and the next struck the next, and so on till they were all awake and staring in every direction but the right one.

"Hi! It's me," said Kotick, bobbing in the surf and looking like a little white **slug**[2].

"Well! May I be—skinned!" said Sea Vitch, and they all looked at Kotick as you can fancy a club full of drowsy old gentlemen would look at a little boy. Kotick did not care to hear any more about skinning just then; he had seen enough of it. So he called out: "Isn't there any place for seals to go where men don't ever come?"

"Go and find out," said Sea Vitch, shutting his eyes. "Run away. We're busy here."

Kotick made his dolphin-jump in the air and shouted as loud as he could: "Clam-eater! Clam-eater!" He knew that Sea Vitch never caught a fish in his life but always rooted for clams and **seaweed**[3]; though he pretended to be a very terrible person. Naturally the Chickies and the Gooverooskies and the Epatkas—the Burgomaster Gulls and the Kittiwakes and the Puffins, who are always looking for a chance to be rude, took up the cry, and—so Limmershin told me—for nearly five minutes you could not have heard a gun fired on Walrus Islet. All the population was yelling and screaming "Clam-eater! Stareek [old man]!" while Sea Vitch rolled from side to side grunting and coughing.

"Now will you tell?" said Kotick, all out of breath.

"Go and ask Sea Cow," said Sea Vitch. "If he is living still, he'll be able to tell you."

"How shall I know Sea Cow when I meet him?" said Kotick, **sheering off**[4].

"He's the only thing in the sea uglier than Sea Vitch," screamed a Burgomaster gull, wheeling under Sea Vitch's nose. "Uglier, and with worse manners! Stareek!"

Kotick swam back to Novastoshnah, leaving the gulls to scream. There

① tusk [tʌsk] *n.*（大象、海象、野猪等的）长牙，獠牙

② slug [slʌg] *n.* 鼻涕虫

③ seaweed ['siːwiːd] *n.* 海草

④ sheer off 躲开，避开

海维奇说："哈！霍！哼！怎么啦？"他的长牙打了旁边的海象一下，把人家给弄醒了，那只海象又打了旁边的另一只海象，就这样一只接一只的，所有的海象全都醒了过来，四处乱瞪，就是没看见该看的。

"嗨！是我呀。"柯迪克说，他在潮水里拱了拱身子，就好像一只小小的白鼻涕虫。

海维奇说："哎呀！我倒是给——剥了皮才好呢！"海象全都看着柯迪克，那光景，你要是能想象的话，就跟满俱乐部的昏昏欲睡的老绅士都看着一个小男孩一样。柯迪克这会儿可再不想听什么剥皮的话了，他已经见得够多了。他喊道："就没有什么海豹可以去又没有人的地方吗？"

海维奇闭上眼睛说："你自己找去吧。滚开。我们忙着呢。"

柯迪克像海豚一样跳到空中，扯着嗓子大喊："吃蛤蜊的家伙！吃蛤蜊的家伙！"他知道海维奇虽然摆出一副很可怕的样子，其实一生当中从来没抓过鱼，总是在泥里翻找蛤蜊和海草。

这下那些一直等着撒野的北极鸥、三趾鸥和角嘴海鸥自然而然地趁机大叫起来，于是一时之间——反正利莫欣是这么跟我说的——海象小岛上吵得几乎有整整五分钟，哪怕鸣枪都听不到。所有的动物都在大喊大叫"吃牡蛎的家伙！老家伙！"海维奇呢，则滚来滚去，不停地嘟哝、咳嗽。

柯迪克气喘吁吁地说："现在你肯说了吗？"

海维奇说："去问问海牛吧，要是他还活着的话，就能告诉你。"

柯迪克转过身去，一边问："我见了海牛怎么才能认出他来呢？"

一只北极鸥在海维奇的鼻子下盘旋，尖叫着说："他是海里唯一一比海维奇还要丑的家伙。更丑不说，还更没礼貌！老东西！"

he found that no one **sympathized**① with him in his little attempt to discover a quiet place for the seals. They told him that men had always driven the holluschickie — it was part of the day's work — and that if he did not like to see **ugly**② things he should not have gone to the killing grounds. But none of the other seals had seen the killing, and that made the difference between him and his friends. Besides, Kotick was a white seal.

"What you must do," said old Sea Catch, after he had heard his son's adventures, "is to grow up and be a big seal like your father, and have a nursery on the beach, and then they will leave you alone. In another five years you ought to be able to fight for yourself." Even gentle Matkah, his mother, said: "You will never be able to stop the killing. Go and play in the sea, Kotick." And Kotick went off and danced the Fire-dance with a very heavy little heart.

That autumn he left the beach as soon as he could, and set off alone because of a notion in his bullet-head. He was going to find Sea Cow, if there was such a person in the sea, and he was going to find a quiet island with good firm beaches for seals to live on, where men could not get at them. So he **explored**③ and explored by himself from the North to the South Pacific, swimming as much as three hundred miles in a day and a night. He met with more adventures than can be told, and narrowly escaped being caught by the Basking Shark, and the Spotted Shark, and the Hammerhead, and he met all the **untrustworthy**④ **ruffians**⑤ that loaf up and down the seas, and the heavy polite fish, and the scarlet spotted scallops that are moored in one place for hundreds of years, and grow very proud of it; but he never met Sea Cow, and he never found an island that he could fancy.

If the beach was good and hard, with a slope behind it for seals to play on, there was always the smoke of a **whaler**⑥ on the horizon, boiling down **blubber**⑦, and Kotick knew what that meant. Or else he could see that seals had once visited the island and been killed off, and Kotick knew that where men had come once they would come again.

He picked up with an old stumpy-tailed **albatross**⑧, who told him that

① sympathize ['simpθaiz]
v. 同情

② ugly ['ʌgli] a. 邪恶的，
丑恶的

③ explore [ik'splɔ:] v. 探
索，探究

④ untrustworthy [ʌn'trʌs(t)
wəːði] a. 靠不住的
⑤ ruffian ['rʌfiən] n. 流氓，
无赖，恶棍

⑥ whaler ['weilə] n. 捕鲸船
⑦ blubber ['blʌbə] n. 鲸脂，
鲸油

⑧ albatross ['ælbətrɔs] n.
【鸟类】信天翁

　　海鸥们继续在那儿乱叫唤，柯迪克则游回诺瓦斯托西纳去。可是他发现没有谁赞同他的计划，愿意和他一起为大家寻找一个安静的地方。他们告诉他人类一直在驱赶单身汉——世道就是如此——如果他不喜欢看见这些丑恶的事情，那他就不该跑到屠宰场那儿去。但是其他的海豹之所以和柯迪克不一样，是因为他们谁也没见过屠杀，再加上只有他是白海豹。

　　听完儿子的冒险经历，老海卡奇说："你要做的就是长大，变成像你父亲这样的大海豹，然后在海滩上找个地方成家，这样他们就不会碰你了。再过五年你就该为自己而战了。"哪怕是他母亲，温柔的玛特卡，也说："你永远也没有办法阻止那些杀戮。去海里玩吧，柯迪克。"于是柯迪克走开了，跳起了火焰舞，但是他小小的心啊，无比沉重。

　　那年秋天他早早地就离开了海滩，独自一人上了路，因为他那子弹头一样的小脑袋里有一个想法：他要去找海牛，如果海里真有这么个东西的话，他还要去找到一个安静的小岛，岛上有非常坚实的海滩可供海豹居住，而且没有人类可以到那儿去抓他们。所以他独自从北太平洋找到南太平洋，一个昼夜可以游上三百英里。他遇到了很多惊险，多得说都说不完，差一点点就被姥鲨、斑点鲨和双髻鲨抓住，他还遇到了所有那些在海里东游西荡、满嘴跑火车的恶棍，也有那些笨重却讲礼的鱼，还有鲜红的斑点扇贝，他们在一个地方待了好几百年，而且对此感到非常自豪，但是他从来也没遇见过海牛，也从来没有找到过一个他喜欢的小岛。

　　有的小岛沙滩很好也很结实，后面还有一个斜坡可以让海豹玩耍，但是地平线上总会有只捕鲸船在冒烟，柯迪克明白那是他们在熬炼鲸油。要不然呢，就是一个岛上曾经有过海豹，但是后来被杀光了，柯迪克知道来过人类的地方总是还会再来的。

　　后来他结识了一只粗尾巴的信天翁，听他说科谷埃

Kerguelen Island was the very place for peace and quiet, and when Kotick went down there he was all but smashed to pieces against some wicked black cliffs in a heavy sleet-storm with lightning and thunder. Yet as he pulled out against the gale he could see that even there had once been a seal nursery. And it was so in all the other islands that he visited.

Limmershin gave a long list of them, for he said that Kotick spent five seasons exploring, with a four months' rest each year at Novastoshnah, when the holluschickie used to make fun of him and his imaginary islands. He went to the Gallapagos, a **horrid**[①] dry place on the Equator, where he was nearly baked to death; he went to the Georgia Islands, the Orkneys, Emerald Island, Little Nightingale Island, Gough's Island, Bouvet's Island, the Crossets, and even to a little speck of an island south of the Cape of Good Hope. But everywhere the People of the Sea told him the same things. Seals had come to those islands once upon a time, but men had killed them all off. Even when he swam thousands of miles out of the Pacific and got to a place called Cape Corrientes (that was when he was coming back from Gough's Island), he found a few hundred mangy seals on a rock and they told him that men came there too.

That nearly broke his heart, and he headed round the Horn back to his own beaches; and on his way north he hauled out on an island full of green trees, where he found an old, old seal who was dying, and Kotick caught fish for him and told him all his **sorrows**[②]. "Now," said Kotick, "I am going back to Novastoshnah, and if I am driven to the killing-pens with the holluschickie I shall not care."

The old seal said, "Try once more. I am the last of the Lost Rookery of Masafuera, and in the days when men killed us by the hundred thousand there was a story on the beaches that some day a white seal would come out of the North and lead the seal people to a quiet place. I am old, and I shall never live to see that day, but others will. Try once more."

And Kotick curled up his mustache (it was a beauty) and said, "I am the only white seal that has ever been born on the beaches, and I am the only seal,

伦岛是个非常安静的地方，于是就去了那儿，可是却赶上一场雨夹雪的大风暴，又是打雷又是闪电的，还差点被一些可恨的黑色峭壁撞成碎片。等他好不容易顶着巨风上了岸，却又发现就连这里也曾有过海豹的育儿场。其余他去过的岛屿也都好不到哪儿去。

利莫欣列举了很多这样的岛屿，因为据他说一连五年，每年除了在诺瓦斯托西纳休息的四个月，其余时间都被柯迪克用来搜寻小岛了。而他每次回到诺瓦斯托西纳，单身汉们总会嘲笑他和他臆想出来的岛屿。他去过加拉帕格斯，赤道上一个干得吓人的地方，在那里他几乎被烤焦了；他去过佐治亚群岛、奥克尼群岛、绿宝石岛、小南丁格尔岛、高夫岛、布维岛和克罗泽群岛；他还去过好望角南边的一个丁点大的小岛。可是所到之处，海民们告诉他的都一样。这些岛屿以前都来过海豹，但是人类把他们都杀光了。甚至有一次他游出太平洋几千英里，到了一个叫作科连特斯角的地方（那是在他从高夫岛回来的路上），他在一片岩石上遇到几百只长了疥癣的海豹，他们说那里也有人类来过。

这几乎让他的心都碎了，他只好又绕回合恩角回自己的海滩去。在往北游的路上他在一个绿树葱茏的岛上靠了岸，在那里发现一头很老很老的海豹快要死了。于是柯迪克替他抓了些鱼，跟他倾诉自己的烦恼。柯迪克说："现在，我要回诺瓦斯托西纳去了。就算我跟其他单身汉一起被赶到屠宰圈里去，我也不管了。"

老海豹说："再试一次吧。我是消失的马萨弗埃拉海豹群的最后一名成员，当年人类成千上万地屠杀我的族群时，海滩上曾经流传着一个故事，据说会有一天，一头白海豹会从北边出来，带领海豹族群找到一个安宁之所。我老啦，我永远也活不到那一天了，但是其他海豹会活下去的。再试一次吧。"

柯迪克翘起他的胡须（它长得可漂亮了）说："我是海滩上降生的唯一一只白海豹，我也是唯一一只想要

① horrid ['hɔrid] a. 可怕的，恐怖的，令人恐惧的

② sorrow ['sɔrəu] n. 苦恼，忧愁

black or white, who ever thought of looking for new islands."

This cheered him **immensely**①; and when he came back to Novastoshnah that summer, Matkah, his mother, begged him to marry and settle down, for he was no longer a holluschick but a full-grown sea-catch, with a curly white mane on his shoulders, as heavy, as big, and as fierce as his father. "Give me another season," he said. "Remember, Mother, it is always the seventh wave that goes farthest up the beach."

Curiously enough, there was another seal who thought that she would **put off**② marrying till the next year, and Kotick danced the Fire-dance with her all down Lukannon Beach the night before he set off on his last exploration. This time he went westward, because he had fallen on the trail of a great **shoal**③ of halibut, and he needed at least one hundred pounds of fish a day to keep him in good condition. He chased them till he was tired, and then he curled himself up and went to sleep on the hollows of the ground swell that sets in to Copper Island. He knew the coast perfectly well, so about midnight, when he felt himself gently bumped on a weed-bed, he said, "Hm, tide's running strong tonight," and turning over under water opened his eyes slowly and stretched. Then he jumped like a cat, for he saw huge things nosing about in the shoal water and browsing on the heavy **fringes**④ of the weeds.

"By the Great Combers of Magellan!" he said, **beneath**⑤ his mustache. "Who in the Deep Sea are these people?"

They were like no walrus, sea lion, seal, bear, whale, shark, fish, **squid**⑥, or scallop that Kotick had ever seen before. They were between twenty and thirty feet long, and they had no hind flippers, but a shovel-like tail that looked as if it had been whittled out of wet leather. Their heads were the most foolish-looking things you ever saw, and they balanced on the ends of their tails in deep water when they weren't grazing, bowing solemnly to each other and waving their front flippers as a fat man waves his arm.

"Ahem!" said Kotick. "Good sport, gentlemen?" The big things answered by bowing and waving their flippers like the Frog Footman. When they began

寻找新岛的海豹，不管是白的还是黑的。"

这让他非常高兴。那年夏天当他回到诺瓦斯托西纳时，他的母亲玛特卡求他结婚安家，因为他已经不再是个单身汉，而是一头成年公海豹了，他肩膀上披着卷曲的白色鬃毛，跟他父亲一样壮硕凶猛。他说："再给我一年的时间吧。要知道，妈妈，在海滩上冲得最远的永远是第七道浪。"

奇怪的是，还有一头海豹也决定要等到来年才结婚。这天晚上柯迪克和她跳了火焰舞，把整个鹿坎农海滩都跳了个遍。第二天他就出发踏上了最后一次探险之旅。这回他往西去，因为恰好跟上了一大群大比目鱼，而他每天需要吃掉至少一百磅的鱼才能保持良好的体格。他追赶鱼群，直到精疲力竭才把身子蜷起来，在涌向铜岛的大浪浪谷里睡了一觉。他对这片海岸了若指掌，快到半夜，他觉得自己轻轻地撞上了一块海草床，他对自己说："嗯，看来今晚的潮水来得挺猛的。"于是他在水下翻了个身，慢慢地睁开眼睛，伸了个懒腰。接着他像猫一样跳了起来，因为他看见在浅滩的水里有好些个头巨大的东西在探头探脑地啃食着海草浓密的边缘。

他从胡子底下发出声音："凭着麦哲伦海峡的大浪起誓，这些究竟是什么玩意儿啊？"

他们不像柯迪克见过的任何动物，无论是海象、海狮、海豹、熊还是鲸鱼、鲨鱼、鱼、章鱼或是扇贝。他们有二十到三十英尺长，没有后鳍肢，只有一根铲状的尾巴，好像用湿皮革削出来似的。他们的脑袋是你见过的最傻里傻气的，不吃草的时候他们用尾巴末端在深水里保持平衡，庄重地向彼此鞠躬，还挥动前鳍，那模样好像胖子在挥手似的。

柯迪克说："啊嘿，绅士们，玩得好吗？"这些大家伙向他鞠了鞠躬，还跟《爱丽丝漫游奇境记》里的青蛙侍者一样挥了挥他们的鳍肢。接着他们又开始进食，只

① immensely [i'mensli]
ad. [口语] 非常，很

② put off 推迟

③ shoal [ʃəul] *n.* 鱼群

④ fringe [frindʒ] *n.* 边缘
⑤ beneath [bi'ni:θ] *ad.* 在下面，在下方

⑥ squid [skwid] *n.*【动物】乌贼

feeding again Kotick saw that their upper lip was split into two pieces that they could twitch apart about a foot and bring together again with a whole bushel of seaweed between the splits. They **tucked**① the stuff into their mouths and chumped **solemnly**②.

"Messy style of feeding, that," said Kotick. They bowed again, and Kotick began to lose his temper. "Very good," he said. "If you do happen to have an extra joint in your front flipper you needn't **show off**③ so. I see you bow gracefully, but I should like to know your names." The split lips moved and twitched; and the glassy green eyes stared, but they did not speak.

"Well!" said Kotick. "You're the only people I've ever met uglier than Sea Vitch—and with worse manners."

Then he remembered in a flash what the Burgomaster gull had screamed to him when he was a little yearling at Walrus Islet, and he tumbled backward in the water, for he knew that he had found Sea Cow at last.

The sea cows went on schlooping and grazing and **chumping**④ in the weed, and Kotick asked them questions in every language that he had picked up in his travels; and the Sea People talk nearly as many languages as human beings. But the sea cows did not answer because Sea Cow cannot talk. He has only six bones in his neck where he ought to have seven, and they say under the sea that that prevents him from speaking even to his companions. But, as you know, he has an extra joint in his foreflipper, and by waving it up and down and about he makes what answers to a sort of clumsy **telegraphic**⑤ code.

By daylight Kotick's mane was standing on end and his temper was gone where the dead crabs go. Then the Sea Cow began to travel northward very slowly, stopping to hold absurd bowing councils from time to time, and Kotick followed them, saying to himself, "People who are such idiots as these are would have been killed long ago if they hadn't found out some safe island. And what is good enough for the Sea Cow is good enough for the Sea Catch. All the same, I wish they'd hurry."

It was **weary**⑥ work for Kotick. The herd never went more than forty or

见他们的上唇裂成两半，扯开来恨不得有一英尺宽，合拢的时候就夹住了一大团水草。然后他们把那一团水草塞进嘴里，认真地嚼起来。

柯迪克说："呃，这种吃法可真够恶心的。"他们又向他鞠躬，搞得柯迪克快要失去耐心了。他说："太好了。就算你们前鳍恰巧多长了个关节，你们也不用这样子炫耀吧。我知道你们鞠躬鞠得很优雅，但是我更想知道你们叫什么。"他们那裂开的唇瓣动了动又抽了抽，呆滞的眼睛瞪得大大的，但还是一言不发。

柯迪克说："好吧！你们算是我见过的最丑的家伙了，比海维奇还要丑——还要没礼貌。"

转瞬之间，他想起来在他还是个一岁大的小毛头时北极鸥在海象小岛冲他吼的那句话，他在水里往后翻了个跟斗，因为他意识到自己终于找到海牛啦。

这群海牛继续大吃大嚼着海草，柯迪克呢，尝试了用他在旅途中学会的各种语言来跟他们提问，而海里的居民使用的语言几乎跟人类的一样多。但是海牛始终没有回答，因为他们不会说话。海牛的脖子里本该有七块骨头，但是他们只有六块，所以海里的动物们就说，这就是为什么海牛甚至连跟自己的同类说话都做不到。但是呢，你知道，海牛的前鳍偏偏多长了个关节，所以他可以上下左右地挥舞自己的前鳍，效果差不多就跟发电报一样，只不过笨点儿罢了。

到天亮的时候，柯迪克的鬃毛都竖起来了，他的脾气也到了爆发的边缘。就在这时海牛开始往北移动，速度非常缓慢，因为他们不时地停下来开个会，点头哈腰的，那模样荒唐极了。柯迪克跟着他们，心里想："要不是找到了安全的岛屿，像他们这样痴呆的家伙肯定早就被杀死了。而且海牛都觉得不错的地方肯定也适合海豹。不过，我希望他们能快点儿。"

对柯迪克来说，跟踪海牛实在是件乏味透顶的差

① tuck [tʌk] v. 把……塞进
② solemnly ['sɔləmli] ad. 庄严地

③ show off 卖弄，炫耀

④ chump [tʃʌmp] v. 用力嚼

⑤ telegraphic [ˌteliˈgræfik] a. 电报的

⑥ weary ['wiəri] a. 令人厌倦的，使人厌烦的

fifty miles a day, and stopped to feed at night, and kept close to the shore all the time; while Kotick swam round them, and over them, and under them, but he could not hurry them up one-half mile. As they went farther north they held a bowing council every few hours, and Kotick nearly bit off his mustache with impatience till he saw that they were following up a warm current of water, and then he respected them more.

One night they sank through the shiny water—**sank**[1] like stones—and for the first time since he had known them began to swim quickly. Kotick followed, and the pace **astonished**[2] him, for he never dreamed that Sea Cow was anything of a swimmer. They headed for a cliff by the shore—a cliff that ran down into deep water, and plunged into a dark hole at the foot of it, twenty fathoms under the sea. It was a long, long swim, and Kotick badly wanted fresh air before he was out of the dark tunnel they led him through.

"My **wig**[3]!" he said, when he rose, gasping and puffing, into open water at the farther end. "It was a long dive, but it was worth it."

The sea cows had separated and were browsing lazily along the edges of the finest beaches that Kotick had ever seen. There were long stretches of smooth-worn rock running for miles, exactly fitted to make seal-nurseries, and there were play-grounds of hard sand sloping inland behind them, and there were rollers for seals to dance in, and long grass to roll in, and sand dunes to climb up and down, and, best of all, Kotick knew by the feel of the water, which never **deceives**[4] a true sea catch, that no men had ever come there.

The first thing he did was to assure himself that the fishing was good, and then he swam along the beaches and counted up the delightful low sandy islands half hidden in the beautiful rolling fog. Away to the northward, out to sea, ran a line of **bars**[5] and shoals and rocks that would never let a ship come within six miles of the beach, and between the islands and the mainland was a stretch of deep water that ran up to the perpendicular cliffs, and somewhere below the

事。海牛群一天走的路绝不超过四五十英里，晚上还要停下来进食，而且从来都不离开岸边。柯迪克一会儿绕着他们游，一会儿在他们头顶或是脚下游，但还是没办法让他们多走半英里。等到了更北边，他们每过几个钟头就会开一次鞠躬会，柯迪克不耐烦得连胡须都要咬断了，直到后来他发现原来他们是在追寻一股暖流，这才对他们产生了一些敬意。

一天夜里，他们从闪闪发光的海面往下沉——就跟石头一样沉下去——而且开始快速地游动，这还是他遇到他们以来的头一遭。柯迪克跟着他们，被他们的速度吓了一跳，因为他做梦也没想到海牛也是游泳的好手。他们朝着岸边的一处悬崖游过去——那悬崖往下一直伸向深深的水底——然后一头扎进崖底的一个黑洞，这时他们离海面已经有二十英寻深了。这段路好长好长，柯迪克跟着他们在黑暗的隧道里游啊游，迫切地想出去吸上一口新鲜的空气。

当他终于从隧道那头钻出来，冒出水面时，他拼命地大口喘气。他说："我的鬃毛啊！这潜得可真够久的，不过还是很值得呀。"

海牛已经分散开来，沿着海滩的边缘懒洋洋地吃草。这是柯迪克见过的最棒的海滩，有大片光滑的岩石，绵延开去长达数英里，正好可以用来做海豹的育儿场，后面还有通向内陆的沙坡，可以做游乐场。这里有卷浪可供海豹跳舞，有长草可以让他们打滚，还有沙丘可以爬上爬下。不过最棒的是，柯迪克凭着水感——真正的成年海豹都能感觉出来——知道这里还从来没有人类来过。

接下来他做的第一件事就是确认这里是否方便捕鱼，然后他沿着海滩游了一圈，数了数那些低矮多沙的小岛，他们半掩在美丽的翻滚的雾气中，一看就让人喜欢。在北边，面向大海的地方有一长溜沙洲、浅滩和礁石，船只永远也无法越过它们靠近海滩六英里以内。而在群岛和大陆之间则隔着一片深海，一直通向那些近乎垂直的

① sink [siŋk] v. 下沉

② astonish [əˈstɔniʃ] v. 使惊讶，使吃惊

③ wig [wig] n. 假发

④ deceive [diˈsiːv] v. 欺骗，哄骗

⑤ bar [bɑː] n. 栅，栏

cliffs was the mouth of the tunnel.

"It's Novastoshnah over again, but ten times better," said Kotick. "Sea Cow must be wiser than I thought. Men can't come down the cliffs, even if there were any men; and the shoals to seaward would knock a ship to **splinters**①. If any place in the sea is safe, this is it."

He began to think of the seal he had left behind him, but though he was in a hurry to go back to Novastoshnah, he thoroughly explored the new country, so that he would be able to answer all questions.

Then he dived and made sure of the mouth of the tunnel, and raced through to the southward. No one but a sea cow or a seal would have dreamed of there being such a place, and when he looked back at the cliffs even Kotick could hardly believe that he had been under them.

He was six days going home, though he was not swimming slowly; and when he hauled out just above Sea Lion's Neck the first person he met was the seal who had been waiting for him, and she saw by the look in his eyes that he had found his island at last.

But the holluschickie and Sea Catch, his father, and all the other seals laughed at him when he told them what he had discovered, and a young seal about his own age said, "This is all very well, Kotick, but you can't come from no one knows where and order us off like this. Remember we've been fighting for our nurseries, and that's a thing you never did. You preferred **prowling**② about in the sea."

The other seals laughed at this, and the young seal began **twisting**③ his head from side to side. He had just married that year, and was making a great **fuss**④ about it.

"I've no nursery to fight for," said Kotick. "I only want to show you all a place where you will be safe. What's the use of fighting?"

"Oh, if you're trying to back out, of course I've no more to say," said the young seal with an ugly **chuckle**⑤.

"Will you come with me if I win?" said Kotick. And a green light came into

悬崖，悬崖底部的某个地方就藏着那条隧道。

柯迪克说："这简直就是另外一个诺瓦斯托西纳，只不过还要好上十倍。海牛肯定比我想的要聪明。就算有人来，他们也没法从那些悬崖上下来；面朝大海的浅滩呢，又能把小船给撞成碎片。如果海里真有什么地方是安全的，那肯定就是这儿了。"

他开始思念他没有带来的那只母海豹，但是尽管他急着赶回诺瓦斯托西纳去，他还是彻彻底底地把这片新的国土探查了一遍，以确保自己能回答所有可能会被问到的问题。

然后他潜到水下，弄清楚了隧道的出口在哪儿，然后就飞速地穿过去往南游。除了海牛或者海豹没人能够想到会有这样的一个地方。当他回望那片悬崖时，柯迪克几乎不敢相信自己刚从那下面经过。

虽然游得不慢，他还是花了六天才回到家。他刚登上"海狮脖"，遇见的第一个人就是一直在等待他的那只海豹。她一看他的眼神就明白他终于找到了他的岛。

但是当柯迪克告诉别人他的发现时，他的父亲海卡奇、单身汉和其他的海豹都嘲笑他。一头跟他差不多大的年轻海豹说："柯迪克，你说的这些好是好，但是你总不能凭空找个谁也不知道的地方，就这样把我们赶过去吧。要知道我们可是一直在为自己的家园战斗，而你却从来也没有过。你更愿意在海里游荡，不是吗？"

其他的海豹听见了都笑起来，那只年轻的海豹也开始把头扭来扭去。他那年刚结的婚，所以巴不得大吹大擂一番。

柯迪克说："我不想争什么育儿地，我只想带你们去一个地方，让你们大家都能够安安全全的地方。我干吗要打架呢？"

"哦，如果你是想要当缩头乌龟的话，我当然无话可说咯。"那只年轻海豹说道，笑得很难听。

柯迪克说："要是我打赢了，你会跟我去吗？"眼看

① splinter ['splintə] n.（木、石、骨等的）碎片

② prowl [praul] v. 徘徊

③ twist [twist] v. 转动

④ fuss [fʌs] n. 奔忙，瞎忙

⑤ chuckle ['tʃʌkl] n. 低声的笑

his eye, for he was very angry at having to fight at all.

"Very good," said the young seal carelessly. "If you win, I'll come."

He had no time to change his mind, for Kotick's head was out and his teeth sunk in the blubber of the young seal's neck. Then he threw himself back on his haunches and hauled his enemy down the beach, shook him, and knocked him over. Then Kotick roared to the seals: "I've done my best for you these five seasons past. I've found you the island where you'll be safe, but unless your heads are dragged off your silly necks you won't believe. I'm going to teach you now. Look out for yourselves!"

Limmershin told me that never in his life—and Limmershin sees ten thousand big seals fighting every year—never in all his little life did he see anything like Kotick's charge into the nurseries. He flung himself at the biggest sea catch he could find, caught him by the throat, **choked**① him and bumped him and banged him till he grunted for **mercy**②, and then threw him aside and attacked the next. You see, Kotick had never fasted for four months as the big seals did every year, and his deep-sea swimming trips kept him in perfect condition, and, best of all, he had never fought before. His curly white mane stood up with rage, and his eyes flamed, and his big dog teeth glistened, and he was **splendid**③ to look at. Old Sea Catch, his father, saw him tearing past, hauling the grizzled old seals about as though they had been halibut, and upsetting the young bachelors in all directions; and Sea Catch gave a roar and shouted: "He may be a fool, but he is the best fighter on the beaches! Don't tackle your father, my son! He's with you!"

Kotick roared in answer, and old Sea Catch waddled in with his mustache on end, blowing like a **locomotive**④, while Matkah and the seal that was going to marry Kotick cowered down and admired their men-folk. It was a gorgeous fight, for the two fought as long as there was a seal that dared lift up his head, and when there were none they paraded grandly up and down the beach side by side, bellowing.

这一架非打不可，他气得不得了，眼睛都闪着绿光。

年轻海豹满不在乎地说："好呀，如果你赢了，我就去。"

他还来不及改主意，柯迪克的脑袋就扑过来了，牙齿深深地陷进他脖子上的那层脂肪里。接着柯迪克往后一仰，把他的敌人拖下海滩，使劲儿摇晃，揍了个四脚朝天。然后他对海豹群咆哮着说："过去的五年里我为你们尽了全力，我已经替你们找到了能够保证你们安全的岛屿，但是你们非要我把你们的脑袋从傻脖子上给揪下来，你们才会相信。我现在就来教训教训你们。你们自个儿小心吧。"

利莫欣告诉我他一辈子——利莫欣每年都能看到一万只大海豹打架——还没见过有谁像柯迪克那样气势汹汹地冲进育儿场里。柯迪克一下扑到个头最大的那只成年海豹身上，咬住他的咽喉，让他都快窒息了，然后又狠命地撞他直到他咕哝着求饶，才把他扔到一边，开始攻击下一个。要知道柯迪克跟这些大海豹不一样，他们每年都有四个月的禁食期，柯迪克可从来没有过，不仅如此，他在深海的多次探险之旅还使他保持了非常健壮的体格，而且最重要的是，他从来没有挨过打。此刻，因为发怒，他那卷曲的白色鬃毛根根直立，双眼喷着怒火，粗大的犬牙闪着幽光，看上去真是威风凛凛。他的父亲老海卡奇，看见他一路横冲直撞，把那些毛发灰白的老海豹拖来甩去好比甩大比目鱼一般，撞得年轻的单身汉东倒西歪。于是海卡奇自己也大声怒喝："他也许是个笨蛋，但他却是海滩上最厉害的斗士！我的儿子，别来揍你的父亲呀！他可是站在你这边儿的！"

柯迪克报以一声大吼，接下来只见老海卡奇也翘着胡须摇摇摆摆地加入了战斗，如同火车头一样发出长鸣，而玛特卡则和那头想跟柯迪克结婚的母海豹一起缩成一团，欣赏着她们丈夫的雄姿。这场战斗真是打得酣畅淋漓，父子俩把所有敢于抬头的海豹都打趴下了，最后他俩肩并肩地在海滩上神气十足地走来走去，一边还

① choke [tʃəuk] v. 使窒息，使不能呼吸，掐住……的脖子

② mercy ['mə:si] n. 宽容

③ splendid ['splendid] a. 极好的，绝妙的

④ locomotive ['ləukə,məutiv] n. 火车头

At night, just as the Northern Lights were **winking**[①] and flashing through the fog, Kotick climbed a bare rock and looked down on the scattered nurseries and the torn and bleeding seals. "Now," he said, "I've taught you your lesson."

"My wig!" said old Sea Catch, **boosting** himself **up**[②] stiffly, for he was fearfully **mauled**[③]. "The Killer Whale himself could not have cut them up worse. Son, I'm proud of you, and what's more, I'll come with you to your island—if there is such a place."

"Hear you, fat pigs of the sea. Who comes with me to the Sea Cow's tunnel? Answer, or I shall teach you again," roared Kotick.

There was a murmur like the ripple of the tide all up and down the beaches. "We will come," said thousands of tired voices. "We will follow Kotick, the White Seal."

Then Kotick dropped his head between his shoulders and shut his eyes proudly. He was not a white seal any more, but red from head to tail. All the same he would have scorned to look at or touch one of his wounds.

A week later he and his army (nearly ten thousand holluschickie and old seals) went away north to the Sea Cow's tunnel, Kotick leading them, and the seals that stayed at Novastoshnah called them idiots. But next spring, when they all met off the fishing banks of the Pacific, Kotick's seals told such tales of the new beaches beyond Sea Cow's tunnel that more and more seals left Novastoshnah. Of course it was not all done at once, for the seals are not very clever, and they need a long time to **turn** things **over**[④] in their minds, but year after year more seals went away from Novastoshnah, and Lukannon, and the other nurseries, to the quiet, **sheltered**[⑤] beaches where Kotick sits all the summer through, getting bigger and fatter and stronger each year, while the holluschickie play around him, in that sea where no man comes.

① wink [wiŋk] *v.* 闪烁

② boost up 向上推,把……抬起

③ maul [mɔːl] *v.* 殴打

④ turn over 仔细考虑,思考,

⑤ sheltered ['ʃeltəd] *a.* 不受风雨袭击的

不断地发出咆哮。

夜里,正当北极光闪烁着穿透雾气时,柯迪克攀上一块裸露的岩石,看着下面七零八落的育儿营,和那些皮开肉绽、鲜血直流的海豹。他说:"好了,这下我可是好好教训了你们一顿。"

老海卡奇有点僵硬地直起身子,因为他也受了很重的伤。他说:"我的鬃毛啊!就是杀人鲸自己来,也不可能把他们揍得更惨啦。儿子,我真为你骄傲,而且,我还要跟你一起去你的岛——如果真有这么个地儿的话。"

柯迪克大吼一声:"听着,你们这些海里的肥猪。谁要跟我去海牛的隧道?回答我,否则我就再教训你们一次。"

一阵低语如同潮水一般漫延开去席卷了整个海滩。成千上万疲惫的声音答道:"我们去。我们都跟着白海豹柯迪克去。"

于是柯迪克把头缩进肩窝里,骄傲地闭上了眼睛。他也不再是白海豹,因为他从头到尾都被染红了。尽管如此,他还是不屑于看一眼或是摸一摸他的伤口。

一周以后,他带领他的部队(差不多有一万只左右,包括单身汉和老海豹)朝北边的海牛隧道去了,留在诺瓦斯托西纳的海豹们说他们都是白痴。但是到了第二年春天,当他们在太平洋的渔场相遇时,柯迪克的海豹们讲了好多海牛隧道那边的新海滩的故事,全都无比诱人,引得越来越多的海豹也离开了诺瓦斯托西纳。当然了,他们也不是一下子都走了,因为海豹本来就不是很聪明,他们需要很长的时间才能想通一件事情,但是年复一年,更多的海豹离开了诺瓦斯托西纳、鹿坎农和其他的育儿滩,来到那片安静的、受到庇护的海滩。在那里,柯迪克整个夏天都坐着,变得越来越大,越来越胖,也越来越壮。在他周围,单身汉们嬉戏玩耍,就在那片无人惊扰的海域。

Lukannon

This is the great deep-sea song that all the St. Paul seals sing when they are heading back to their beaches in the summer. It is a sort of very sad seal National Anthem.

*I met my **mates**① in the morning (and, oh, but I am old!)*
*Where roaring on the **ledges**② the summer ground-swell rolled;*
*I heard them lift the **chorus**③ that drowned the breakers' song—*
The Beaches of Lukannon—two million voices strong.

The song of pleasant stations beside the salt lagoons,
The song of blowing squadrons that shuffled down the dunes,
*The song of midnight dances that **churned**④ the sea to flame—*
The Beaches of Lukannon—before the sealers came!

I met my mates in the morning (I'll never meet them more!);
They came and went in legions that darkened all the shore.
And o'er the foam-flecked offing as far as voice could reach
*We **hailed**⑤ the landing-parties and we sang them up the beach.*

鹿坎农之歌

这是一首动听的深海之歌，圣保罗所有海豹在夏季重返他们的海滩时都会唱。这是一首非常悲伤的海豹赞美诗。

① mate [meit] *n.* 同伴
② ledge [ledʒ] *n.* 岩礁
③ chorus ['kɔːrəs] *n.* 合唱

清晨我遇见我的同伴（而且，噢，可是我老了！）
他们夏天在波涛汹涌的暗礁上吵闹；
我听见他们的歌声淹没了碎浪的声响——
鹿坎农的海滩啊——有两百万个声音在同时歌唱。

咸水湖畔舒适栖息地的歌谣，
吹散沙丘那鼓风队的歌谣，
把海水搅成火焰的午夜舞蹈歌谣——
鹿坎农的海滩啊——在捕海豹的人还没到来之时！

④ churn [tʃəːn] *v.* 用力搅拌

清晨我遇见我的同伴（我再也不会遇见他们了！）
他们成群结队来来往往，黑压压盖住了整片海滩。
在远方泡沫斑驳的大海，声音能传到的远处，
我们欢迎登陆的队伍，我们为他们踏上海滩而歌唱。

⑤ hail [heil] *v.* 向……致敬

The Beaches of Lukannon—the winter wheat so tall—
The dripping, crinkled **lichens**①, and the sea-fog **drenching**② all!
The platforms of our playground, all shining smooth and worn!
The Beaches of Lukannon—the home where we were born!

I met my mates in the morning, a broken, scattered band.
Men shoot us in the water and club us on the land;
Men drive us to the Salt House like silly sheep and **tame**③,
And still we sing Lukannon—before the **sealers**④ came.

Wheel down, wheel down to southward; oh, Gooverooska, go!
And tell the Deep-Sea Viceroys the story of our **woe**⑤;
Ere, empty as the shark's egg the tempest flings ashore,
The Beaches of Lukannon shall know their sons no more!

① lichen ['laikən] n.【植物】
地衣
② drench [drentʃ] v. 浸湿，
使湿透

③ tame [teim] a. 驯服的
④ sealer ['si:lə] n. 猎海豹
的船或人

⑤ woe [wəu] n. 深沉的悲
哀

鹿坎农的海滩啊——冬日的小麦长得那么高——
地衣湿淋淋、皱巴巴，海雾把一切全裹包！
我们玩耍的台地，全都磨得一片平滑，闪着金光！
鹿坎农的海滩啊——我们出生的地方！

清晨我遇见我的同伴，一支溃散的队伍。
我们在海里时人们向我们开火，我们在陆地时人们
敲打我们的头；
人们把我们像蠢绵羊一样赶到盐场去驯服，
但我们仍唱着鹿坎农的歌——在捕海豹的人还没到
来之时！

掉头吧，掉头往南走吧，噢，海豹们，走吧！
向深海之王倾诉我们的悲伤吧。
从前，如鲨鱼卵那样空空荡荡，暴风雨猛冲上岸，
鹿坎农的海滩啊，再也不认识他们的子孙！

"Rikki-Tikki-Tavi"

At the hole where he went in
Red-Eye called to Wrinkle-Skin.
Hear what little Red-Eye saith:
"Nag, come up and dance with death!"

Eye to eye and head to head,
 (Keep the measure, Nag.)
This shall end when one is dead;
 (At thy pleasure, Nag.)
Turn for turn and twist for twist—
 (Run and hide thee, Nag.)
Hah! The hooded Death has missed!
 (Woe betide thee, Nag!)

This is the story of the great war that Rikki-tikki-tavi fought single-handed, through the bath-rooms of the big **bungalow**① in Segowlee **cantonment**②. Darzee, the Tailorbird, helped him, and Chuchundra, the musk-rat, who never comes out into the middle of the floor, but always creeps round by the wall, gave him advice, but Rikki-tikki did the real fighting.

"瑞奇－迪奇－塔维"

在他走进的洞穴里，
红眼睛的对皱皮肤的说，
听小红眼睛在说什么吧：
"纳格，出来和死神共舞！"

眼对眼、头碰头，
（保持距离，纳格。）
当一方死去，舞蹈就会结束；
（如你所愿，纳格。）
转来转去，扭东扭西——
（逃吧躲吧，纳格。）
哈！戴兜帽的死神失手了！
（灾难降临，纳格。）

　　这个故事讲的是瑞奇－迪奇－塔维单打独斗的那场大战，战场跨越了瑟枸里军营那座大平房的好几个浴室。虽然有缝叶莺达吉帮了他一把，还有从不敢跑到地板中央、总沿着墙根儿爬行的麝鼠楚蔷德拉也给他出了出主意，但是瑞奇－迪奇才是真正打架的那个。

① bungalow ['bʌŋɡələu] *n.*（印度的有廊的）平房
② cantonment [kæn'tuːnmənt] *n.*（临时性的）军营，兵营

He was a **mongoose**①, rather like a little cat in his fur and his tail, but quite like a **weasel**② in his head and his habits. His eyes and the end of his restless nose were pink. He could scratch himself anywhere he pleased with any leg, front or back, that he chose to use. He could **fluff up**③ his tail till it looked like a bottle brush, and his war cry as he scuttled through the long grass was: "Rikk-tikk-tikki-tikki-tchk!"

One day, a high summer flood washed him out of the burrow where he lived with his father and mother, and carried him, kicking and **clucking**④, down a roadside ditch. He found a little wisp of grass floating there, and clung to it till he lost his senses. When he revived, he was lying in the hot sun on the middle of a garden path, very draggled indeed, and a small boy was saying, "Here's a dead mongoose. Let's have a funeral."

"No," said his mother, "let's take him in and dry him. Perhaps he isn't really dead."

They took him into the house, and a big man picked him up between his finger and thumb and said he was not dead but half choked. So they wrapped him in cotton **wool**⑤, and warmed him over a little fire, and he opened his eyes and sneezed.

"Now," said the big man (he was an Englishman who had just moved into the bungalow), "don't frighten him, and we'll see what he'll do."

It is the hardest thing in the world to frighten a mongoose, because he is eaten up from nose to tail with curiosity. The **motto**⑥ of all the mongoose family is "Run and find out," and Rikki-tikki was a true mongoose. He looked at the cotton wool, decided that it was not good to eat, ran all round the table, sat up and put his fur in order, scratched himself, and jumped on the small boy's shoulder.

"Don't be frightened, Teddy," said his father. "That's his way of making friends."

"Ouch! He's tickling under my chin," said Teddy.

Rikki-tikki looked down between the boy's collar and neck, **snuffed**⑦ at his

① mongoose ['mɔŋguːs] *n.*【动物】猫鼬

② weasel ['wiːzəl] *n.*【动物学】鼬属

③ fluff up 拍松，抖松（枕头、坐垫等）

④ cluck [klʌk] *v.*（人用舌头）发咯咯声（表示关心或同意）

⑤ wool [wul] *n.* 绵羊毛

⑥ motto ['mɔtəu] *n.* 座右铭

⑦ snuff [snʌf] *v.* 嗅，闻

　　他是一只猫鼬，他的毛和尾巴看上去像只小猫，但是他的脑袋和习惯却更像一只黄鼠狼。他的眼睛和总是东嗅西嗅的鼻子尖儿都是粉粉的。他会随时随地用任意一条腿儿给自己挠痒痒，不管是前腿还是后腿，他想用就用了。他还会让尾巴上的毛都竖起来，看上去就跟个奶瓶刷一样。当他在长长的草间急速飞奔时，他会发出战斗的呼喊："瑞克－迪克－迪奇－迪奇－忒克！"

　　原先他跟爸妈住在一个地洞里，后来有一天，一场夏天的大洪水把他从洞里冲了出去。他一路叫唤，使劲儿踢腾，最后还是被洪水冲到了路边的一条沟里。那儿漂着一小捆草，他就紧紧地抓着它直到失去了知觉。等他醒过来时，发现自己躺在一条花园的小径上，暴晒在阳光下，浑身脏兮兮的，一个小男孩在说："这儿有只死了的猫鼬。咱们给他弄个葬礼吧。"

　　小男孩的母亲说："不，咱们把他拿进去，给他弄干。也许他还没死呢。"

　　于是他们把他带进屋子里，一个大个子男人用拇指和食指把他拎起来，说他没有死，只是被水呛着了。然后他们用棉絮把他裹起来，放在一小堆火上烤烤，直到他睁开眼睛，打了个喷嚏。

　　大个儿男人（他是个英国人，刚搬进这个平房里来）说："好了，别吓着他了，让咱们看看他要干什么。"

　　要想吓住一只猫鼬，这恐怕是世界上最难的事情了，因为他从鼻子到尾巴都透着股好奇劲儿。猫鼬家族的座右铭是"奔跑不息，发现不止"，而瑞奇－迪奇可是一只地地道道的猫鼬。他看了看棉絮，觉得那应该不会好吃，于是就在桌上跑了一圈，又坐直身子理了理毛，挠了挠痒，接着就跳到了小男孩的肩上。

　　男孩的父亲说："别害怕，泰迪。他是想跟你交朋友呢。"

　　泰迪说："哎呀！他在挠我的下巴。"

　　瑞奇－迪奇从男孩的衣领和脖子间望下去，闻了闻

ear, and climbed down to the floor, where he sat rubbing his nose.

"Good gracious," said Teddy's mother, "and that's a wild creature! I suppose he's so tame because we've been kind to him."

"All mongooses are like that," said her husband. "If Teddy doesn't pick him up by the tail, or try to put him in a cage, he'll run in and out of the house all day long. Let's give him something to eat."

They gave him a little piece of raw meat. Rikki-tikki liked it immensely, and when it was finished he went out into the **veranda**① and sat in the sunshine and fluffed up his fur to make it dry to the roots. Then he felt better.

"There are more things to find out about in this house," he said to himself, "than all my family could find out in all their lives. I shall certainly stay and find out."

He spent all that day **roaming**② over the house. He nearly drowned himself in the bath-tubs, put his nose into the ink on a writing table, and burned it on the end of the big man's **cigar**③, for he climbed up in the big man's lap to see how writing was done. At nightfall he ran into Teddy's nursery to watch how **kerosene**④ lamps were lighted, and when Teddy went to bed Rikki-tikki climbed up too. But he was a restless companion, because he had to get up and attend to every noise all through the night, and find out what made it. Teddy's mother and father came in, the last thing, to look at their boy, and Rikki-tikki was awake on the pillow. "I don't like that," said Teddy's mother. "He may bite the child." "He'll do no such thing," said the father. "Teddy's safer with that little beast than if he had a **bloodhound**⑤ to watch him. If a snake came into the nursery now—"

But Teddy's mother wouldn't think of anything so awful.

Early in the morning Rikki-tikki came to early breakfast in the veranda riding on Teddy's shoulder, and they gave him banana and some boiled egg. He sat on all their laps one after the other, because every well-brought-up mongoose always hopes to be a house mongoose some day and have rooms to run about in; and Rikki-tikki's mother (she used to live in the general's house at Segowlee)

他的耳朵，又爬下来，坐在地板上揉了揉自己的鼻子。

泰迪的母亲说："天啊，他真的是野生的吗？我猜他是因为我们对他很好才会这么乖的吧。"

她的丈夫说："所有的猫鼬都是这样的。只要泰迪不抓他的尾巴，或者想要把他关到笼子里去，他就会整天屋里屋外地跑来跑去。咱们给他弄点儿吃的吧。"

他们给了他一小片生肉。瑞奇－迪奇非常喜欢，吃完以后他就跑到外面的阳台①上，坐在太阳底下，把毛都给蓬起来好彻底晒干。然后他觉得舒服多了。

他对自己说："这座房子里值得瞧瞧的东西比我们一家一辈子能发现的还要多。我一定得留下来好好看看。"

他花了一整天的时间在屋子里游荡②。他一会儿差点在浴缸里淹死，一会儿把鼻子伸进写字台上的墨水里，后来又爬上大个子男人的膝盖去看他怎么写字，结果鼻头被男人的雪茄③给烫了一下。天黑的时候，他又跑进泰迪的房间里看煤油④灯是怎么点燃的，等泰迪上床时，瑞奇－迪奇也爬了上去。但他可不会安安生生地陪在旁边，整个晚上但凡哪里有点动静他就会爬起来去看个究竟。最后，泰迪的父母进来看看他们的儿子，发现瑞奇－迪奇清醒地躺在枕头上。泰迪的母亲说："我不喜欢这样。他也许会咬伤孩子的。"父亲说："他不会干这种事的。泰迪跟这个小东西在一起再安全不过了，哪怕有猎犬看着也比不上呢。如果现在有条蛇爬进房间里——"

泰迪的母亲没让他说完，因为她无法想象如此可怕的场景。

一大早瑞奇－迪奇骑在泰迪的肩头上到阳台上来吃早餐。他们给了瑞奇－迪奇一些香蕉和白煮蛋。他挨个儿在这家人的大腿上坐了个遍，因为凡是有教养的猫鼬都渴望有朝一日能够成为家养的猫鼬，这样就能在各个房间里跑来跑去。瑞奇－迪奇的妈妈曾经在瑟枸里的将军家住过，她很仔细地告诉过瑞奇－迪奇要是碰上白人

① veranda [vəˈrændə] n. 阳台

② roam [rəum] v. 闲逛

③ cigar [siˈgɑ:] n. 雪茄烟

④ kerosene [ˈkerəsi:n] n. 煤油，火油

⑤ bloodhound [ˈblʌdhaund] n.【动物】寻血猎犬

had carefully told Rikki what to do if ever he came across white men.

Then Rikki-tikki went out into the garden to see what was to be seen. It was a large garden, only half cultivated, with bushes, as big as summer-houses, of Marshal Niel roses, **lime**① and orange trees, clumps of bamboos, and thickets of high grass. Rikki-tikki licked his lips. "This is a splendid hunting-ground," he said, and his tail grew bottle-brushy at the thought of it, and he **scuttled**② up and down the garden, snuffing here and there till he heard very sorrowful voices in a thorn-bush.

It was Darzee, the Tailorbird, and his wife. They had made a beautiful nest by pulling two big leaves together and stitching them up the edges with **fibers**③, and had filled the hollow with cotton and downy **fluff**④. The nest **swayed**⑤ to and fro, as they sat on the rim and cried.

"What is the matter?" asked Rikki-tikki.

"We are very miserable," said Darzee. "One of our babies fell out of the nest yesterday and Nag ate him."

"H'm!" said Rikki-tikki, "that is very sad—but I am a stranger here. Who is Nag?"

Darzee and his wife only cowered down in the nest without answering, for from the thick grass at the foot of the bush there came a low hiss—a horrid cold sound that made Rikki-tikki jump back two clear feet. Then inch by inch out of the grass rose up the head and spread hood of Nag, the big black cobra, and he was five feet long from tongue to tail. When he had lifted one-third of himself clear of the ground, he stayed balancing to and fro exactly as a **dandelion**⑥ tuft balances in the wind, and he looked at Rikki-tikki with the wicked snake's eyes that never change their expression, whatever the snake may be thinking of.

"Who is Nag?" said he. "I am Nag. The great God Brahm put his mark upon all our people, when the first cobra spread his hood to keep the sun off Brahm as he slept. Look, and be afraid!"

He spread out his hood more than ever, and Rikki-tikki saw the spectacle-mark on the back of it that looks exactly like the eye part of a hook-and-eye

了该怎么办。

然后瑞奇－迪奇跑进花园里去查看有什么可看的。这个花园很大，但是打理得并不精心，种了些尼埃尔元帅玫瑰，花丛长得跟凉亭一样高大，还有酸橙、甜橙、竹子和一蓬蓬的高草。瑞奇－迪奇舔舔嘴唇，说："这里真是个再好不过的狩猎场。"他一想到这个，尾巴又变得跟奶瓶刷一样了。他在花园里飞快地跑来跑去，这儿嗅嗅那儿闻闻，直到他听见荆棘丛里发出非常悲痛的哭声。

那是缝叶莺达吉和他的老婆。他们之前用两片大叶子做了一个漂亮的鸟巢，叶子的边都用纤维缝合起来，里面还塞上了棉絮和绒毛。现在他俩坐在巢边上哭，鸟巢就来回地晃着。

瑞奇－迪奇问道："这是怎么回事？"

达吉说："我们太惨了。昨天我们的一个宝宝从窝里掉出去，被纳格吃掉了。"

瑞奇－迪奇说："嗯！这是够惨的，不过我刚来，谁也不认识。谁是纳格呢？"

达吉和他的老婆不作声了，在鸟巢里蜷缩成一团，因为从荆棘丛底部密密的草丛里传来低沉的嘶嘶声，这个声音冰冷可怕，把瑞奇－迪奇吓得往后直跳了两英尺远。只见一条黑色大眼镜蛇的头和膨大的颈部一点一点地从草里冒出来，这就是纳格，他从头到脚足足有五英尺长。当他把三分之一的身体都抬离地面时，他来回地摇晃着身躯以保持平衡，活像一朵蒲公英在风中摇曳。他用那双恶毒的蛇眼盯着瑞奇－迪奇，谁也不知道他到底在想些什么，因为他眼睛里的神情从来都没有变化。

他说："谁是纳格？我就是纳格。想当初第一条眼镜蛇撑起兜帽为睡着的大梵天神遮挡太阳时，伟大的梵天神就把他的印记留在我们所有的族民身上了。看吧，恐惧吧！"

他把兜帽撑得比什么时候都要开，瑞奇－迪奇就看见兜帽的背面有着眼镜形状的花纹，就跟搭扣的扣眼一

① lime [laim] n.【植物】酸橙树
② scuttle ['skʌtl] v. 破坏，毁坏

③ fiber ['faibə] n. 纤维
④ fluff [flʌf] n.（织物上的）绒毛，软毛
⑤ sway [swei] v. 摇动，摆动

⑥ dandelion ['dændilaiən] n.【植物】蒲公英

fastening. He was afraid for the minute, but it is impossible for a mongoose to stay frightened for any length of time, and though Rikki-tikki had never met a live cobra before, his mother had fed him on dead ones, and he knew that all a grown mongoose's business in life was to fight and eat snakes. Nag knew that too and, at the bottom of his cold heart, he was afraid.

"Well," said Rikki-tikki, and his tail began to fluff up again, "marks or no marks, do you think it is right for you to eat **fledglings**① out of a nest?"

Nag was thinking to himself, and watching the least little movement in the grass behind Rikki-tikki. He knew that mongooses in the garden meant death sooner or later for him and his family, but he wanted to get Rikki-tikki off his guard. So he dropped his head a little, and put it on one side.

"Let us talk," he said. "You eat eggs. Why should not I eat birds?"

"Behind you! Look behind you!" sang Darzee.

Rikki-tikki knew better than to waste time in staring. He jumped up in the air as high as he could go, and just under him **whizzed**② by the head of Nagaina, Nag's wicked wife. She had crept up behind him as he was talking, to make an end of him. He heard her savage hiss as the stroke missed. He came down almost across her back, and if he had been an old mongoose he would have known that then was the time to break her back with one bite; but he was afraid of the terrible lashing return **stroke**③ of the cobra. He bit, indeed, but did not bite long enough, and he jumped clear of the **whisking**④ tail, leaving Nagaina torn and angry.

"Wicked, wicked Darzee!" said Nag, lashing up as high as he could reach toward the nest in the thorn-bush. But Darzee had built it out of reach of snakes, and it only swayed to and fro.

Rikki-tikki felt his eyes growing red and hot (when a mongoose's eyes grow red, he is angry), and he sat back on his tail and hind legs like a little **kangaroo**⑤, and looked all round him, and chattered with rage. But Nag and Nagaina had disappeared into the grass. When a snake misses its stroke, it never

模一样。瑞奇－迪奇害怕了一会会儿，但是猫鼬从来都不会一直害怕下去。再说了，尽管瑞奇－迪奇以前从没见过活生生的眼镜蛇，他的妈妈倒是喂他吃了不少死的，所以他知道成年的猫鼬一辈子都在打蛇、吃蛇。纳格当然也知道，在纳格冰冷的内心深处，他才是害怕的那个。

瑞奇－迪奇的尾巴上的毛又竖起来了，他说："喂，不管你有没有印记，你觉得把鸟窝里掉出来的幼鸟给吃了，这样好吗？"

① fledgling ['fledʒliŋ] *n.* 刚生羽毛（或刚会飞）的小鸟

纳格一边思索，一边密切地注视着瑞奇－迪奇身后草丛里的动静。他明白一旦花园里有了猫鼬，那他们一家子也就离死不远了，但是他想让瑞奇－迪奇放松警惕，所以就把头低下来一点点，往一边偏了偏。

他说："咱们谈谈吧。你吃鸡蛋。我为什么就不能吃鸟呢？"

达吉叫起来："你后面！看你后面！"

② whizz [wiz] *v.* 使发嗖嗖声

瑞奇－迪奇压根就没工夫去看。他奋力一下跳到空中，纳盖娜的头就从他身下一掠而过，她是纳格的老婆，最是可恶了。趁着瑞奇－迪奇在说话，她就从背后偷偷地扑上来，想要结果他的性命。瑞奇－迪奇听见她扑空时发出凶狠的嘶嘶声。他落地时几乎掠过纳盖娜的背部。要是瑞奇－迪奇是一头老猫鼬的话，就会知道这是一口咬断她脊背的最佳时机。但是瑞奇－迪奇害怕眼镜蛇转身时威力吓人的回抽，所以他咬是咬了，可是只咬了一下下就闪过身子好躲开甩过来的蛇尾。纳盖娜身上被撕开一道口子，气得不得了。

③ stroke [strəuk] *n.* 打，击，敲
④ whisk [wisk] *v.* 飞快地掠过

纳格说："坏达吉，太坏了！"他纵身一跃，想去攻击荆棘丛上的鸟窝，但是达吉把窝修得很高，蛇根本就够不着，所以鸟窝只是来回晃动了几下。

⑤ kangaroo [,kæŋgə'ru:] *n.*【动物】袋鼠

瑞奇－迪奇觉得自己的眼睛开始变得又红又热（当猫鼬的眼睛变红时，表示他生气了），他往后坐在尾巴和后腿上，像只小袋鼠一样，然后环顾四周，把牙齿咬得咯咯作响。但是纳格和纳盖娜都钻进草丛不见了。蛇

says anything or gives any sign of what it means to do next. Rikki-tikki did not care to follow them, for he did not feel sure that he could manage two snakes at once. So he trotted off to the gravel path near the house, and sat down to think. It was a serious matter for him.

If you read the old books of natural history, you will find they say that when the mongoose fights the snake and happens to get bitten, he runs off and eats some **herb**① that cures him. That is not true. The victory is only a matter of quickness of eye and quickness of foot—snake's **blow**② against mongoose's jump—and as no eye can follow the motion of a snake's head when it strikes, this makes things much more wonderful than any magic herb. Rikki-tikki knew he was a young mongoose, and it made him all the more pleased to think that he had managed to escape a blow from behind. It gave him confidence in himself, and when Teddy came running down the path, Rikki-tikki was ready to be **petted**③.

But just as Teddy was stooping, something wriggled a little in the dust, and a tiny voice said: "Be careful. I am Death!" It was Karait, the dusty brown snakeling that lies for choice on the dusty earth; and his bite is as dangerous as the cobra's. But he is so small that nobody thinks of him, and so he does the more harm to people.

Rikki-tikki's eyes grew red again, and he danced up to Karait with the peculiar rocking, swaying motion that he had **inherited**④ from his family. It looks very funny, but it is so perfectly balanced a **gait**⑤ that you can fly off from it at any angle you please, and in dealing with snakes this is an advantage. If Rikki-tikki had only known, he was doing a much more dangerous thing than fighting Nag, for Karait is so small, and can turn so quickly, that unless Rikki bit him close to the back of the head, he would get the return stroke in his eye or his lip. But Rikki did not know. His eyes were all red, and he rocked back and forth, looking for a good place to hold. Karait struck out. Rikki jumped sideways and tried to run in, but the wicked little dusty gray

进攻失败时，从来也不会说些什么或者做些什么让人知道接下来的打算。瑞奇－迪奇也并不想去追踪他们，因为他没有把握自己能一下子对付两条蛇。所以他只是跑到房子附近的碎石小路上，蹲在那儿开始思考。对他来说，这可是件大事。

如果你读过一些自然史的古老著作，你就会发现它们都说猫鼬和蛇打架被咬了，会跑去找些能治伤的草药来吃。事实并非如此。对付蛇的进攻，猫鼬完全是凭跳跃的功夫，能够取胜靠的仅仅是眼疾脚快，而正因为没有什么眼睛能跟得上蛇头攻击时的动作，猫鼬的本事才显得比任何魔草更加不可思议。瑞奇－迪奇知道自己尚且年幼，刚才能够躲过来自背后的攻击，实在很了不起，所以他非常高兴，也对自己更有信心。所以等看见泰迪沿着小路跑过来时，瑞奇－迪奇已经做好准备享受一番爱抚。

可是泰迪正弯下腰时，尘土里有什么东西蠕动了一下，一个细细的声音说道："小心。我是死神！"那是卡莱特，一条棕色的灰扑扑的小蛇，他故意趴在满是灰尘的地面上。虽然他的毒牙和眼镜蛇一样厉害，但是因为他太小了，很难被注意到，所以他的危害其实更大。

瑞奇－迪奇的双眼又变得血红一片，他迈着一种特别的来回摇摆的步伐朝着卡莱特走去。这种步态是他从家族那里继承来的，虽然看上去很可笑，但是却非常平衡，能够从任意角度飞出去，这在和蛇类打交道时无疑是个绝佳的优势。要是瑞奇－迪奇懂行的话，他就会知道自己是在干一件远比挑战纳格更加危险的事情，因为卡莱特是如此细小，又能如此迅捷地转身，所以除非瑞奇－迪奇能够一下咬到靠近蛇头背部的部位，否则他的眼睛或者嘴唇就会被蛇的反击击中。但是瑞奇－迪奇并不知道这一点。他的眼睛涨得通红，来回晃动着身子寻找一个合适的位置。卡莱特发动了进攻。瑞奇－迪奇往旁边一跃，正要迎上去，但是卡莱特恶毒的灰扑扑的小脑袋猛地扑了过来，差一点

① herb [həːb] n.【植物学】草本植物

② blow [bləu] n. 突然袭击

③ pet [pet] v. 宠爱

④ inherit [in'herit] v. 获得性格（或特征等）中的遗传

⑤ gait [geit] n. 步态，步法

head lashed within a fraction of his shoulder, and he had to jump over the body, and the head followed his heels close.

Teddy shouted to the house: "Oh, look here! Our mongoose is killing a snake." And Rikki-tikki heard a scream from Teddy's mother. His father ran out with a **stick**①, but by the time he came up, Karait had **lunged**② out once too far, and Rikki-tikki had sprung, jumped on the snake's back, dropped his head far between his forelegs, bitten as high up the back as he could get hold, and rolled away. That bite **paralyzed**③ Karait, and Rikki-tikki was just going to eat him up from the tail, after the custom of his family at dinner, when he remembered that a full meal makes a slow mongoose, and if he wanted all his strength and quickness ready, he must keep himself thin.

He went away for a dust bath under the castor-oil bushes, while Teddy's father beat the dead Karait. "What is the use of that?" thought Rikki-tikki. "I have settled it all;" and then Teddy's mother picked him up from the dust and hugged him, crying that he had saved Teddy from death, and Teddy's father said that he was a **providence**④, and Teddy looked on with big scared eyes. Rikki-tikki was rather amused at all the fuss, which, of course, he did not understand. Teddy's mother might just as well have petted Teddy for playing in the dust. Rikki was thoroughly enjoying himself.

That night at dinner, walking to and fro among the wine-glasses on the table, he might have **stuffed**⑤ himself three times over with nice things. But he remembered Nag and Nagaina, and though it was very pleasant to be patted and petted by Teddy's mother, and to sit on Teddy's shoulder, his eyes would get red from time to time, and he would go off into his long war cry of "Rikk-tikk-tikki-tikki-tchk!"

Teddy carried him off to bed, and insisted on Rikki-tikki sleeping under his chin. Rikki-tikki was too well bred to bite or scratch, but as soon as Teddy was asleep he went off for his nightly walk round the house, and in the dark he ran up against Chuchundra, the musk-rat, creeping around by the wall.

就咬中他的肩膀，瑞奇－迪奇只好从蛇身上跳过去，可是
蛇头紧追着他的脚踝不放。

泰迪朝着屋子大喊："哦，过来看啊！我们的猫鼬
在杀一条蛇呢。"瑞奇－迪奇听到泰迪的母亲尖叫了一
声。他的父亲拿着棍子跑出来，但是等他赶过来时，卡
莱特已经又扑了过来，只不过这次他扑过了头，瑞奇－
迪奇一下子弹起来，跳到蛇背上，头从前腿中间使劲儿
扎下去，朝蛇背上靠近头部的地方狠狠咬下去，然后滚
到一边。这一咬把卡莱特弄瘫了，瑞奇－迪奇正打算按
照他们家进餐的习惯，从尾巴开始把蛇全部吃掉，又突
然想起来饱餐一顿以后他的行动就会迟缓，而如果他想
保持体力和速度，他就必须让自己始终苗条。

瑞奇－迪奇走到蓖麻树丛下打算洗个土浴，这时泰
迪的父亲开始用棍子抽打死掉的卡莱特，瑞奇－迪奇想：
"这有什么用呢？我都已经把事情搞定了啊。"接下来泰
迪的母亲把瑞奇－迪奇从尘土里捞起来，拥抱他，哭着
说他救了泰迪的命，泰迪的父亲也说他是上帝派来的天
使，泰迪呢，则瞪着两只大大的惊恐的眼睛在一边看着。
瑞奇－迪奇倒是觉得他们这般大惊小怪挺有意思的，但
他并不明白他们为什么这么做，在他看来，泰迪的母亲
还不如因为看见泰迪在土里玩而去爱抚泰迪。瑞奇－迪
奇自己就玩得非常开心。

那天晚上吃饭的时候，瑞奇－迪奇在餐桌上的酒杯
之间踱来踱去，肚子里塞满了好东西，兴许比他平时的
食量还多两倍。但是他记得纳格和纳盖娜，所以虽然他
很享受泰迪母亲的爱抚，也很高兴坐在泰迪的肩上，他
的眼睛还是时不时就红一下，还会发出长长的战斗的呐
喊："瑞克－迪克－迪奇－迪奇－忒克！"

泰迪把他带到床上，坚持让他睡在自己下巴颏下
面。瑞奇－迪奇很有教养，所以他并没有咬孩子，也没
有抓他，只是等泰迪一睡着，他就跑掉了，在屋子里进
行夜间巡视。黑暗中他撞上了正在墙边偷偷摸摸爬的麝

① stick [stik] *n.* 杆，杖，棍，棒

② lunge [lʌndʒ] *v.* 扑

③ paralyze ['pærəlaiz] *v.* 使麻痹

④ providence ['prɔvidəns] *n.* 天意，神的眷顾

⑤ stuff [stʌf] *v.* 把……塞满

Chuchundra is a broken-hearted little beast. He whimpers and cheeps all the night, trying to make up his mind to run into the middle of the room. But he never gets there.

"Don't kill me," said Chuchundra, almost weeping. "Rikki-tikki, don't kill me!"

"Do you think a snake-killer kills **muskrats**①?" said Rikki-tikki scornfully.

"Those who kill snakes get killed by snakes," said Chuchundra, more sorrowfully than ever. "And how am I to be sure that Nag won't mistake me for you some dark night?"

"There's not the least danger," said Rikki-tikki. "But Nag is in the garden, and I know you don't go there."

"My cousin Chua, the rat, told me—" said Chuchundra, and then he stopped.

"Told you what?"

"H'sh! Nag is everywhere, Rikki-tikki. You should have talked to Chua in the garden."

"I didn't—so you must tell me. Quick, Chuchundra, or I'll bite you!"

Chuchundra sat down and cried till the tears rolled off his whiskers. "I am a very poor man," he sobbed. "I never had spirit enough to run out into the middle of the room. H'sh! I mustn't tell you anything. Can't you hear, Rikki-tikki?"

Rikki-tikki listened. The house was as still as still, but he thought he could just catch the faintest scratch-scratch in the world—a noise as faint as that of a wasp walking on a window-pane—the dry scratch of a snake's scales on brick-work.

"That's Nag or Nagaina," he said to himself, "and he is crawling into the bath-room **sluice**②. You're right, Chuchundra; I should have talked to Chua."

He stole off to Teddy's bath-room, but there was nothing there, and then to Teddy's mother's bathroom. At the bottom of the smooth **plaster**③ wall

鼠楚强德拉。楚强德拉是个伤心的小家伙，他每天晚上都为了下定决心跑去房间中央而不停地呜咽叫唤，可是他从来没有成功过。

楚强德拉几乎哭了出来，他说："别杀我，瑞奇－迪奇，别杀我！"

瑞奇－迪奇满是不屑地说："你以为杀蛇的勇士会杀麝鼠吗？"

楚强德拉却说："那些杀蛇的最后都被蛇杀死了。"他听上去无比哀伤。"再说了，我又怎么知道纳格哪天夜里不会把我错认成你呢？"

瑞奇－迪奇说："那哪会呢？纳格在花园里，我知道你是不会去那儿的。"

"我的表哥，老鼠楚阿，告诉过我——"楚强德拉没有说完就停下来了。

"告诉过你什么？"

"嘘！瑞奇－迪奇，纳格无处不在。你早该跟园子里的楚阿聊聊。"

"我没有——所以现在你得告诉我。快点，楚强德拉，要不我就咬你了！"

楚强德拉坐下来开始哭泣，泪珠子都从胡须上滚落下来。他抽抽搭搭地说："我是个很可怜的人。我从来没有勇气跑到房间中央去。嘘！我什么都不能告诉你。瑞奇－迪奇，你难道听不见吗？"

瑞奇－迪奇倾听着。屋子里静悄悄的，但是他觉得自己听见了世界上最最轻微的抓挠声——这声音轻到好像一只马蜂在窗玻璃上走一样——这正是蛇的鳞片在砖墙上摩擦时发出的干沙沙的声音。

他告诉自己："这应该是纳格或者纳盖娜。他正在往卫生间的下水道里爬。楚强德拉，你说得对，我本应该找楚阿聊聊的。"

他悄悄地跑进泰迪的卫生间，但是那里什么也没有，于是他又去了泰迪母亲的卫生间。就在光滑的石膏

① muskrat ['mʌskræt] *n.* 【动物】麝鼠

② sluice [sluːs] *n.* 闸门，水闸

③ plaster ['plɑːstə] *n.* (涂墙等用的）灰泥，灰浆

there was a brick pulled out to make a sluice for the bath water, and as Rikki-tikki stole in by the **masonry**① **curb**② where the bath is put, he heard Nag and Nagaina whispering together outside in the moonlight.

"When the house is emptied of people," said Nagaina to her husband, "he will have to go away, and then the garden will be our own again. Go in quietly, and remember that the big man who killed Karait is the first one to bite. Then come out and tell me, and we will hunt for Rikki-tikki together."

"But are you sure that there is anything to be gained by killing the people?" said Nag.

"Everything. When there were no people in the bungalow, did we have any mongoose in the garden? So long as the bungalow is empty, we are king and queen of the garden; and remember that as soon as our eggs in the **melon**③ bed hatch (as they may tomorrow), our children will need room and quiet."

"I had not thought of that," said Nag. "I will go, but there is no need that we should hunt for Rikki-tikki afterward. I will kill the big man and his wife, and the child if I can, and come away quietly. Then the bungalow will be empty, and Rikki-tikki will go."

Rikki-tikki **tingled**④ all over with rage and **hatred**⑤ at this, and then Nag's head came through the sluice, and his five feet of cold body followed it. Angry as he was, Rikki-tikki was very frightened as he saw the size of the big cobra. Nag coiled himself up, raised his head, and looked into the bathroom in the dark, and Rikki could see his eyes glitter.

"Now, if I kill him here, Nagaina will know; and if I fight him on the open floor, the odds are in his favor. What am I to do?" said Rikki-tikki-tavi.

Nag waved to and fro, and then Rikki-tikki heard him drinking from the biggest water-jar that was used to fill the bath. "That is good," said the snake. "Now, when Karait was killed, the big man had a stick. He may have that stick still, but when he comes in to bathe in the morning he will not have a stick. I shall wait here till he comes. Nagaina—do you hear me?—I shall wait here in the cool till daytime."

墙底部，有一块砖头被抽了出来好让洗澡水流出去。正当瑞奇－迪奇沿着放澡盆的砖槽溜进去的时候，他听见纳格和纳盖娜在屋外的月光下小声说话。

纳盖娜对丈夫说："等屋子里没人住了，他也就只好走了，到时候花园又会是我们的啦。悄悄地进去，记住，先咬打死卡莱特的那个大个子。然后你出来告诉我，咱俩一起去对付瑞奇－迪奇。"

纳格说："可是你确信杀死这些人会有什么好处吗？"

"好处大着呢。要是平房里不住人了，花园里还会有猫鼬吗？只要平房是空的，咱俩就是花园的主子。还有，等咱们瓜田里的蛋一孵化——明天就有可能——咱们的孩子就会需要更多的空间和一个清清静静的家呀。"

纳格说："这我倒是没有想到。好吧，我去，但是咱们过后没必要再去猎杀瑞奇－迪奇。我会杀死大个子和他老婆，还有那个孩子，要是我有机会的话，然后我就悄悄地离开。接下来平房就没人住了，瑞奇－迪奇自然就会走了。"

听了他们的话，瑞奇－迪奇又气又恨，浑身热血沸腾。只见纳格的脑袋从排水口里探出来，紧接着是他五英尺长的冰凉的身子。尽管此刻满怀怒火，瑞奇－迪奇看见眼镜蛇庞大的身躯时还是非常恐惧。纳格把身子盘了起来，抬起头，在黑暗中打量着浴室。瑞奇－迪奇能看见蛇的眼睛在闪闪发光。

瑞奇－迪奇想道："要是我在这里杀死他，纳盖娜就会知道；要是我在开阔的地上跟他斗，他的胜算就更大。我该怎么办呢？"

纳格摇晃着身子，接下来瑞奇－迪奇又听见他从那个最大的装洗澡水的罐子里喝水，蛇还说道："这倒是不错。听着，之前卡莱特被打死的时候，大个子有根棍子。说不定他现在还拿着呢，但是等他早上进来洗澡，他肯定不会带着那根棍子的。我就在这里等着，等他进来。纳盖娜——你听见了吗？——我就在这阴凉地儿等到白天。"

① masonry ['meisənri] n. 石造（或砖砌）建筑
② curb [kə:b] n. 缘饰，边饰

③ melon ['melən] n.【植物】瓜（指西瓜、甜瓜等）

④ tingle ['tiŋgl] v. 激动
⑤ hatred ['heitrid] n. 憎恨，仇恨

There was no answer from outside, so Rikki-tikki knew Nagaina had gone away. Nag coiled himself down, coil by **coil**①, round the **bulge**② at the bottom of the water jar, and Rikki-tikki stayed still as death. After an hour he began to move, muscle by muscle, toward the jar. Nag was asleep, and Rikki-tikki looked at his big back, wondering which would be the best place for a good hold. "If I don't break his back at the first jump," said Rikki, "he can still fight. And if he fights—O Rikki!" He looked at the thickness of the neck below the **hood**③, but that was too much for him; and a bite near the tail would only make Nag savage.

"It must be the head," he said at last, "the head above the hood. And, when I am once there, I must not let go."

Then he jumped. The head was lying a little clear of the water jar, under the curve of it; and, as his teeth met, Rikki braced his back against the bulge of the red earthenware to hold down the head. This gave him just one second's purchase, and he made the most of it. Then he was **battered**④ to and fro as a rat is shaken by a dog—to and fro on the floor, up and down, and around in great circles, but his eyes were red and he held on as the body cart-whipped over the floor, upsetting the tin dipper and the soap dish and the flesh brush, and banged against the tin side of the bath. As he held he closed his jaws tighter and tighter, for he made sure he would be banged to death, and, for the honor of his family, he preferred to be found with his teeth locked. He was dizzy, aching, and felt shaken to pieces when something went off like a **thunderclap**⑤ just behind him. A hot wind knocked him senseless and red fire singed his fur. The big man had been wakened by the noise, and had fired both barrels of a **shotgun**⑥ into Nag just behind the hood.

Rikki-tikki held on with his eyes shut, for now he was quite sure he was dead. But the head did not move, and the big man picked him up and said, "It's the mongoose again, Alice. The little **chap**⑦ has saved our lives now."

Then Teddy's mother came in with a very white face, and saw what was left of Nag, and Rikki-tikki dragged himself to Teddy's bedroom and spent half the rest of the night shaking himself tenderly to find out whether he really was

① coil [kɔil] v. 卷, 盘绕
② bulge [bʌldʒ] n. 凸出部分, 隆起物

③ hood [hud] n. 头巾, 兜帽

④ batter ['bætə] v. 连续猛击

⑤ thunderclap ['θʌndəklæp] n. 雷鸣

⑥ shotgun ['ʃɔtgʌn] n. 猎枪, 滑膛枪

⑦ chap [tʃæp] n. 家伙

外面并没有任何回音, 瑞奇－迪奇明白纳盖娜已经离开了。纳格蜷起身子, 在大水罐凸起的底部绕了一圈又一圈。瑞奇－迪奇一动也不动, 等到一个钟头以后, 他才开始一点一点地朝着水罐挪动。纳格已经睡熟了, 瑞奇－迪奇审视着蛇宽阔的后背, 思考哪里才是进攻的最佳位置。他想: "要是我不能第一跳就咬断他的背, 那他就还会跟我打。而他要是打起来的话——哦, 瑞奇－迪奇!"他看看蛇兜帽下面粗粗的脖子, 那对他来说太厚了; 可是如果在靠近尾巴的地方咬一下, 那又只会让纳格发狂。

他终于跟自己说: "只能是头了, 就在兜帽上面, 脑袋那里。而且, 一旦我爬上去了, 就不能松手。"

于是他跳了起来。蛇的脑袋没有紧挨着水罐, 而是搁在水罐肚子下面。瑞奇－迪奇一合上牙齿, 就弓起背紧紧地抵着红色瓦罐突出的腹部, 以便压着蛇头。这让他能够牢牢地抓住大蛇, 虽然只有一秒钟, 但他也充分地利用了这一秒的优势。接下来他就像被狗叼着乱摇的老鼠一样, 在地板上来来回回、上上下下、绕着大圈摔来打去, 他双眼通红, 始终不松口, 那蛇身像马车鞭子一样抽打地板, 碰翻了锡勺、肥皂盒和搓澡刷, 又撞上了锡制的澡盆。他抓住蛇身的同时也把牙关越收越紧, 因为他打定主意哪怕是被摔死, 也不能被人发现是大张着嘴巴死的, 那样的话可就把他们家族的脸给丢光了。瑞奇－迪奇头晕目眩, 浑身疼痛, 觉得自己都快散架了, 这时什么东西在他身后像响雷一样炸开, 一股热浪把他击倒了, 红色的火焰燎着了他的皮毛。原来是大个子被他们吵醒了, 拿起猎枪连击两发, 全都击中了纳格的兜帽后面。

瑞奇－迪奇紧闭着双眼仍然没有松口, 因为此刻他相当确信自己已经死了。但是蛇头并没有动, 大个子把他抱起来, 说: "爱丽丝, 又是猫鼬。这小家伙救了我们的命。"

broken into forty pieces, as he fancied.

When morning came he was very stiff, but well pleased with his doings. "Now I have Nagaina to settle with, and she will be worse than five Nags, and there's no knowing when the eggs she spoke of will hatch. Goodness! I must go and see Darzee," he said.

Without waiting for breakfast, Rikki-tikki ran to the **thornbush**① where Darzee was singing a song of **triumph**② at the top of his voice. The news of Nag's death was all over the garden, for the **sweeper**③ had thrown the body on the rubbish-heap.

"Oh, you stupid tuft of feathers!" said Rikki-tikki angrily. "Is this the time to sing?"

"Nag is dead—is dead—is dead!" sang Darzee. "The **valiant**④ Rikki-tikki caught him by the head and held fast. The big man brought the bang-stick, and Nag fell in two pieces! He will never eat my babies again."

"All that's true enough. But where's Nagaina?" said Rikki-tikki, looking carefully round him.

"Nagaina came to the bathroom sluice and called for Nag," Darzee went on, "and Nag came out on the end of a stick—the sweeper picked him up on the end of a stick and threw him upon the rubbish heap. Let us sing about the great, the red-eyed Rikki-tikki!" And Darzee filled his throat and sang.

"If I could get up to your nest, I'd roll your babies out!" said Rikki-tikki. "You don't know when to do the right thing at the right time. You're safe enough in your nest there, but it's war for me down here. Stop singing a minute, Darzee."

"For the great, the beautiful Rikki-tikki's sake I will stop," said Darzee. "What is it, O Killer of the terrible Nag?"

"Where is Nagaina, for the third time?"

"On the rubbish heap by the **stables**⑤, mourning for Nag. Great is Rikki-tikki with the white teeth."

"Bother my white teeth! Have you ever heard where she keeps her eggs?"

于是泰迪的母亲苍白着脸走进来，看着地上纳格残留的躯体。瑞奇－迪奇拖着身子回到泰迪的卧室，整个后半夜他都在轻轻地晃动着身体，好确信自己并不是像想象那样碎成了四十片渣渣。

第二天清晨，尽管他浑身僵硬，但是他对自己的壮举非常满意。他想："现在就剩纳盖娜了，她可能比五个纳格加起来还要厉害，而且谁也不知道她提过的那些蛋什么时候就会孵化。天啊，我得去看看达吉去。"

等不及吃早饭，瑞奇－迪奇就跑到荆棘丛那儿，达吉正在放声高唱胜利之歌。纳格的死讯已经传遍了花园，因为清洁工把他的尸体扔到了垃圾堆上。

瑞奇－迪奇生气地说："噢，你这个愚蠢的羽毛团儿！现在是唱歌的时候吗？"

达吉唱道："纳格死啦，死啦，死啦！英勇的瑞奇－迪奇抓住了他的头，抓得紧紧的。大个子拿来了砰砰响的棍子，纳格断成了两段！他再也吃不了我的宝宝啦！"

瑞奇－迪奇小心地看看四周，说："你说的都没错，可是纳盖娜在哪儿？"

达吉接下去说："纳盖娜去浴室的排水口呼唤纳格，纳格吊在棍子尖儿上出来了——清洁工用棍子的一头把他挑了起来，扔到了垃圾堆上。让我们歌颂伟大的、红眼睛的瑞奇－迪奇！"达吉大吸了一口气，开始唱起来。

瑞奇－迪奇说："我要是能够得着你的鸟窝，就会把你的宝贝儿们都给扔出去！你压根儿不知道什么时候该做什么事。你在你的鸟窝里倒是安全了，可是我在下面却有一场仗要打啊。闭嘴吧，达吉。"

达吉说："看在伟大的、俊美的瑞奇－迪奇的分上，我不唱了。哦，可怕的纳格的终结者，您有什么事啊？"

"这是第三遍了，纳盖娜到底在哪儿？"

"在马厩边上的垃圾堆那儿哀悼纳格呢。白牙齿的瑞奇－迪奇真伟大啊！"

"我才不管什么白牙齿呢！你听说过她把蛋藏在哪儿吗？"

① thornbush ['θɔːnbuʃ] n.【植物】山楂林

② triumph ['traiəmf] n. 凯旋，胜利

③ sweeper ['swiːpə] n. 打扫的人，清洁工

④ valiant ['væljənt] a. 英勇的，勇敢的

⑤ stable ['steibl] n. 畜舍，马厩

"In the melon bed, on the end nearest the wall, where the sun strikes nearly all day. She hid them there weeks ago."

"And you never thought it worth while to tell me? The end nearest the wall, you said?"

"Rikki-tikki, you are not going to eat her eggs?"

"Not eat exactly; no. Darzee, if you have a grain of sense you will fly off to the stables and pretend that your wing is broken, and let Nagaina chase you away to this bush. I must get to the melon-bed, and if I went there now she'd see me."

Darzee was a feather-brained little **fellow**① who could never hold more than one idea at a time in his head. And just because he knew that Nagaina's children were born in eggs like his own, he didn't think at first that it was fair to kill them. But his wife was a sensible bird, and she knew that cobra's eggs meant young cobras later on. So she flew off from the nest, and left Darzee to keep the babies warm, and continue his song about the death of Nag. Darzee was very like a man in some ways.

She **fluttered**② in front of Nagaina by the rubbish heap and cried out, "Oh, my wing is broken! The boy in the house threw a stone at me and broke it." Then she fluttered more desperately than ever.

Nagaina lifted up her head and hissed, "You warned Rikki-tikki when I would have killed him. Indeed and truly, you've chosen a bad place to be lame in." And she moved toward Darzee's wife, slipping along over the dust.

"The boy broke it with a stone!" shrieked Darzee's wife.

"Well! It may be some **consolation**③ to you when you're dead to know that I shall settle accounts with the boy. My husband lies on the rubbish heap this morning, but before night the boy in the house will lie very still. What is the use of running away? I am sure to catch you. Little fool, look at me!"

Darzee's wife knew better than to do that, for a bird who looks at a snake's eyes gets so frightened that she cannot move. Darzee's wife fluttered on, **piping**④ sorrowfully, and never leaving the ground, and Nagaina quickened her pace.

"在瓜田里，就在最靠近墙的那头儿，那儿几乎整天都能晒着太阳。她把蛋藏在那儿好几个星期了。"

"你就从来没想过应该告诉我吗？你是说最靠近墙的那头儿？"

"瑞奇－迪奇，你不会是要去吃掉她的蛋吧？"

"不是真的吃掉，不是。达吉，要是你有哪怕一点点脑子的话，你就飞到马厩那儿去，假装你的翅膀断了，然后让纳盖娜来追你，追到这边的灌木丛来。我得去瓜田那儿，可要是我现在过去的话，她会发现我的。"

达吉是个没什么脑子的小东西，他的脑袋里一次只能装下一个念头。正因为他知道纳盖娜的孩子是从蛋里孵出来的，就跟他自己的孩子一样，所以他一开始并不觉得杀死他们是件正大光明的事情。但是他的老婆比他聪明得多，她明白眼镜蛇的蛋意味着将来会有很多的小眼镜蛇。所以她从鸟窝里飞出去，留下达吉给孩子们暖着窝，继续歌唱纳格的死亡。达吉在某些方面确实很像男人。

她在垃圾堆边上遇到了纳盖娜，在她面前拍打着翅膀，一边喊道："噢，我的翅膀断了！屋子里的男孩儿朝我扔了一块石头，打折了我的翅膀。"然后她就扑扇得更厉害了。

纳盖娜抬起头，冲她发出嘶嘶声："我本来可以杀死瑞奇－迪奇的，都是你警告了他。说真的，你的翅膀断得太不是地方啦！"她朝着达吉的老婆追过去，从尘土上一路滑过。

达吉的老婆尖叫着说："那个男孩用石头把它打折了！"

"好啊！等你死了，我会去跟那个孩子算账的，这样你会高兴点儿吧。今天早上我的丈夫躺在垃圾堆上，可是过不了今晚，屋里的那个孩子就会躺着一动也不动了。逃跑有什么用呢？我肯定会抓住你的。看着我，小笨蛋！"

达吉的老婆当然不会看她啦，因为直视蛇的眼睛会让鸟儿吓得丝毫也不能动弹。达吉的老婆继续扑扇着翅膀，发出悲鸣，却始终不离开地面，这让纳盖娜加快了速度。

① fellow ['feləu] n. 家伙

② flutter ['flʌtə] v.（鸟）鼓翼，振翅

③ consolation [ˌkɔnsə'leiʃən] n. 安慰，慰藉

④ pipe [paip] v. 尖声叫嚷

· 209 ·

Rikki-tikki heard them going up the path from the stables, and he raced for the end of the melon patch near the wall. There, in the warm **litter**① above the melons, very cunningly hidden, he found twenty-five eggs, about the size of a **bantam**②'s eggs, but with **whitish**③ skin instead of shell.

"I was not a day too soon," he said, for he could see the baby cobras curled up inside the skin, and he knew that the minute they were hatched they could each kill a man or a mongoose. He bit off the tops of the eggs as fast as he could, taking care to crush the young cobras, and turned over the litter from time to time to see whether he had missed any. At last there were only three eggs left, and Rikki-tikki began to chuckle to himself, when he heard Darzee's wife **screaming**④:

"Rikki-tikki, I led Nagaina toward the house, and she has gone into the veranda, and—oh, come quickly—she means killing!"

Rikki-tikki smashed two eggs, and **tumbled**⑤ backward down the melon-bed with the third egg in his mouth, and scuttled to the veranda as hard as he could put foot to the ground. Teddy and his mother and father were there at early breakfast, but Rikki-tikki saw that they were not eating anything. They sat stone-still, and their faces were white. Nagaina was coiled up on the matting by Teddy's chair, within easy striking distance of Teddy's **bare**⑥ leg, and she was swaying to and fro, singing a song of triumph.

"Son of the big man that killed Nag," she hissed, "stay still. I am not ready yet. Wait a little. Keep very still, all you three! If you move I strike, and if you do not move I strike. Oh, foolish people, who killed my Nag!"

Teddy's eyes were fixed on his father, and all his father could do was to whisper, "Sit still, Teddy. You mustn't move. Teddy, keep still."

Then Rikki-tikki came up and cried, "Turn round, Nagaina. Turn and fight!"

"All in good time," said she, without moving her eyes. "I will settle my account with you presently. Look at your friends, Rikki-tikki. They are still and white. They are afraid. They dare not move, and if you come a step nearer I strike."

① litter ['litə] *n.* (供牲畜睡眠或防植物受冻的）褥草

② bantam ['bæntəm] *n.* （尤指产于爪哇的）万丹鸡，矮脚鸡

③ whitish ['waitiʃ] *a.* 略带白色的，发白的

④ scream [skri:m] *v.* 尖叫

⑤ tumble ['tʌmbl] *v.* 跌倒，摔倒

⑥ bare [bɛə] *a.* 赤裸的

瑞奇－迪奇听见他们从马厩那边的小路过来了，他赶紧跑到靠墙的那一处瓜田。就在那里，他找到了被晒得暖暖和和的一窝蛋，非常巧妙地藏在瓜上，一共有二十五只，个头跟矮脚鸡的蛋差不多大，但是没有壳，取而代之的是一层灰白色的皮。

"我来得不早也不晚。"他想，因为他看见蛋皮里蜷缩着的小眼镜蛇，他明白一旦他们孵出来，每一条都能杀死一个人或者一只猫鼬。他飞快地咬掉每只蛋的顶部，小心翼翼地把那些幼蛇都压死，然后不时地翻翻蛇窝，看看还有没有遗漏的。终于只剩下三只蛋了，瑞奇－迪奇咯咯地笑起来，这时他听见达吉的老婆尖叫着说："瑞奇－迪奇，我把纳盖娜引到房子那边去了，她进了阳台，——啊，快来啊——她要杀人啦！"

瑞奇－迪奇又压碎了两只蛋，然后把第三只蛋叼在嘴里，往后一翻，从瓜田上滚下来，朝着阳台几乎脚不沾地地急速飞奔。泰迪和父母正在吃早餐，但是瑞奇－迪奇看见他们什么也没吃，他们如同石像一般僵坐着，脸色都煞白煞白的。纳盖娜在泰迪椅子边的地席上盘起身子，轻而易举就能咬到泰迪裸着的小腿，她来回地摇晃着身体，唱着胜利之歌。

她嘶嘶地说："杀死纳格的大个子的儿子啊，你别动。我还没准备好呢。再等一会儿。你们三个，谁都别动一下！你们动我就咬，你们不动我也咬。噢，愚蠢的人啊，你们竟然杀死了我的纳格！"

泰迪盯着他的父亲，而他父亲能做的只是悄悄地跟他说："泰迪，坐好了别动。你不能动啊。泰迪，别动。"

这时瑞奇－迪奇过来，叫道："转过身来，纳盖娜。转过来跟我打啊！"

"不用着急，"她说，连眼珠子都没动一下。"我很快就去跟你算账。瑞奇－迪奇，看看你的朋友们吧。他们都僵了，脸也白了。他们害怕极了。他们不敢动，你要是过来一步我就咬他们。"

"Look at your eggs," said Rikki-tikki, "in the melon bed near the wall. Go and look, Nagaina!"

The big snake turned half around, and saw the egg on the veranda. "Ah-h! Give it to me," she said.

Rikki-tikki put his paws one on each side of the egg, and his eyes were blood-red. "What price for a snake's egg? For a young cobra? For a young king cobra? For the last—the very last of the **brood**①? The **ants**② are eating all the others down by the melon bed."

Nagaina spun clear round, forgetting everything for the sake of the one egg. Rikki-tikki saw Teddy's father shoot out a big hand, catch Teddy by the shoulder, and drag him across the little table with the tea-cups, safe and out of reach of Nagaina.

"Tricked! Tricked! Tricked! Rikk-tck-tck!" chuckled Rikki-tikki. "The boy is safe, and it was I—I—I that caught Nag by the hood last night in the bathroom." Then he began to jump up and down, all four feet together, his head close to the floor. "He threw me to and fro, but he could not shake me off. He was dead before the big man blew him in two. I did it! Rikki-tikki-tck-tck! Come then, Nagaina. Come and fight with me. You shall not be a **widow**③ long."

Nagaina saw that she had lost her chance of killing Teddy, and the egg lay between Rikki-tikki's paws. "Give me the egg, Rikki-tikki. Give me the last of my eggs, and I will go away and never come back," she said, lowering her hood.

"Yes, you will go away, and you will never come back. For you will go to the rubbish heap with Nag. Fight, widow! The big man has gone for his gun! Fight!"

Rikki-tikki was bounding all round Nagaina, keeping just out of reach of her stroke, his little eyes like hot **coals**④. Nagaina gathered herself together and flung out at him. Rikki-tikki jumped up and backward. Again and again and again she struck, and each time her head came with a **whack**⑤ on the matting of the veranda and she gathered herself together like a watch spring. Then Rikki-

瑞奇－迪奇说："看看你的蛋吧，就在靠墙的瓜田里。去看一眼吧，纳盖娜！"

大蛇转过一半的身子，看见了阳台上的蛋，她说："啊——！把它给我！"

瑞奇－迪奇把两只爪子放在蛋的两边，他的眼睛一片血红。"一只蛇蛋值多少钱啊？一条小眼镜蛇呢？一条小眼镜王蛇呢？最后一只——这一窝仅剩的一只蛋呢？现在瓜田那儿的蚂蚁正在吃掉其他的蛋哦。"

纳盖娜一下子转过身来，为了这只蛋把什么都抛在脑后了。瑞奇－迪奇看见泰迪的父亲如闪电般伸出一只大手，抓住泰迪的肩膀把他从放着茶杯的小桌子上一把扯了过来，安全地脱离了纳盖娜能够着的范围。

瑞奇－迪奇咯咯笑着说："上当啦，上当啦！男孩安全了。而且昨天晚上是我——我——我在浴室里抓住了纳格的兜帽。"他开始四条腿一起跳上跳下，脑袋却靠着地板。"他把我甩来甩去，却怎么也甩不掉我。在大个子把他轰成两半之前，他就已经死啦。是我干的！瑞奇－迪奇克－迪克－迪奇－迪奇－忒克！来啊，纳盖娜，来和我打啊。你想当寡妇也当不久啦。"

纳盖娜眼看已经丧失了杀死泰迪的机会，而她的蛋还待在瑞奇－迪奇的两爪之间。她放下兜帽，说："把蛋给我吧，瑞奇－迪奇。把我最后的这只蛋还给我，我就离开这里，再也不回来。"

"是的，你会离开，你再也不会回来，因为你会跟纳格一起待在垃圾堆上。寡妇，开打吧！大个子已经去拿他的枪了！打啊！"

瑞奇－迪奇绕着纳盖娜蹦蹦跳跳，恰好在她能够得着的距离之外，他的小眼睛红得就跟烧红的煤块一样。纳盖娜打起精神朝他猛扑过去。瑞奇－迪奇往上一蹦，又朝后一躲。她一次又一次地发起攻击，每次她的脑袋都重重地砸在阳台的地席上，可是接着她又像表簧一样重新弹起来。然后瑞奇－迪奇跳了一圈跑

① brood [bruːd] *n.* (动物，尤指鸟或家禽如雏鸡的）一窝

② ant [ænt] *n.*【昆虫】蚂蚁

③ widow ['widəu] *n.* 寡妇

④ coal [kəul] *n.* 煤，煤炭

⑤ whack [wæk] *n.* 重击

tikki danced in a circle to get behind her, and Nagaina spun round to keep her head to his head, so that the rustle of her tail on the matting sounded like dry leaves blown along by the wind.

He had forgotten the egg. It still lay on the veranda, and Nagaina came nearer and nearer to it, till at last, while Rikki-tikki was drawing breath, she caught it in her mouth, turned to the veranda steps, and flew like an **arrow**① down the path, with Rikki-tikki behind her. When the cobra runs for her life, she goes like a whip-lash flicked across a horse's neck.

Rikki-tikki knew that he must catch her, or all the trouble would begin again. She headed straight for the long grass by the thorn-bush, and as he was running Rikki-tikki heard Darzee still singing his foolish little song of triumph. But Darzee's wife was wiser. She flew off her nest as Nagaina came along, and flapped her wings about Nagaina's head. If Darzee had helped they might have turned her, but Nagaina only lowered her hood and went on. Still, the instant's delay brought Rikki-tikki up to her, and as she plunged into the rat-hole where she and Nag used to live, his little white teeth were **clenched**② on her tail, and he went down with her—and very few mongooses, however wise and old they may be, care to follow a cobra into its hole. It was dark in the hole; and Rikki-tikki never knew when it might open out and give Nagaina room to turn and strike at him. He held on savagely, and stuck out his feet to act as **brakes**③ on the dark slope of the hot, moist earth.

Then the grass by the mouth of the hole stopped waving, and Darzee said, "It is all over with Rikki-tikki! We must sing his death song. Valiant Rikki-tikki is dead! For Nagaina will surely kill him underground."

So he sang a very **mournful**④ song that he made up on the **spur**⑤ of the minute, and just as he got to the most touching part, the grass quivered again, and Rikki-tikki, covered with dirt, dragged himself out of the hole leg by leg, licking his whiskers. Darzee stopped with a little shout. Rikki-tikki shook some of the dust out of his fur and sneezed. "It is all over," he said. "The widow will never come out again." And the red ants that live between the grass stems heard

到她身后去，纳盖娜也嗖地转过身去，脑袋紧跟着他的脑袋，她的尾巴在地席上摩擦的声音听上去就跟枯叶被风吹过一样。

瑞奇 - 迪奇忘记了那只蛋。它还搁在阳台上，纳盖娜离它越来越近，终于，当瑞奇 - 迪奇还在吸气的时候，她一下子用嘴把它叼起来，转身朝着阳台台阶下面箭①一般地蹿过去，沿着小路飞奔，而瑞奇 - 迪奇就跟在她后面紧追不舍。眼镜蛇逃命时，速度快得就跟马鞭啪的一声掠过马脖子一般。

瑞奇 - 迪奇明白自己必须抓住纳盖娜，不然所有的麻烦又会卷土重来。她朝着荆棘丛旁边的长草直奔过去，瑞奇 - 迪奇一边跑，还一边听见达吉还在唱着他那荒唐的胜利之歌。但是达吉的老婆更有理智。她飞出鸟窝，迎向纳盖娜，在蛇的头上拍打翅膀。如果达吉也来帮忙的话，他们也许能把她赶回去，但是纳盖娜只是放下兜帽，继续朝前赶路。不过，就因为她耽搁了那么一下，瑞奇 - 迪奇趁机赶了上来，眼看着她一头就要扎进她和纳格住的那个鼠洞里去，瑞奇 - 迪奇的白牙一下子咬住②了她的尾巴，跟着她进了洞——很少有猫鼬愿意跟着眼镜蛇钻进洞里去，不管他们有多聪明或者多老到。洞里黑漆漆的，瑞奇 - 迪奇丝毫也不清楚什么时候会碰到一片开阔点儿的地方，那时纳盖娜就能转过身来攻击他了。他只能拼命地咬着她，脚伸出去时就像刹车③一样刮在闷热、潮湿、黑暗的斜坡上。

接下来，洞口的草丛停止颤动，达吉说："瑞奇 - 迪奇完了！我们要为他唱挽歌。英勇的瑞奇 - 迪奇死了！纳盖娜肯定在地底下把他杀死了。"

于是他唱了一首非常悲哀④的歌，这是他即兴编出来的。可是正当他唱到最哀婉的部分时，草丛又开始颤动了，瑞奇 - 迪奇一条腿一条腿地从洞里挤了出来，他舔着自己的胡须，浑身都是泥土。达吉低叫了一声，停下歌唱。瑞奇 - 迪奇抖抖身上的土，打了个喷嚏。他说：

① arrow ['ærəu] *n.* 箭，矢

② clench [klentʃ] *v.* 咬紧（牙齿等）

③ brake [breik] *n.*【植物】欧洲蕨

④ mournful ['mɔːnful] *a.* 悲哀的，悲伤的

⑤ spur [spəː] *n.* 踢马刺，靴刺

him, and began to troop down one after another to see if he had spoken the truth.

Rikki-tikki curled himself up in the grass and slept where he was—slept and slept till it was late in the afternoon, for he had done a hard day's work.

"Now," he said, when he awoke, "I will go back to the house. Tell the Coppersmith, Darzee, and he will tell the garden that Nagaina is dead."

The Coppersmith is a bird who makes a noise exactly like the beating of a little **hammer**① on a **copper**② pot; and the reason he is always making it is because he is the town crier to every Indian garden, and tells all the news to everybody who cares to listen. As Rikki-tikki went up the path, he heard his "attention" notes like a tiny dinner **gong**③, and then the steady "Ding-dong-tock! Nag is dead—dong! Nagaina is dead! Ding-dong-tock!" That set all the birds in the garden singing, and the frogs croaking, for Nag and Nagaina used to eat frogs as well as little birds.

When Rikki got to the house, Teddy and Teddy's mother (she looked very white still, for she had been fainting) and Teddy's father came out and almost cried over him; and that night he ate all that was given him till he could eat no more, and went to bed on Teddy's shoulder, where Teddy's mother saw him when she came to look late at night.

"He saved our lives and Teddy's life," she said to her husband. "Just think, he saved all our lives."

Rikki-tikki woke up with a jump, for the mongooses are light sleepers.

"Oh, it's you," said he. "What are you bothering for? All the cobras are dead. And if they weren't, I'm here."

Rikki-tikki had a right to be **proud**④ of himself. But he did not grow too proud, and he kept that garden as a mongoose should keep it, with tooth and jump and **spring**⑤ and bite, till never a cobra dared show its head inside the walls.

"都结束了。寡妇再也不会出来了。"住在草茎间的红蚂蚁听了他的话，开始一个接一个地排队下去，看看他说的是不是真的。

瑞奇－迪奇在草里蜷成一团，就地睡着了，他睡啊睡啊，一直睡到了黄昏，这一天他可是干了不少辛苦活儿。

他醒来以后说："现在，我要回屋子那儿去。达吉，你去跟铜匠说，让他告诉花园里所有的动物纳盖娜死了。"

① hammer ['hæmə] *n.* 锤子，槌，榔头

② copper ['kɔpə] *a.* 铜制的

③ gong [gɔŋ] *n.* 铜锣，锣

铜匠是一只小鸟，他发出的叫声就跟小锤子敲在铜壶上一模一样，而且他总是一刻不停地在叫，因为他就像个街头公告员，专门给每个印度花园传递消息，一有什么新闻他就会告诉所有想听的人。于是，当瑞奇－迪奇沿着小路走过去时，他就听见了铜匠"播报"的声音，像个小小的宣布开饭的锣在敲似的，响了一遍又一遍："叮咚呛！纳格死了——咚！纳盖娜死了！叮咚呛！"这个消息让园子里所有的鸟儿都开始歌唱，所有的青蛙也都开始呱呱叫，因为纳格和纳盖娜不但吃小鸟也吃青蛙。

当瑞奇－迪奇走到房子那儿时，泰迪和他母亲（她的脸色还是惨白的，因为她之前吓晕过去了）还有父亲出来迎接他，他们差点要搂着他痛哭一场。当晚，瑞奇－迪奇把所有给他的食物全都吃光了，直到他再也吃不下为止。他坐在泰迪的肩上去睡觉，等到晚些时候泰迪的母亲去看他们时发现他还趴在那儿呢。

泰迪的母亲对丈夫说："他救了我们的命，还有泰迪的命。想想看啊，他救了我们大家。"

瑞奇－迪奇动弹了一下，醒了过来，他们猫鼬睡觉都很警醒。

④ proud [praud] *a.* 自豪的，骄傲的

⑤ spring [spriŋ] *n.* 跳跃，蹦跳

他说："哦，是你们啊。你们在这儿操什么心呢？所有的眼镜蛇都死了。就算没有，还有我呢。"

瑞奇－迪奇当然有理由如此骄傲。但是他也没有变得太骄傲，而且就像所有猫鼬都会做的那样，他用尖牙利齿和一身腾跳的本领把花园守护得好好的，再也没有哪条眼镜蛇敢把头伸进墙里来。

Darzee's Chant

(Sung in honor of Rikki-tikki-tavi)

*Singer and **tailor**① am I—*
  Doubled the joys that I know—
*Proud of my **lilt**② to the sky,*
  *Proud of the house that I **sew**③—*
*Over and under, so **weave**④ I my music—so weave I the house that I sew.*

Sing to your fledglings again,
  Mother, oh lift up your head!
*Evil that plagued us is **slain**⑤,*
  Death in the garden lies dead.
Terror that hid in the roses is impotent—flung on the dung-hill and dead!

Who has delivered us, who?
  Tell me his nest and his name.
Rikki, the valiant, the true,
  Tikki, with eyeballs of flame,
Rikk-tikki-tikki, the ivory-fanged, the hunter with eyeballs of flame!

达吉之歌

（为瑞奇-迪奇-塔维而唱）

我是歌手和裁缝——
能让我享受双重喜悦——
为我的调子比天高而自豪，
为我缝好的鸟巢而骄傲——
忽上忽下，就这样谱写我的乐曲——就这样我缝好
我的鸟巢。

再次为你们的幼鸟歌唱，
母亲，噢，仰起你的头！
祸害我们的恶魔被杀了，
花园死神再也不会复生。
藏在玫瑰里的恐惧萎缩了——挂在垃圾堆上死掉了！

是谁拯救了我们，是谁？
告诉我他的巢穴和姓名。
瑞奇，他勇猛而精准，
迪奇，他眼珠似火焰，
瑞奇—迪奇—迪奇，这个猎手白牙尖利，眼珠放火！

① tailor ['teilə] *n.*（尤指缝制男子外衣的）裁缝,成衣工
② lilt [lilt] *n.* 轻快活泼的歌曲（或曲调,旋律）
③ sew [səu] *v.* 缝,缝合
④ weave [wi:v] *v.* 织

⑤ slain [slein] *v.*（slay 的过去分词）杀死,杀害

Give him the Thanks of the Birds,
    Bowing with tail feathers spread!
Praise[1] him with **nightingale**[2] words—
    Nay, I will praise him instead.
Hear! I will sing you the praise of the bottle-tailed Rikki, with **eyeballs**[3] of
    red!

(Here Rikki-tikki interrupted, and the rest of the song is lost.)

向他致以鸟儿们的感激，
展开尾巴上的羽毛向他鞠躬，
用夜莺般的歌声赞颂他——
不，是我要来将他歌颂。
听啊！我要为你歌唱，尾巴缩拢、眼珠涨红的瑞奇。

（唱到这里，瑞奇-迪奇打断了达吉的歌声，歌曲剩下的部分已遗失。）

① praise [preiz] v. 赞扬，表扬
② nightingale ['naitiŋgeil] n.【鸟类】夜莺
③ eyeball ['aibɔ:l] n. 眼球，眼珠子

Toomai of the Elephants

*I will remember what I was, I am sick of **rope**[①] and **chain**[②]—*
  I will remember my old strength and all my forest affairs.
I will not sell my back to man for a bundle of sugar-cane:
  *I will go out to my own kind, and the wood-folk in their **lairs**[③].*

I will go out until the day, until the morning break—
  *Out to the wind's **untainted**[④] kiss, the water's clean **caress**[⑤];*
I will forget my ankle-ring and snap my picket stake.
  I will revisit my lost loves, and playmates masterless!

Kala Nag, which means Black Snake, had served the Indian Government in every way that an elephant could serve it for forty-seven years, and as he was fully twenty years old when he was caught, that makes him nearly seventy—a ripe age for an elephant. He remembered pushing, with a big leather pad on his forehead, at a gun stuck in deep mud, and that was before the Afghan War of 1842, and he had not then come to his full strength.

His mother Radha Pyari,—Radha the darling,—who had been caught

象群的图迈

① rope [rəup] *n.* 绳，索
② chain [tʃein] *n.* 链，链条

③ lair [lɛə] *n.* 巢穴，窝

④ untainted [ʌn'teintid] *a.* 无污点的
⑤ caress [kə'res] *n.* 爱抚

我会牢记我以前的身份，我已经受够了绳索和铁链——

我会牢记我过去的力量和丛林的生活。

我不会为了一捆甘蔗让人类骑在我的脊梁上：

我要出去寻找我的同胞，还有所有安于巢穴的森林民众。

我要出去，一直走到拂晓，直到天亮——

去感受清风纯净的亲吻和流水干净的抚摸。

我会忘记我的脚镣，挣断我的木桩。

我要回去寻找我失去的爱人和自由自在的玩伴！

卡拉·纳格（这个名字是黑蛇的意思）已经为印度政府工作了四十七年，凡是大象能干的活儿他都干过。因为他刚被抓住时已经满二十岁，所以现在差不多得有七十岁了，这对大象来说正是壮年。他还记得当年自己额头上顶着块儿大大的皮垫子，使劲儿去推深陷在泥里的一门大炮，那还是在 1842 年的阿富汗战争之前，那时他的力气还没有达到巅峰呢。

他的母亲拉达·皮亚丽——亲爱的拉达——是和

in the same drive with Kala Nag, told him, before his little milk tusks had dropped out, that elephants who were afraid always got hurt. Kala Nag knew that that advice was good, for the first time that he saw a shell burst he backed, screaming, into a stand of piled **rifles**①, and the bayonets pricked him in all his softest places. So, before he was twenty-five, he gave up being afraid, and so he was the best-loved and the best-looked-after elephant in the service of the Government of India. He had carried **tents**②, twelve hundred pounds' weight of tents, on the march in Upper India. He had been **hoisted**③ into a ship at the end of a steam crane and taken for days across the water, and made to carry a **mortar**④ on his back in a strange and rocky country very far from India, and had seen the Emperor Theodore lying dead in Magdala, and had come back again in the steamer entitled, so the soldiers said, to the Abyssinian War medal. He had seen his fellow elephants die of cold and **epilepsy**⑤ and starvation and **sunstroke**⑥ up at a place called Ali Musjid, ten years later; and afterward he had been sent down thousands of miles south to haul and pile big balks of teak in the timberyards at Moulmein. There he had half killed an insubordinate young elephant who was shirking his fair share of work.

After that he was taken off timber-hauling, and employed, with a few score other elephants who were trained to the business, in helping to catch wild elephants among the Garo hills. Elephants are very strictly preserved by the Indian Government. There is one whole department which does nothing else but hunt them, and catch them, and break them in, and send them up and down the country as they are needed for work.

Kala Nag stood ten fair feet at the shoulders, and his tusks had been cut off short at five feet, and bound round the ends, to prevent them splitting, with bands of copper; but he could do more with those stumps than any untrained elephant could do with the real sharpened ones. When, after weeks and weeks of cautious driving of scattered elephants across the hills, the forty or fifty wild monsters were driven into the last **stockade**⑦, and the big drop gate, made of tree trunks lashed together, jarred down behind them, Kala Nag, at the word of

① rifle ['raifl] *n.* 步枪

② tent [tent] *n.* 帐篷,帐棚
③ hoist [hɔist] *v.*（尤指用机械装置等）吊起

④ mortar ['mɔːtə] *n.* 砂浆,灰浆

⑤ epilepsy ['epilepsi] *n.*【病理学】癫痫,羊痫风

⑥ sunstroke ['sʌnstrəuk] *n.* 中暑

⑦ stockade [stɔ'keid] *n.*（防御用的）栅栏,围桩

卡拉·纳格一起被捕捉的。在卡拉·纳格的小乳牙脱落之前，母亲曾告诉他害怕的大象总会受伤。卡拉·纳格知道她说的是对的，因为他第一次看见炸弹爆炸时，吓得尖叫着后退，跌进一排步枪里，结果身上最娇嫩的地方都被刺刀扎了个遍。所以他还不到二十五岁时，就已经不再害怕了，他也因此成为所有为印度政府服役的大象中最受喜爱、最受呵护的一头大象。他曾经在北印度的行军中搬运过重达一千二百磅的帐篷。他也曾被一架蒸汽吊车送到轮船上，在水上航行了好多天，又在那片远离印度的多岩的陌生国度运送一门迫击炮，然后亲眼看到西奥多皇帝死在马格达拉的战场上，最后又坐着蒸汽轮船回到印度。据士兵们说，他坐的那艘船还被授予了阿比西尼亚战争勋章。那之后过了十年，在一个叫作阿里·马斯基德的地方他又见过其他的大象因为寒冷、癫痫、饥饿和中暑而死去，后来他被送到几千英里以南的马尔梅因，在一个又一个的木材场里搬运、堆放大根的柚木。在那里他差点儿杀死了一头不听话的年轻大象，因为那个懒蛋不肯好好干自己该干的活儿。

再后来，人们不让他运木头了，又派他和其他几十头受过训练的大象一起去伽罗山帮忙捕捉野生大象。印度政府对大象的管制非常严格，有整整一个部门别的什么也不干，专门负责捕捉、驯化大象，然后按照需求把大象送往全国各地去完成各种各样的工作。

卡拉·纳格直立时两肩离地面足足有十英尺高，他的象牙被截短了，只剩五英尺长，顶端被铜带裹起来以免开裂，但是就凭这两截残牙他能干的事情也比任何真正拥有尖牙的大象要多得多，因为那些大象没有受过训练。经过长达数周小心的驱赶，从各处被赶来的四五十头野象翻过群山，被赶进最后一个围栏，然后用树干捆在一起做成的巨大吊闸会在这些野蛮的猛兽背后落下。这时卡拉·纳格就会服从命令，走进乱吼乱叫的象群

command, would go into that flaring, trumpeting **pandemonium**① (generally at night, when the flicker of the torches made it difficult to judge distances), and, picking out the biggest and wildest tusker of the mob, would hammer him and hustle him into quiet while the men on the backs of the other elephants roped and tied the smaller ones.

There was nothing in the way of fighting that Kala Nag, the old wise Black Snake, did not know, for he had stood up more than once in his time to the charge of the wounded tiger, and, curling up his soft trunk to be out of harm's way, had knocked the springing **brute**② sideways in mid-air with a quick sickle cut of his head, that he had invented all by himself; had knocked him over, and kneeled upon him with his huge knees till the life went out with a gasp and a **howl**③, and there was only a fluffy striped thing on the ground for Kala Nag to pull by the tail.

"Yes," said Big Toomai, his driver, the son of Black Toomai who had taken him to Abyssinia, and grandson of Toomai of the Elephants who had seen him caught, "there is nothing that the Black Snake fears except me. He has seen three generations of us feed him and **groom**④ him, and he will live to see four."

"He is afraid of me also," said Little Toomai, standing up to his full height of four feet, with only one rag upon him. He was ten years old, the eldest son of Big Toomai, and, according to custom, he would take his father's place on Kala Nag's neck when he grew up, and would handle the heavy iron **ankus**⑤, the elephant **goad**⑥, that had been worn smooth by his father, and his grandfather, and his great-grandfather.

He knew what he was talking of; for he had been born under Kala Nag's shadow, had played with the end of his trunk before he could walk, had taken him down to water as soon as he could walk, and Kala Nag would no more have dreamed of disobeying his shrill little orders than he would have dreamed of killing him on that day when Big Toomai carried the little brown baby under Kala Nag's tusks, and told him to **salute**⑦ his master that was to be.

① pandemonium [,pændə'məuniəm] *n.* 喧嚣；嘈杂

② brute [bru:t] *n.* 兽，野兽

③ howl [haul] *n.*（狼等的）嗥叫，凄厉的长嚎

④ groom [gru:m] *v.* 梳刷（马、狗等）

⑤ ankus ['æŋkəs] *n.*（尤指有尖钉和钩的印度的）驯象（用）刺棒

⑥ goad [gəud] *n.*（赶牛用的）刺棒

⑦ salute [sə'lju:t] *v.* 向……致意

（通常都是晚上，因为在火把跳跃的光下很难判断清楚距离），然后挑出其中个头最大、最野的大象，把他一通暴打，逼他安静下来。与此同时，骑着大象进来的人们会把剩下的个子小点儿的大象一一绑缚起来。

说到打架，没有什么事情是卡拉·纳格这头聪明的老"黑蛇"所不知道的。他曾经不止一次面对过受伤的老虎的进攻。他把柔软的象鼻卷起来以免碰伤，然后在老虎跃至半空时，脑袋迅速一摆，用一记巧妙的镰刀切，就把老虎撞飞了——这个招式还是他自己发明的呢——把老虎撞翻以后，他就用硕大的膝盖跪在老虎身上，直到对方咽最后一口气、哀嚎一声死去，地上就只剩下一摊带条纹的毛茸茸的东西，卡拉·纳格只需卷着他的尾巴把他拖走就行了。

他的象夫大图迈说："是的，'黑蛇'什么都不怕，除了我以外。我们一家已经有三代人喂养、照顾过他了，等我儿子长大成人时，他肯定还活着。"大图迈的爸爸是黑图迈，卡拉·纳格就是跟着他去的阿比西尼亚，爷爷是"象群的图迈"，大图迈的爷爷亲眼看见卡拉·纳格被捕捉。

"他还怕我呢。"小图迈说，尽管他站起来只有四英尺高，身上只裹着条破布。他是大图迈的大儿子，今年十岁了。根据惯例，长大以后他会取代父亲坐在卡拉·纳格的脖子上，还将接管沉重的象棒，那是一根铁做的刺棍，这根刺棍已经被他的父亲、祖父和曾祖父用得非常光滑了。

他知道自己在说什么，因为他就出生在卡拉·纳格的影子里，还不会走路的时候就跟卡拉·纳格的鼻子一起玩耍，刚会走路就带卡拉·纳格去水边，所以卡拉·纳格做梦也不会违背他那尖尖的小嗓子发出的命令，就像当年大图迈把还是棕色小婴儿的小图迈放到他的象牙底下，让他对未来的主人敬礼时，卡拉·纳格也压根没有动过想把这个小孩杀死的念头。

"Yes," said Little Toomai, "he is afraid of me," and he took long strides up to Kala Nag, called him a fat old pig, and made him lift up his feet one after the other.

"Wah!" said Little Toomai, "thou art a big elephant," and he **wagged**① his fluffy head, quoting his father. "The Government may pay for elephants, but they belong to us **mahouts**②. When thou art old, Kala Nag, there will come some rich **rajah**③, and he will buy thee from the Government, on account of thy size and thy manners, and then thou wilt have nothing to do but to carry gold earrings in thy ears, and a gold howdah on thy back, and a red cloth covered with gold on thy sides, and walk at the head of the **processions**④ of the King. Then I shall sit on thy neck, O Kala Nag, with a silver ankus, and men will run before us with golden sticks, crying, `Room for the King's elephant!' That will be good, Kala Nag, but not so good as this hunting in the jungles."

"Umph!" said Big Toomai. "Thou art a boy, and as wild as a buffalo-calf. This running up and down among the hills is not the best Government service. I am getting old, and I do not love wild elephants. Give me brick elephant lines, one stall to each elephant, and big stumps to tie them to safely, and flat, broad roads to exercise upon, instead of this come-and-go camping. Aha, the Cawnpore barracks were good. There was a **bazaar**⑤ close by, and only three hours' work a day."

Little Toomai remembered the Cawnpore elephant-lines and said nothing. He very much preferred the camp life, and hated those broad, flat roads, with the daily grubbing for grass in the forage reserve, and the long hours when there was nothing to do except to watch Kala Nag fidgeting in his pickets.

What Little Toomai liked was to scramble up bridle paths that only an elephant could take; the dip into the valley below; the glimpses of the wild elephants **browsing**⑥ miles away; the rush of the frightened pig and peacock under Kala Nag's feet; the blinding warm rains, when all the hills and valleys smoked; the beautiful misty mornings when nobody knew where they would camp that night; the steady, cautious drive of the wild elephants, and the mad

小图迈说："是的，他怕我。"他大步走到卡拉·纳格跟前，管他叫老肥猪，还命令他把腿一条一条地抬起来。

小图迈说："哇！你可真是头大——象啊。"他摇晃着毛乎乎的脑袋，背诵父亲说过的话："大象也许是政府花钱养的，但是他们却归我们象夫所有。卡拉·纳格，等你老了，就会有个有钱的王公来把你从政府手里买走，因为你又大又懂礼貌，然后你就可以啥事也不用做，只需要在耳朵上戴着金耳环，背上驮个金轿子，身上披着绣满金线的红布，走在国王仪仗队伍的最前面。哦，卡拉·纳格，那时我会拿着银象棒骑在你的脖子上，咱们前面跑着些拿金棍子的男人们，他们边跑边喊：'给国王的大象让道啊！'卡拉·纳格，那样可真不错，不过，还是没有现在在丛林里打猎好。"

大图迈说："哼！你就是个孩子，还跟小牛犊一样野。像这样在山里面跑来跑去可不是什么美差。我上了年纪了，也不喜欢什么野象。让我住砖砌的象栏，每头大象一个隔间，配着大树桩好把他们拴得牢牢的，还有平坦、宽阔的马路可供他们训练。我才不要现在这种来了又走的露营呢。啊哈，像考恩坡军营就很不错嘛，那儿附近有个集市，而且每天只需要干三个小时。"

小图迈当然记得考恩坡的象营，但是他什么也没说。他更喜欢露营的生活，他讨厌那些宽阔、平坦的大马路，每天都要在草料堆里翻掘干草，剩下的漫长时间里除了看着卡拉·纳格在象栏里走来走去以外无所事事。

小图迈喜欢的是爬上只有大象可以走的象道，或是跳进下面的山谷，或是眺望几英里外觅食的野象群，或是在卡拉·纳格脚下受惊乱跑的猪和孔雀，或是温暖的大雨倾盆而下时轻烟弥漫的群山和山谷，或是薄雾笼罩的美丽的清晨，尽管谁也不知道晚上将在哪里扎营，再或是经过一夜的狂奔乱冲、火光喧天和闹闹嚷嚷之后，终于能够平稳小心地驱赶野象，头天夜里

① wag [wæg] v. 摇摆，摇动

② mahout [mə'haut] n.（印度及东印度群岛的）管象人

③ rajah ['rɑːdʒə] n.（印度的）王公

④ procession [prə'seʃən] n. 行列，游行

⑤ bazaar [bə'zɑː] n.（东方国家的）市场，集市

⑥ browse [brauz] v. 吃草

rush and blaze and hullabaloo of the last night's drive, when the elephants poured into the stockade like boulders in a landslide, found that they could not get out, and flung themselves at the heavy posts only to be driven back by **yells**[1] and flaring torches and **volleys**[2] of blank **cartridge**[3].

Even a little boy could be of use there, and Toomai was as useful as three boys. He would get his torch and wave it, and yell with the best. But the really good time came when the driving out began, and the Keddah—that is, the stockade—looked like a picture of the end of the world, and men had to make signs to one another, because they could not hear themselves speak. Then Little Toomai would climb up to the top of one of the quivering stockade posts, his sun-bleached brown hair flying loose all over his shoulders, and he looking like a goblin in the torch-light. And as soon as there was a **lull**[4] you could hear his high-pitched yells of encouragement to Kala Nag, above the trumpeting and crashing, and snapping of ropes, and groans of the **tethered**[5] elephants. "Mael, mael, Kala Nag! (Go on, go on, Black Snake!) Dant do! (Give him the tusk!) Somalo! Somalo! (Careful, careful!) Maro! Mar! (Hit him, hit him!) Mind the post! Arre! Arre! Hai! Yai! Kya-a-ah!" he would shout, and the big fight between Kala Nag and the wild elephant would sway to and fro across the Keddah, and the old elephant catchers would wipe the sweat out of their eyes, and find time to nod to Little Toomai wriggling with joy on the top of the posts.

He did more than **wriggle**[6]. One night he slid down from the post and slipped in between the elephants and threw up the loose end of a rope, which had dropped, to a driver who was trying to get a purchase on the leg of a kicking young calf (calves always give more trouble than full-grown animals). Kala Nag saw him, caught him in his trunk, and handed him up to Big Toomai, who slapped him then and there, and put him back on the post.

Next morning he gave him a scolding and said, "Are not good brick elephant lines and a little tent carrying enough, that thou must needs go elephant catching on thy own account, little worthless? Now those foolish hunters, whose pay is less than my pay, have spoken to Petersen Sahib of the

① yell [jel] *n.* 叫喊
② volley ['vɔli] *n.* 齐射出的子弹（或炮弹、箭等）
③ cartridge ['kɑ:tridʒ] *n.* 子弹

④ lull [lʌl] *n.*（风、雨等的）暂时平息,暂时平静
⑤ tether ['teðə] *v.*（用绳、链等）拴

⑥ wriggle ['rigl] *n.* 蠕动

大象们如同泥石流里的巨石一般冲进围栏时，发现自己无路可走因此拼命地用身子去撞击沉重的围栏，但是最终还是被人们用呐喊、火把和连续发射的空弹给驱赶回去。

在那样的场合，即使是一个小孩也能派上用场，而图迈一个能顶三个男孩使。他会举着火把挥舞，尽力大声地呼喊。但是对他来说，最精彩的时刻还是在把野象赶出围栏时。那时，象栏周围的一切看上去就像一幅世界末日的图景，男人们互相打着手势，因为实在太吵了，他们连自己说话都听不见。小图迈会爬上一根不断颤动的柱子，坐在顶上，他那一头被阳光晒成了棕色的头发胡乱地披散在肩头，火光下他整个人看上去就跟个地精一样。只要稍微安静下来，你就会听到小图迈尖尖的叫声，它远远高出周围的吼叫和撞击声、绳子的抽打声，还有被拴住的大象的呻吟声。那是他在给卡拉·纳格打气："加油，加油，黑蛇！用牙顶他！小心！小心！打他，打他！小心柱子！啊嘿！啊嘿！哈咦！呀！驾——！"在他的叫喊声中，卡拉·纳格和野象之间的大战就从象栏的这头打到那头，那些老的捕象人会擦掉眼睛周围的汗水，一边抽空朝着小图迈赞许地点点头，而小图迈呢，则在柱子的顶端高兴地扭来扭去。

小图迈当然不是只会扭来扭去。有天晚上，他还从柱子上滑下来，溜进大象中间，捡起绳子松开的一头，递给一个象夫，当时那个象夫本想要抓住一头胡乱踢腾的小象的腿（幼崽总是比成年动物要麻烦得多），结果把绳子弄掉了。卡拉·纳格看见了小图迈，及时用鼻子把他卷起来，递给了大图迈。大图迈当场就给了他一巴掌，然后把他重新放到柱子上去。

第二天早上，大图迈教训了他一顿："你这个没用的小东西，上好的砖砌象圈对你来说还不够吗？搬搬帐篷不就可以了吗？你居然还要自己去抓大象？好嘛，那些愚蠢的捕象人，他们的工资还没我的多，现在他们已

matter." Little Toomai was frightened. He did not know much of white men, but Petersen Sahib was the greatest white man in the world to him. He was the head of all the Keddah operations—the man who caught all the elephants for the Government of India, and who knew more about the ways of elephants than any living man.

"What—what will happen?" said Little Toomai.

"Happen! The worst that can happen. Petersen Sahib is a **madman**①. Else why should he go hunting these wild **devils**②? He may even require thee to be an elephant catcher, to sleep anywhere in these fever-filled jungles, and at last to be trampled to death in the Keddah. It is well that this nonsense ends safely. Next week the catching is over, and we of the plains are sent back to our stations. Then we will **march on**③ smooth roads, and forget all this hunting. But, son, I am angry that thou shouldst **meddle**④ in the business that belongs to these dirty Assamese jungle folk. Kala Nag will obey none but me, so I must go with him into the Keddah, but he is only a fighting elephant, and he does not help to rope them. So I sit at my ease, as befits a mahout,—not a mere hunter,—a mahout, I say, and a man who gets a pension at the end of his service. Is the family of Toomai of the Elephants to be trodden underfoot in the dirt of a Keddah? Bad one! Wicked one! Worthless son! Go and wash Kala Nag and attend to his ears, and see that there are no thorns in his feet. Or else Petersen Sahib will surely catch thee and make thee a wild hunter—a follower of elephant's foot tracks, a jungle bear. Bah! Shame! Go!"

Little Toomai went off without saying a word, but he told Kala Nag all his **grievances**⑤ while he was examining his feet. "No matter," said Little Toomai, turning up the fringe of Kala Nag's huge right ear. "They have said my name to Petersen Sahib, and perhaps—and perhaps—and perhaps—who knows? Hai! That is a big thorn that I have pulled out!"

The next few days were spent in getting the elephants together, in walking the newly caught wild elephants up and down between a couple of tame ones to

经去跟皮特森·萨黑布报告了这件事情。"小图迈害怕了。他对白人了解得不多，但是对他来说，皮特森·萨黑布是世界上最伟大的白人。皮特森负责领导所有的捕象业务，所有给印度政府服役的大象都是他抓来的，他也比当时的任何人都更加了解大象的习性。

小图迈问："那——那接下来会怎么样呢？"

"怎么样？你死定了！皮特森·萨黑布是个疯子。不然他怎么会去猎捕这些可怕的野兽？他甚至有可能让你去抓大象，睡在到处都会染上热病的丛林里，最后在象圈里被大象踩死。当然了，这场闹剧最后也有可能安全收场。下个星期捕象就会结束，我们这些从平原来的人又可以回到我们的象营。然后我们就可以走在平路上，把捕猎的这档子事全部忘掉。但是，儿子，你居然去掺和本来该这些肮脏的阿萨姆丛林土著干的事情，我很生气。卡拉·纳格只听我的，所以我才不得不跟他到象圈里去，但他是头战象，他不用帮忙去拴那些大象。所以我可以舒舒服服地坐着，因为这才符合我们象夫的身份。象夫和捕象人可不一样，我告诉你，我们退休的时候是有养老金可以拿的。象群的图迈家族难道是在象圈的泥巴里面被踩来踩去的吗？坏孩子！野孩子！没用的家伙！去，给卡拉·纳格洗洗，看看他的耳朵，检查一下他的脚上有没有扎刺儿。不然的话，皮特森·萨黑布肯定会抓住你，把你变成个野蛮的捕象人，这样你只配去追踪大象的脚印，活得跟丛林里的熊一样。呸！丢脸！滚！"

小图迈一言不发走开了，但是后来他给卡拉·纳格检查脚掌的时候却把自己的满腹委屈都讲给了大象听。他抓住卡拉·纳格大大的右耳，一边翻开耳朵边缘，一边说："没关系。就算他们把我的名字告诉了皮特森·萨黑布，那又怎样——也许——也许，谁知道呢？哈！看我拔出来的这根大刺儿！"

后来的几天，大家忙着把大象聚到一起，把新抓来的野象赶到几只温驯的大象中间，好让他们在接下来去

① madman ['mædmən] n. 疯子，精神失常者

② devil ['devəl] n. 魔鬼，恶魔

③ march on 行进，向前进

④ meddle ['medl] v. 干预，干涉

⑤ grievance ['gri:vəns] n. 委屈

· 233 ·

prevent them giving too much trouble on the downward march to the plains, and in taking stock of the blankets and ropes and things that had been worn out or lost in the forest.

Petersen Sahib came in on his clever she-elephant Pudmini; he had been paying off other camps among the hills, for the season was coming to an end, and there was a native clerk sitting at a table under a tree, to pay the drivers their wages. As each man was paid he went back to his elephant, and joined the line that stood ready to start. The catchers, and hunters, and beaters, the men of the regular Keddah, who stayed in the jungle year in and year out, sat on the backs of the elephants that belonged to Petersen Sahib's permanent force, or leaned against the trees with their guns across their arms, and made fun of the drivers who were going away, and laughed when the newly caught elephants broke the line and ran about.

Big Toomai went up to the **clerk**[①] with Little Toomai behind him, and Machua Appa, the head **tracker**[②], said in an undertone to a friend of his, "There goes one piece of good elephant stuff at least. 'Tis a pity to send that young jungle-cock to **molt**[③] in the plains."

Now Petersen Sahib had ears all over him, as a man must have who listens to the most silent of all living things—the wild elephant. He turned where he was lying all along on Pudmini's back and said, "What is that? I did not know of a man among the plains-drivers who had wit enough to rope even a dead elephant."

"This is not a man, but a boy. He went into the Keddah at the last drive, and threw Barmao there the rope, when we were trying to get that young calf with the **blotch**[④] on his shoulder away from his mother."

Machua Appa pointed at Little Toomai, and Petersen Sahib looked, and Little Toomai bowed to the earth.

"He throw a rope? He is smaller than a picket-pin. Little one, what is thy name?" said Petersen Sahib.

Little Toomai was too frightened to speak, but Kala Nag was behind him,

平原的路上少惹点麻烦。人们还清点了毯子、绳索和其他杂物，看看有哪些磨损了或者丢失在森林里。

皮特森·萨黑布骑着他那头聪明的母象普德米妮过来了，他之前到山里的其他营区去发工钱了，因为今年的捕象季已经走到尾声。一个管账的当地人坐在树下的小桌子后面，给象夫们发放工资。每个人领到钱以后就走回自己的大象那儿，排成一队准备出发。那些负责追踪、抓捕、鞭打大象的人呢，因为是象圈的固定员工，所以他们常年待在丛林里。他们有的骑在大象——这些都属于皮特森·萨黑布的常规军——背上，有的靠着树干，胳膊上架着猎枪，一齐嘲笑那些将要离开的象夫，每当有新抓来的大象脱离队伍到处乱跑时，他们又爆发出一阵阵的大笑。

① clerk [klɑːk] *n.* 职员，事务员
② tracker ['trækə] *n.* 纤夫
③ molt [məult] *v.*【动物学】蜕皮

大图迈走到管账员跟前，他身后跟着小图迈。跟踪大象的猎人头领，马楚阿·阿帕对一个朋友低声说："看，那边那个总算是个像样的捕象人。真可惜，这么好的一个丛林小公鸡，却要被送到平原上去换羽毛啦。"

作为一个能够察知野象动静的人（野象可以说是所有生物当中最悄无声息的了），皮特森·萨黑布当然拥有超常的听力。他本来是平躺在普德米妮的背上的，这时他转过身来问道："什么？平原上来的象夫哪怕连死的大象都套不住，我还没听说过他们有谁这么聪明呢？"

"不是象夫，是个男孩。上次赶象时，他跑到象圈里去了。我们当时正在把那头肩膀上长了块斑的小象从他妈妈身边拖走，就是这个小孩把绳子扔给巴茂的。"

④ blotch [blɔtʃ] *n.*（皮肤上的）红斑，斑点

马楚阿·阿帕指指小图迈，皮特森·萨黑布看过去，小图迈深深鞠了一躬。

皮特森·萨黑布问："他扔的绳子？他还没有围栏的插销个头大呢。小家伙，你叫什么名字？"

小图迈吓得不敢张口，但是卡拉·纳格正站在他的

and Toomai made a sign with his hand, and the elephant caught him up in his trunk and held him level with Pudmini's **forehead**①, in front of the great Petersen Sahib. Then Little Toomai covered his face with his hands, for he was only a child, and except where elephants were concerned, he was just as **bashful**② as a child could be.

"Oho!" said Petersen Sahib, smiling underneath his mustache, "and why didst thou teach thy elephant that trick? Was it to help thee steal green corn from the roofs of the houses when the ears are put out to dry?"

"Not green corn, Protector of the Poor, — melons," said Little Toomai, and all the men sitting about broke into a roar of laughter. Most of them had taught their elephants that trick when they were boys. Little Toomai was hanging eight feet up in the air, and he wished very much that he were eight feet underground.

"He is Toomai, my son, Sahib," said Big Toomai, **scowling**③. "He is a very bad boy, and he will end in a **jail**④, Sahib."

"Of that I have my doubts," said Petersen Sahib. "A boy who can face a full Keddah at his age does not end in jails. See, little one, here are four annas to spend in **sweetmeats**⑤ because thou hast a little head under that great thatch of hair. In time thou mayest become a hunter too." Big Toomai scowled more than ever. "Remember, though, that Keddahs are not good for children to play in," Petersen Sahib went on.

"Must I never go there, Sahib?" asked Little Toomai with a big gasp.

"Yes." Petersen Sahib smiled again. "When thou hast seen the elephants dance. That is the proper time. Come to me when thou hast seen the elephants dance, and then I will let thee go into all the Keddahs."

There was another roar of laughter, for that is an old joke among elephant-catchers, and it means just never. There are great cleared flat places hidden away in the forests that are called elephants' ball-rooms, but even these are only found by accident, and no man has ever seen the elephants dance. When

身后，于是小图迈打了个手势，大象就用鼻子把他卷起来，举到空中和普德米妮的额头①齐平的地方，让他面对着伟大的皮特森·萨黑布。小图迈用手捂住脸，他还是个孩子，所以如果不是面对跟大象有关的事情的时候，还是跟普通小孩一样害羞②。

皮特森·萨黑布抿着胡子笑了，他说："哦呵！你为什么教你的大象玩这一招呢？是为了帮你从房顶上偷晾晒的青玉米吗？"

小图迈回答说："穷人的守护者，不是偷青玉米，是——西瓜。"坐在周围的所有人都哄堂大笑，因为他们当中大多数人小的时候也都教自己的大象这么干过。小图迈悬在空中离地八英尺高，此刻他却恨不得自己是在地下八英尺深的地方。

大图迈皱③着眉头说："萨黑布，他叫图迈，是我的儿子。我这个孩子太调皮了，萨黑布，他将来肯定会进监狱④的。"

皮特森·萨黑布却说："这我倒是有点怀疑。像他这么大的男孩竟然敢于面对一整个象圈，这样的孩子可进不了监狱。看，小家伙，这儿有四安纳，你可以拿去买果脯⑤吃，因为你那一头乱蓬蓬的头发下面倒是有个聪明的小脑袋。将来你可能也会成为一个猎手呢。"大图迈的眉头皱得更厉害了。皮特森·萨黑布又接着说："但是，你要记住，象圈可不是小孩玩的地方。"

小图迈大吸了一口气，问："那我永远也不能去那儿了吗，萨黑布？"

皮特森·萨黑布又笑了："是的，除非你能看到大象跳舞，那时你就可以去了。等你真的见到象舞了，你来找我，我就会允许你去所有的象圈。"

人群中又爆发出一阵笑声，因为这是个捕象人都知道的老笑话，意思就是这事永远也不可能发生。据说在丛林里隐藏着一些开阔的空地，叫作大象的舞池，但是人们也只是偶尔才会发现这些地方，并没有人真的见过大象跳

① forehead ['fɔ:hed] n. 前额，额

② bashful ['bæʃful] a. 胆怯的

③ scowl [skaul] v. 皱眉头
④ jail [dʒeil] n. 监狱

⑤ sweetmeat ['swi:tmi:t] n. 糖果

a driver boasts of his skill and bravery the other drivers say, "And when didst thou see the elephants dance?"

Kala Nag put Little Toomai down, and he bowed to the earth again and went away with his father, and gave the **silver**① four-anna piece to his mother, who was nursing his baby brother, and they all were put up on Kala Nag's back, and the line of grunting, **squealing**② elephants rolled down the hill path to the plains. It was a very lively march on account of the new elephants, who gave trouble at every **ford**③, and needed **coaxing**④ or beating every other minute.

Big Toomai **prodded**⑤ Kala Nag spitefully, for he was very angry, but Little Toomai was too happy to speak. Petersen Sahib had noticed him, and given him money, so he felt as a private soldier would feel if he had been called out of the ranks and praised by his commander-in-chief.

"What did Petersen Sahib mean by the elephant dance?" he said, at last, softly to his mother.

Big Toomai heard him and grunted. "That thou shouldst never be one of these hill buffaloes of trackers. That was what he meant. Oh, you in front, what is blocking the way?"

An Assamese driver, two or three elephants ahead, turned round angrily, crying: "Bring up Kala Nag, and knock this youngster of mine into good behavior. Why should Petersen Sahib have chosen me to go down with you **donkeys**⑥ of the rice fields? Lay your beast alongside, Toomai, and let him prod with his tusks. By all the Gods of the Hills, these new elephants are possessed, or else they can smell their companions in the jungle." Kala Nag hit the new elephant in the ribs and knocked the wind out of him, as Big Toomai said, "We have swept the hills of wild elephants at the last catch. It is only your carelessness in driving. Must I keep order along the whole line?"

"Hear him!" said the other driver. "We have swept the hills! Ho! Ho! You are very wise, you plains people. Anyone but a mud-head who never saw the jungle would know that they know that the drives are ended for the season.

舞。当一个象夫夸耀自己技术高超或是勇气非凡的时候，其他象夫就会说："那你什么时候见过大象跳舞啊？"

卡拉·纳格把小图迈放下来，他再次深深鞠了一躬，然后跟着父亲离开了。他把那个四安纳的银币交给了正在给他小弟弟哺乳的母亲，然后他们都爬上卡拉·纳格的背，接下来排成一队的大象就哼哼唧唧、不时尖叫着顺着山路往平原走去。因为那些新来的大象的缘故，队伍里热闹极了，他们每经过一个浅滩都会惹出些乱子来，时时刻刻都需要人哄着、打着。

大图迈满腔怒火，恶狠狠地用象棒捅着卡拉·纳格，而小图迈却乐得连话都说不出来。皮特森·萨黑布不但注意到他，还给了他钱，所以他的感觉就像一个士兵被叫出队列，接受长官的表扬一样。

过了好一会儿，他才轻声地问母亲："皮特森·萨黑布说的象舞是什么意思呀？"

大图迈听见了，哼了一声，说道："意思是你永远也不可能像这些山里的蛮牛一样去追踪野象。这就是他的意思。噢，前面的那个，你，怎么不走了？"

在他们前面，隔着两三头大象那么远，一个阿萨姆象夫转过身来怒气冲冲地喊道："把卡拉·纳格带过来，好好揍揍我这头小崽子，教他听话。皮特森·萨黑布干吗要让我跟着你们这群稻田的蠢驴下山呢？图迈，让你的畜生靠过来，让他用象牙好好戳戳。群山的众神啊，这些新来的大象简直是中邪了，要不然就是他们闻到了丛林里的同伴的气味。"卡拉·纳格用牙顶了那头新象的肋部，打得他气都喘不上来。这时大图迈说道："我们最后这次抓捕已经把这片山里的野象都抓光了。是你自己赶象不够小心而已。难道还要我来维持整个队伍的秩序吗？"

那个象夫说："听听他说的！我们已经把山林都清空了。哈，哈！你们这些平原人，你们可真聪明啊。除了从没见过丛林的傻子以外，谁都知道大象们都清楚这

① silver ['silvə] *n.* 银，白银

② squeal [skwi:l] *v.* 发出长而尖锐的刺耳叫声

③ ford [fɔ:d] *n.* 浅滩
④ coax [kəuks] *v.* 哄，劝诱
⑤ prod [prɔd] *v.*（用手指、棍棒等）刺

⑥ donkey ['dɔŋki] *n.*【动物】驴

Therefore all the wild elephants to-night will—but why should I waste wisdom on a river-turtle?"

"What will they do?" Little Toomai called out.

"Ohe, little one. Art thou there? Well, I will tell thee, for thou hast a cool head. They will dance, and it **behooves**① thy father, who has swept all the hills of all the elephants, to double-chain his pickets to-night."

"What talk is this?" said Big Toomai. "For forty years, father and son, we have tended elephants, and we have never heard such **moonshine**② about dances."

"Yes; but a **plainsman**③ who lives in a **hut**④ knows only the four walls of his hut. Well, leave thy elephants unshackled tonight and see what comes. As for their dancing, I have seen the place where—Bapree-bap! How many **windings**⑤ has the Dihang River? Here is another ford, and we must swim the **calves**⑥. Stop still, you behind there."

And in this way, talking and wrangling and splashing through the rivers, they made their first march to a sort of receiving camp for the new elephants. But they lost their tempers long before they got there.

Then the elephants were chained by their hind legs to their big **stumps**⑦ of pickets, and extra ropes were fitted to the new elephants, and the fodder was piled before them, and the hill drivers went back to Petersen Sahib through the afternoon light, telling the plains drivers to be extra careful that night, and laughing when the plains drivers asked the reason.

Little Toomai attended to Kala Nag's supper, and as evening fell, wandered through the camp, unspeakably happy, in search of a **tom-tom**⑧. When an Indian child's heart is full, he does not run about and make a noise in an irregular fashion. He sits down to a sort of **revel**⑨ all by himself. And Little Toomai had been spoken to by Petersen Sahib! If he had not found what he wanted, I believe he would have been ill. But the sweetmeat seller in the camp lent him a little tom-tom—a drum beaten with the flat of the hand—and he sat down, cross-legged, before Kala Nag as the stars began to come out, the tom-tom in his lap,

一季的抓捕已经结束了。所以今晚所有的野象都会——不过我干吗要跟一只王八费口舌呢？"

小图迈喊道："他们都会干什么？"

"哦呵，小家伙。你在那儿吗？好吧，我可以告诉你，因为你脑子清醒。他们会跳舞。而你的爸爸，他不是才把这山里的大象都扫荡了吗？但是今晚，他可得把象栏加上两道铁链才行呢。"

大图迈说："这都是什么话呀？我们家几代人照管大象都有四十年了，还从来没听说过什么大象跳舞的鬼话。"

"是啊，住在茅屋里的平原人当然只认识自己屋子的四面墙喽。嗯，要不你今晚就别给大象带上脚镣，看看会发生什么事。说到大象跳舞，我可是见过有个地方，那儿——啊噶呸！狄航河到底有几道弯啊？又是一个浅滩，我们得让象恩游过去。后面的，停下来。"

于是，他们就这样一路说着、吵着、踩着水过了河，终于来到了一个专门接待新象的营地。但是早在抵达之前，人们就已经失去了耐性。

大象的后腿都用铁链拴在了象栏的大木桩上，新象还都额外配备了绳索，草料也都摆放在大象跟前。山里来的象夫趁着午后返回皮特森·萨黑布那里，走之前告诫平原的象夫们当晚要多加小心，但是在被问到为什么时却只是笑笑。

小图迈照顾卡拉·纳格吃完晚餐，夜幕降临时，他在营地里走来走去想找一个手鼓，心里说不出的高兴。当一个印度小孩心里乐开花儿时，他不会到处乱跑，毫无章法地大喊大叫。他会一个人坐着自我陶醉一番。皮特森·萨黑布跟小图迈说话了！要是他没有找着想要的东西，我相信他会生病的。但是营地里的一个卖果脯的小贩借给了他一个小小的手鼓——这是一种用手掌拍打的鼓——于是当星星开始出来时，他在卡拉·纳格面前盘着腿坐下来，大腿间放着手鼓，然后他拍

① behoove [bi'hu:v] v. 对（某人）来说有必要
② moonshine ['mu:nʃain] n. 空谈，妄想
③ plainsman ['pleinzmən] n. 平原居民
④ hut [hʌt] n.（避雨）茅屋，（简陋的）小屋
⑤ winding ['waindiŋ] n. 蜿蜒的道路
⑥ calf [kɑ:f] n. 小牛，犊
⑦ stump [stʌmp] n. 树桩，树墩
⑧ tom-tom ['tɔmtɔm] n.（美洲印第安人、印度、非洲部落等地用的狭长）手鼓
⑨ revel ['revəl] n. 狂欢

and he thumped and he thumped and he thumped, and the more he thought of the great honor that had been done to him, the more he **thumped**①, all alone among the elephant fodder. There was no tune and no words, but the thumping made him happy.

The new elephants strained at their ropes, and squealed and trumpeted from time to time, and he could hear his mother in the camp hut putting his small brother to sleep with an old, old song about the great God Shiv, who once told all the animals what they should eat. It is a very soothing **lullaby**②, and the first verse says:

> *Shiv, who poured the harvest and made the winds to blow,*
> *Sitting at the doorways of a day of long ago,*
> *Gave to each his portion, food and toil and fate,*
> *From the King upon the guddee to the Beggar at the gate.*
>   *All things made he—Shiva the Preserver.*
> *Mahadeo! Mahadeo! He made all—*
> *Thorn for the camel, fodder for the kine,*
> *And mother's heart for sleepy head, O little son of mine!*

Little Toomai came in with a **joyous**③ tunk-a-tunk at the end of each verse, till he felt sleepy and stretched himself on the **fodder**④ at Kala Nag's side. At last the elephants began to lie down one after another as is their custom, till only Kala Nag at the right of the line was left standing up; and he rocked slowly from side to side, his ears put forward to listen to the night wind as it blew very slowly across the hills. The air was full of all the night noises that, taken together, make one big silence—the click of one bamboo stem against the other, the rustle of something alive in the undergrowth, the scratch and **squawk**⑤ of a half-waked bird (birds are awake in the night much more often than we imagine), and the fall of water ever so far away. Little Toomai slept for some time, and when he waked it was brilliant moonlight, and Kala Nag was still standing up with his

啊拍啊拍啊，一边回想他受到的光荣待遇，想得越多拍得越起劲，尽管就他一个人孤零零地坐在大象的草料中间，尽管他拍的没调也没词，但光是鼓声就已经让他无比快乐了。

新来的大象不断拉扯他们身上的绳索，还不时发出尖叫和怒吼。他听见母亲在小屋里给小弟弟唱歌哄他睡觉，母亲唱的是一首很老很老的歌，讲的是伟大的湿婆告诉众生他们该吃什么食物。这是一首很能安神的摇篮曲，第一段是这样唱的：

> 湿婆啊，是他予我们丰收，是他让大风呼啸，
> 很久很久以前的一天，他坐在门口，
> 赐予众生各自应有的食物、劳动和命运，
> 无论是王座上的国王还是门口的乞丐。
> 湿婆，万物的保护者，他创造了万物。
> 湿婆！湿婆！他创造了一切。
> 荆棘给骆驼，草料给黄牛，
> 母亲的胸口给犯困的小脑袋，哦，我的小宝贝哟！

小图迈拍着鼓在每段歌的结尾都加上一个欢快的伴奏，直到他困了，在卡拉·纳格身边的草料堆上躺了下来。终于，大象们也按照习惯一只接一只地躺下来，最后只剩象栏右边的卡拉·纳格还站着。他轻轻地左右摇晃，伸出两只耳朵倾听夜风缓缓地从山间吹过。空中满是夜晚的各种响声，汇在一起反而分外宁静，这些响动里有竹竿互相碰撞的声音，有某种活物在草丛里窸窸窣窣的声音，有鸟儿在半梦半醒间抓挠和尖叫的声音（鸟类在夜间醒来的次数比我们想象的多得多），还有远处山涧的声音。小图迈睡了一会儿，当他醒来时，月色正好，卡拉·纳格还竖着耳朵站在那儿。小图迈翻翻身，在草料堆里蹭了蹭，卡拉·纳格巨大的背部轮廓挡住了夜空一半的星星。他一边看着一边

① thump [θʌmp] v. 重击，捶击

② lullaby ['lʌləbai] n. 摇篮曲

③ joyous ['dʒɔiəs] a. 快乐的，欢乐的
④ custom ['kʌstəm] n. 习惯

⑤ squawk [skwɔːk] n. 粗厉的尖叫声

ears cocked. Little Toomai turned, rustling in the fodder, and watched the curve of his big back against half the stars in heaven, and while he watched he heard, so far away that it sounded no more than a **pinhole**① of noise pricked through the stillness, the "hoot-toot" of a wild elephant.

All the elephants in the lines jumped up as if they had been shot, and their grunts at last waked the sleeping mahouts, and they came out and drove in the picket pegs with big **mallets**②, and tightened this rope and knotted that till all was quiet. One new elephant had nearly grubbed up his picket, and Big Toomai took off Kala Nag's leg chain and shackled that elephant fore-foot to hind-foot, but slipped a loop of grass string round Kala Nag's leg, and told him to remember that he was tied fast. He knew that he and his father and his grandfather had done the very same thing hundreds of times before. Kala Nag did not answer to the order by gurgling, as he usually did. He stood still, looking out across the moonlight, his head a little raised and his ears spread like fans, up to the great folds of the Garo hills.

"Tend to him if he grows restless in the night," said Big Toomai to Little Toomai, and he went into the hut and slept. Little Toomai was just going to sleep, too, when he heard the coir string snap with a little "tang," and Kala Nag rolled out of his pickets as slowly and as silently as a cloud rolls out of the mouth of a valley. Little Toomai pattered after him, barefooted, down the road in the moonlight, calling under his breath, "Kala Nag! Kala Nag! Take me with you, O Kala Nag!" The elephant turned, without a sound, took three strides back to the boy in the moonlight, put down his **trunk**③, swung him up to his neck, and almost before Little Toomai had settled his knees, slipped into the forest.

There was one blast of **furious**④ trumpeting from the lines, and then the silence shut down on everything, and Kala Nag began to move. Sometimes a **tuft**⑤ of high grass washed along his sides as a wave washes along the sides of a ship, and sometimes a cluster of wild-pepper vines would scrape along his back, or a bamboo would creak where his shoulder touched it. But between those times he moved absolutely without any sound, drifting through the thick Garo forest as

听到从远处传来的野象的"呼——嘟——"声，那声音如此遥远，就像在无边的寂静上刺破了一个针尖大小的洞那样一丁丁点响声。

象栏里的大象全都仿佛中了枪一般跳了起来，他们的咕哝声终于惊醒了象夫们。人们走出来，用大木槌把围栏的楔子锤进去，绳索该上紧的上紧、该打结的打结，直到最后一切重新安静下来。一头新象差点把拴他的桩子给翻起来了，大图迈将卡拉·纳格的腿链解下来，用这条链子把那头大象的前腿和后腿给锁在一起。他又在卡拉·纳格的腿上戴了个草环，告诉他要记住自己是被拴得牢牢的。大图迈知道不光他自己，他的父亲还有祖父也都这样干过好几百次。卡拉·纳格没有像往常那样用咯咯声来回应他的命令。他静静地站着，脑袋稍稍抬起，耳朵张开如同蒲扇，透过月光向外张望，看向重峦叠嶂的伽罗山。

大图迈对小图迈说："好好看着他，要是他今晚不安分的话。"然后他就走进茅棚里去睡了。小图迈本来也正要去睡，突然听见用椰子壳纤维编的那根草环轻轻"咔嗒"一声断开了，卡拉·纳格从围栏里一摇一摆地走出来，慢慢的，静悄悄的，就好像一朵云从山谷口飘出来一样。小图迈跟在他后面，光着脚板啪嗒啪嗒地跑在月光下的小路上，压着嗓子喊："卡拉·纳格！卡拉·纳格！带我一起去，噢，卡拉·纳格！"大象转过身来，一声也不吭，几个大步迈向月下的小男孩，放下鼻子，把男孩一下甩到自己脖子上，还不等小图迈在上面坐好就一溜烟地跑向了丛林。

象栏那里爆发出一声愤怒的咆哮，然后一切重又归于寂静。卡拉·纳格开始移动。有时一簇高草擦过他的身体一侧，如同波浪冲刷着船身，有时一丛野椒藤刮过他的背部，还有的时候一根竹子被他的肩膀碰着了咯吱咯吱地响。但是除了这些声音以外，他完全是悄无声息地在茂密的伽罗山林间快速地穿行，宛如一股轻烟一

① pinhole ['pinhəul] *n.* 针刺的孔，小孔

② mallet ['mælit] *n.* 槌

③ trunk [trʌŋk] *n.* 树干

④ furious ['fjuːriəs] *a.* 巨大的，强烈的

⑤ tuft [tʌft] *n.*（头发、羽毛、草等的）一簇，一束，一丛

though it had been smoke. He was going uphill, but though Little Toomai watched the stars in the rifts of the trees, he could not tell in what direction.

Then Kala Nag reached the **crest**[1] of the ascent and stopped for a minute, and Little Toomai could see the tops of the trees lying all speckled and furry under the moonlight for miles and miles, and the blue-white mist over the river in the hollow. Toomai leaned forward and looked, and he felt that the forest was awake below him—awake and alive and crowded. A big brown fruit-eating bat brushed past his ear; a **porcupine**[2]'s quills rattled in the thicket; and in the darkness between the tree stems he heard a hog-bear digging hard in the moist warm earth, and snuffing as it digged.

Then the branches closed over his head again, and Kala Nag began to go down into the valley—not quietly this time, but as a runaway gun goes down a steep bank—in one rush. The huge limbs moved as steadily as **pistons**[3], eight feet to each stride, and the wrinkled skin of the elbow points rustled. The undergrowth on either side of him ripped with a noise like torn **canvas**[4], and the saplings that he heaved away right and left with his shoulders sprang back again and banged him on the flank, and great trails of **creepers**[5], all matted together, hung from his tusks as he threw his head from side to side and plowed out his pathway. Then Little Toomai laid himself down close to the great neck lest a swinging bough should sweep him to the ground, and he wished that he were back in the lines again.

The grass began to get squashy, and Kala Nag's feet sucked and squelched as he put them down, and the night mist at the bottom of the valley chilled Little Toomai. There was a splash and a **trample**[6], and the rush of running water, and Kala Nag strode through the bed of a river, feeling his way at each step. Above the noise of the water, as it swirled round the elephant's legs, Little Toomai could hear more splashing and some trumpeting both upstream and down—great grunts and angry snortings, and all the mist about him seemed to be full of rolling, wavy shadows.

"Ai!" he said, half aloud, his teeth chattering. "The elephant-folk are out tonight. It is the dance, then!"

① crest [krest] *n.* 山顶，最高峰

② porcupine ['pɔ:kjupain] *n.* 【动物】豪猪

③ piston ['pistən] *n.* 活塞，柱塞

④ canvas ['kænvəs] *n.*（制作帐篷、船帆等的）粗帆布

⑤ creeper ['kri:pə] *n.* 爬行者

⑥ trample ['træmpl] *n.* 践踏声

般。他一直在往山上走，但是尽管小图迈观察着树枝间露出的星星，他并不知道大象到底在朝哪个方向走。

卡拉·纳格来到山顶，停下来歇了一会儿，小图迈看见月光下斑斑点点、仿佛毛茸茸的树林远远地蔓延开去，山谷间的河流被笼罩在一层蓝白色的薄雾之中。图迈往前倾下身看着，觉得他脚下的森林好像是醒着的——清醒的、活生生的，又是拥挤的。一只巨大的棕色果蝠从他耳旁掠过，一只箭猪的刺在灌木丛里飒飒作响，透过树枝他听见黑暗中有一头猪熊在奋力地挖掘温暖潮湿的泥土，一边挖还一边吸着鼻子。

然后树枝再次在他头上合拢。卡拉·纳格又开始往下面的山谷走去——这次不再是静悄悄的了，而是像一架失去控制的猎枪一样一口气狂冲下陡峭的河岸。他那硕大的四肢如同活塞一样平稳地运动，每一步都跨出去八英尺远，关节处的褶皱不断摩擦沙沙作响。他两旁的灌木丛哗啦一声分开，好似把帆布撕裂了一样，被他用肩膀挤到左右两边的小树又弹回来砰地撞到他身上。为了开路，他把头摆来摆去，大团大团的藤蔓密密麻麻地搅在一起，挂在他的象牙上。小图迈不得不俯下身紧紧地挨着硕大的象颈，以免被晃荡的树枝扫到地上去，此刻他巴不得回到象栏。

草丛这时变得又湿又软，卡拉·纳格每踩一步，脚都会被吸住，发出扑哧的声音，山谷底部的夜雾让小图迈觉得好冷。他听见哗啦一声响，然后是踩水的声音，还有流水哗哗的响声，卡拉·纳格正在河床上走，每一步都小心翼翼。河水在大象的腿周围打着旋，在一片水声之上，小图迈还听见了更多的溅水声和象吼声，从上游和下游纷纷传来——有大声的咕哝，还有生气的喷鼻子声，将他包裹的薄雾仿佛就像不断翻滚的波浪一般。

"啊！"他几乎叫出声来，牙齿都在咯咯打战。他说："今晚大象们都出来了。这就是说，他们要跳舞啦！"

Kala Nag swashed out of the water, blew his trunk clear, and began another climb. But this time he was not alone, and he had not to make his path. That was made already, six feet wide, in front of him, where the bent jungle-grass was trying to recover itself and stand up. Many elephants must have gone that way only a few minutes before. Little Toomai looked back, and behind him a great wild tusker with his little pig's eyes glowing like hot coals was just lifting himself out of the misty river. Then the trees closed up again, and they went on and up, with trumpetings and crashings, and the sound of breaking branches on every side of them.

At last Kala Nag stood still between two tree-trunks at the very top of the hill. They were part of a circle of trees that grew round an irregular space of some three or four acres, and in all that space, as Little Toomai could see, the ground had been trampled down as hard as a brick floor. Some trees grew in the center of the clearing, but their **bark**① was **rubbed away**②, and the white wood beneath showed all shiny and polished in the patches of moonlight. There were creepers hanging from the upper branches, and the bells of the flowers of the creepers, great **waxy**③ white things like **convolvuluses**④, hung down fast asleep. But within the limits of the clearing there was not a single blade of green—nothing but the trampled earth.

The moonlight showed it all iron gray, except where some elephants stood upon it, and their shadows were inky black. Little Toomai looked, holding his breath, with his eyes starting out of his head, and as he looked, more and more and more elephants swung out into the open from between the tree trunks. Little Toomai could only count up to ten, and he counted again and again on his fingers till he lost count of the tens, and his head began to swim. Outside the clearing he could hear them crashing in the undergrowth as they worked their way up the hillside, but as soon as they were within the circle of the tree trunks they moved like ghosts.

There were white-tusked wild males, with fallen leaves and nuts and twigs lying in the wrinkles of their necks and the folds of their ears; fat, slow-footed

卡拉·纳格摇晃着身体从水里走出来，把象鼻里的水都喷干净了，然后开始再次攀登。但是这一次不止他一个在爬，他也不用自己开路了。路已经开好了，就在他的前方，足有六英尺宽，上面的丛林草被压弯了又不断地直起来。肯定有很多大象几分钟前刚从那里走过。小图迈回头看见自己身后一头壮硕的野象刚从雾气弥漫的河里走出来，他那小小的眼睛亮得跟红彤彤的炭火似的。接着树丛又合上了，他们继续往上走，周围不停地传来吼叫声、撞击声和树枝断裂的声音。

终于，卡拉·纳格在山顶上停下来，站在两棵大树中间。这两棵树和其他一些树一起组成了一个大圈，中间是一块大约三四英亩的不规则形状的空地。小图迈看见这么大的一片空间，地面都被踩得严严实实，好像砖铺的地板一样。空地中央也有些树，但是树皮都被蹭掉了，露出下面白色光滑的木头，在斑斑驳驳的月色下闪闪发光。从上层的树枝间垂下一些藤蔓，上面像旋花一样结着好多硕大的白色蜡质的花朵，它们的花钟紧紧闭合，悬垂下来。但是其他地方一片绿叶也没有——只有被踏平的地面。

月光下，空地上一片铁灰色，除了有大象站着的地方以外，大象的影子则如墨般漆黑。小图迈屏息凝视，眼珠子都快瞪出来了，就在他这样看着的当儿，越来越多、越来越多的大象从树干间摇摆着身子走出来，走到空地上去。小图迈数数儿只会数到十，所以他扳着手指数来数去，最后脑袋都晕了，也记不清到底数了多少个"十"。从空地外面还不时传来大象爬山时挤开灌木丛的声音，但是一等他们走进树圈，他们的动作就轻得跟幽灵一样。

他们当中有的是长着白白象牙的野公象，脖子上和耳朵上的皱纹里夹着落叶、坚果和小树枝；有的是肥

① bark [bɑːk] n.【植物学】树皮
② rub away 磨去
③ waxy ['wæksi] a. 蜡制的
④ convolvulus [kən'vɔlvjuləs] n.【植物】旋花属植物

she-elephants, with restless, little pinky black calves only three or four feet high running under their stomachs; young elephants with their tusks just beginning to show, and very proud of them; **lanky**①, scraggy old-maid elephants, with their hollow anxious faces, and trunks like rough bark; savage old bull elephants, scarred from shoulder to flank with great weals and cuts of **bygone**② fights, and the caked dirt of their **solitary**③ mud baths dropping from their shoulders; and there was one with a broken tusk and the marks of the full-stroke, the terrible drawing scrape, of a tiger's claws on his side.

They were standing head to head, or walking to and fro across the ground in couples, or rocking and swaying all by themselves—scores and **scores of**④ elephants.

Toomai knew that so long as he lay still on Kala Nag's neck nothing would happen to him, for even in the rush and scramble of a Keddah drive a wild elephant does not **reach up**⑤ with his trunk and drag a man off the neck of a tame elephant. And these elephants were not thinking of men that night. Once they started and put their ears forward when they heard the chinking of a leg iron in the forest, but it was Pudmini, Petersen Sahib's **pet**⑥ elephant, her chain snapped short off, grunting, snuffling up the hillside. She must have broken her pickets and come straight from Petersen Sahib's camp; and Little Toomai saw another elephant, one that he did not know, with deep rope galls on his back and breast. He, too, must have run away from some camp in the hills about.

At last there was no sound of any more elephants moving in the forest, and Kala Nag rolled out from his station between the trees and went into the middle of the crowd, clucking and **gurgling**⑦, and all the elephants began to talk in their own tongue, and to move about.

Still lying down, Little Toomai looked down upon scores and scores of broad backs, and wagging ears, and tossing trunks, and little rolling eyes. He heard the click of tusks as they crossed other tusks by accident, and the dry rustle of trunks twined together, and the chafing of enormous sides and shoulders in the crowd, and the **incessant**⑧ flick and hissh of the great tails. Then a cloud

① lanky ['læŋki] *a.* 骨瘦如柴的

② bygone ['baigɔn] *a.* 过去的，从前的

③ solitary ['sɔlitəri] *a.* 单个的，唯一的

④ scores of 许多，大量

⑤ reach up 举起（手等）

⑥ pet [pet] *n.* 供玩赏的动物，爱畜

⑦ gurgle ['gəːgl] *v.* 作咯咯声

⑧ incessant [in'sesənt] *a.* 不停的，持续不断的

胖、缓慢的母象，她们那些小小的黑中透粉的幼崽只有三到四英尺高，不停地在母亲的肚子下面跑来跑去；有的是年轻的小象，因为自己刚刚长出来的象牙而骄傲得不行；有的是从没有生育过的老母象，她们瘦得皮包骨，面颊干瘪，神情焦虑，鼻子粗糙得跟干树皮一样；有的是凶猛的老公象，从肩到腹都是过去打架留下的巨大的伤痕，肩头上还不时掉下些硬结的土块，那是他们独自泡完泥浴以后带出来的；还有一头大象断了一根象牙，身体一侧还留着老虎全力一挥所制造的可怕抓痕。

他们头碰头地站着，或是成双成对地在空地上走来走去，或是自个儿摇晃着身体——总共有好几十头大象。

图迈清楚只要自己趴在卡拉·纳格的脖子上一动不动就什么事情都没有，因为即使是在野象被驱赶进象栏时那样激烈喧闹的场合下，野象也绝不会抬起鼻子去把象夫从驯化的大象脖子上扯下来。更何况这天晚上这些大象在意的显然不是人类。只有一回当他们听到森林里传来脚镣撞击的声音时，他们受了一惊，支起耳朵倾听，后来才发现那不过是帕德米妮——皮特森·萨黑布的骑宠——带着一截挣断的铁链，一边咕哝一边吸着鼻子在爬山而已。她肯定是冲破了围栏从皮特森·萨黑布的营地直接过来的。小图迈还看到另一头以前没见过的大象，背上和胸部都是绳子勒出的深深的印痕。这头大象肯定也是从附近山里的某个营地逃跑过来的。

终于再也没有大象在树林里移动的响声了，卡拉·纳格从两棵大树间一摇一摆地走出来，走到象群的中央，一边发出咯咯的喉音，接着所有的大象都开始用他们的语言交谈，一边走来走去。

小图迈依旧趴着，朝下看着周围一打又一打宽阔的象背、扑扇的耳朵、舞动的象鼻和滴溜溜转的小眼睛。他听见象牙不小心碰到一起发出的咔啦声，象鼻缠绕在一起摩擦的沙沙声，巨大的侧腹和肩膀互相挨挤时发出的窸窸窣窣声，还有大尾巴不断挥动、抽打的嘶嘶声。

came over the moon, and he sat in black darkness. But the quiet, steady hustling and pushing and gurgling went on just the same. He knew that there were elephants all round Kala Nag, and that there was no chance of backing him out of the assembly; so he set his teeth and shivered. In a Keddah at least there was torchlight and shouting, but here he was all alone in the dark, and once a trunk came up and touched him on the knee.

Then an elephant trumpeted, and they all took it up for five or ten terrible seconds. The **dew**① from the trees above spattered down like rain on the unseen backs, and a dull booming noise began, not very loud at first, and Little Toomai could not tell what it was. But it grew and grew, and Kala Nag lifted up one forefoot and then the other, and brought them down on the ground—one-two, one-two, as steadily as trip-hammers. The elephants were stamping all together now, and it sounded like a war drum beaten at the mouth of a cave. The dew fell from the trees till there was no more left to fall, and the booming went on, and the ground rocked and shivered, and Little Toomai put his hands up to his ears to shut out the sound. But it was all one **gigantic**② jar that ran through him—this stamp of hundreds of heavy feet on the raw earth. Once or twice he could feel Kala Nag and all the others surge forward a few strides, and the thumping would change to the crushing sound of **juicy**③ green things being bruised, but in a minute or two the boom of feet on hard earth began again. A tree was creaking and **groaning**④ somewhere near him. He put out his arm and felt the bark, but Kala Nag moved forward, still tramping, and he could not tell where he was in the **clearing**⑤. There was no sound from the elephants, except once, when two or three little calves squeaked together. Then he heard a thump and a shuffle, and the booming went on. It must have lasted fully two hours, and Little Toomai ached in every nerve, but he knew by the smell of the night air that the dawn was coming.

The morning broke in one sheet of pale yellow behind the green hills, and the booming stopped with the first ray, as though the light had been an

然后一朵云过来遮住了月亮，小图迈在一片黑暗中坐着，然而他四周那默默持续的挤碰和咕哝声始终没有停歇。他知道卡拉·纳格周围全是大象，现在也根本不可能让卡拉·纳格退出象群，所以他只好咬紧牙关浑身发抖。在象栏里至少还有火把和人们的吆喝，但是这里他全然是独自一人困于黑暗当中，中间有一次还有一根象鼻挨上来碰了碰他的膝盖。

① dew [dju:] *n.* 露水，露

突然一头大象放声高吼，接着所有的大象都大吼起来足足持续了五到十秒钟的时间。露珠如雨一般从头顶的树叶上洒落下来，打湿了那些看不见的脊背，然后是一阵低低的闷雷般的声音，刚开始并不是很响，所以小图迈分辨不清到底是什么声音。但是这响声变得越来越大，卡拉·纳格抬起一条前腿，又抬起另一条，然后两条腿一起放下——"一二"、"一二"，活像夹板锤那样有规律的节拍。很快，所有的大象都在一齐跺脚，好似在一个洞口擂响了战鼓。露珠不断从树上落下直到掉光，可是这雷鸣般的声

② gigantic [ˌdʒaiˈgæntik] *a.* 巨大的

③ juicy [ˈdʒuːsi] *a.* 多汁的

音一直在持续，地面也在颤动、在摇晃，小图迈不得不用两手捂住耳朵。但是这巨大的震动直接穿透了他的身体——这可是数百只沉重的象脚一齐踩在裸露的地面上啊。有那么一两回他感觉到卡拉·纳格和其他大象一齐朝前冲出去几步，于是跺脚声变成了多汁的绿色植物被踩烂的声音，可是不到一两分钟，又响起了脚踩在坚实的地面上的

④ groan [grəun] *v.* （受重压而）吱嘎作响，发吱嘎声

⑤ clearing [ˈkliəriŋ] *n.* （林中无树木的）空地

声音。他身旁某个地方有棵树断了，发出咯吱咯吱的呻吟声，他伸出胳膊想摸摸树皮，但这时卡拉·纳格一边跺着脚一边往前移动了，所以小图迈也搞不清自己到底在空地的哪个位置。大象们一声也不吭，除了有一次，两三头象崽一起尖叫了一下，接着是一声碰撞和挪动脚步的声音，再接着就又是雷鸣声了。这一切持续了应该有整整两个钟头，小图迈每根神经都疼得厉害，但是他从夜风的气味判断出黎明就要到来了。

淡黄色的晨曦从苍翠的山峦背后露出来，当第一缕光射过来时，雷鸣声戛然而止，仿佛是那晨光下达了命

order. Before Little Toomai had got the ringing out of his head, before even he had shifted his position, there was not an elephant in sight except Kala Nag, Pudmini, and the elephant with the rope-galls, and there was neither sign nor rustle nor whisper down the hillsides to show where the others had gone.

Little Toomai stared again and again. The clearing, as he remembered it, had grown in the night. More trees stood in the middle of it, but the undergrowth and the jungle grass at the sides had been rolled back. Little Toomai stared once more. Now he understood the trampling. The elephants had stamped out more room—had stamped the thick grass and juicy **cane**[①] to trash, the trash into slivers, the slivers into tiny fibers, and the fibers into hard earth.

"Wah!" said Little Toomai, and his eyes were very heavy. "Kala Nag, my lord, let us **keep by**[②] Pudmini and go to Petersen Sahib's camp, or I shall drop from thy neck."

The third elephant watched the two go away, snorted, wheeled round, and took his own path. He may have belonged to some little native king's establishment, fifty or sixty or a hundred miles away.

Two hours later, as Petersen Sahib was eating early breakfast, his elephants, who had been double chained that night, began to trumpet, and Pudmini, **mired**[③] to the shoulders, with Kala Nag, very **footsore**[④], shambled into the camp. Little Toomai's face was gray and **pinched**[⑤], and his hair was full of leaves and drenched with dew, but he tried to salute Petersen Sahib, and cried faintly: "The dance—the elephant dance! I have seen it, and—I die!" As Kala Nag sat down, he slid off his neck in a dead faint.

But, since native children have no nerves worth speaking of, in two hours he was lying very contentedly in Petersen Sahib's **hammock**[⑥] with Petersen Sahib's shooting-coat under his head, and a glass of warm milk, a little brandy, with a dash of **quinine**[⑦], inside of him, and while the old hairy, scarred hunters of the jungles sat three deep before him, looking at him as though he were a spirit, he told his tale in short words, as a child will, and wound up with:

令。小图迈的脑袋还在嗡嗡作响，他甚至都没来得及换个姿势，就发现周围的大象都不见了，只剩下卡拉·纳格、帕德米妮和那头有绳印的大象。周围的山坡也都静悄悄的，没有丝毫动静显示其余的大象都去了哪儿。

小图迈瞪着眼睛看了又看。他记忆中的空地已经在一夜之间变大了许多。现在空地中央有了更多的树，但是周围一圈的灌木丛和丛林草都往后倒了。小图迈又使劲儿看了看。现在他明白大象为什么跺脚了。他们踩出了更多的空地，他们把浓密的草丛和多汁的藤条踩塌了，踩成了碎片，又把碎片踩成了渣滓，最后把渣滓踩成了硬实的地面。

此时小图迈眼睛都快睁不开了，他说："哇！卡拉·纳格，我的主人啊，咱们跟着帕德米妮去皮特森·萨黑布的营地吧，要不我就会从你的脖子滚下来了。"

剩下的那头大象看着他们走开，喷了喷鼻子，也转过身去独自走了。他也许曾经属于某个当地的小领主，那人的领地可能就在五十、六十或者一百英里以外。

两个小时以后，皮特森·萨黑布正在吃早餐，他那些头天晚上被双重铁链拴牢的大象突然开始吼起来。肩膀以下都是泥的帕德米妮还有四肢酸痛的卡拉·纳格跟跟跄跄地走进了营地。小图迈面色灰白、憔悴，头发上满是树叶，还被露水打湿了。他还是用尽力气对皮特森·萨黑布行了个礼，虚弱地喊道："舞——象舞！我看见了，然后——我要死了！"卡拉·纳格坐下来，小图迈从他脖子上滑下来，陷入了昏迷。

不过，当地人的孩子一点儿也不娇气，所以两个小时以后他就心满意足地躺在皮特森·萨黑布的帐篷里，头底下垫着皮特森·萨黑布的猎装，肚子里也已经灌了一杯热牛奶、一点儿白兰地和少许奎宁，而他周围则坐了三圈人，都是那些毛发浓密、脸上有疤的老丛林猎手，他们看着他就好像看着一个幽灵一样。他用一些简短的词句讲述了自己的故事，就像小孩通常会做的那样，结尾的时候他说：

① cane [kein] n. 有长而有节的茎的植物

② keep by 身边有（某物）

③ mire ['maiə] v. 使溅满泥污

④ footsore ['futsɔ:] a.（因走路过久而）脚痛的，走痛了脚的，脚酸的

⑤ pinched [pintʃt] a.（脸等）皱缩的，下陷的

⑥ hammock ['hæmək] n. 吊床

⑦ quinine [kwi'ni:n] n.【药物】奎宁

"Now, if I lie in one word, send men to see, and they will find that the elephant folk have trampled down more room in their dance-room, and they will find ten and ten, and many times ten, tracks leading to that dance-room. They made more room with their feet. I have seen it. Kala Nag took me, and I saw. Also Kala Nag is very leg-weary!"

Little Toomai lay back and slept all through the long afternoon and into the twilight, and while he slept Petersen Sahib and Machua Appa followed the track of the two elephants for fifteen miles across the hills. Petersen Sahib had spent eighteen years in catching elephants, and he had only once before found such a dance-place. Machua Appa had no need to look twice at the clearing to see what had been done there, or to scratch with his **toe**[1] in the packed, **rammed**[2] earth.

"The child speaks truth," said he. "All this was done last night, and I have counted seventy tracks crossing the river. See, Sahib, where Pudmini's leg-iron cut the bark of that tree! Yes; she was there too."

They looked at one another and up and down, and they wondered. For the ways of elephants are beyond the **wit**[3] of any man, black or white, to fathom.

"Forty years and five," said Machua Appa, "have I followed my lord, the elephant, but never have I heard that any child of man had seen what this child has seen. By all the Gods of the Hills, it is—what can we say?" and he shook his head.

When they got back to camp it was time for the evening meal. Petersen Sahib ate alone in his tent, but he gave orders that the camp should have two sheep and some **fowls**[4], as well as a double ration of **flour**[5] and rice and salt, for he knew that there would be a feast.

Big Toomai had come up **hotfoot**[6] from the camp in the plains to search for his son and his elephant, and now that he had found them he looked at them as though he were afraid of them both. And there was a feast by the blazing campfires in front of the lines of picketed elephants, and Little Toomai was the

"现在，我要是有一个字撒了谎，你们可以派人去看，他们会发现大象把舞池踩得更大了，他们还会发现十条和十条，还有好多倍的十条那么多的象径通往那个舞池。他们是用脚踩出来那些新的空地的。我看见的。卡拉·纳格带我去的，我看见了。卡拉·纳格的脚都走累了。"

小图迈躺下去，睡了整整一个漫长的下午，直到黄昏时分才醒。他睡觉的时候，皮特森·萨黑布和马楚阿·阿帕沿着两头大象的脚印找了十五英里，翻了一座又一座山。皮特森·萨黑布捕捉野象已经有十八年了，但是他也只见过一次这样的舞池。马楚阿·阿帕只看了一眼就明白这里发生了什么，他都懒得用脚趾去刮刮那已经被踩得结结实实的地面。

他说："那孩子没说假话。这都是昨天晚上干的，我还数了数，一共有七十头大象过河留下的脚印。你看，萨黑布，那是帕德米妮的脚镣把树皮给划破了的印子！是的，她昨晚也在这儿。"

他们互相对视一眼，又四下看了看，觉得简直不可思议。的确，没有人，不管是白人还是黑人，能够猜透大象的行为。

马楚阿·阿帕又说："我追随我的主人，也就是大象，已经有四十五年了，我还从没听说过哪个人类的小孩看见过这个小孩见过的事情。我以群山的众神起誓，这真是——怎么说好呢？"他摇了摇头。

他俩回到营地时已经是吃晚饭的时候了。皮特森·萨黑布一个人在他的帐篷里吃饭，但是他吩咐给营里的人准备两头羊、几只鸡，还有比平时多一倍的面粉、大米和盐，因为他知道晚上将会有一场盛宴。

早些时候，大图迈从平原的营地马不停蹄地赶来寻找他的儿子和大象，现在虽然找到了他们，可是他看着他们的眼神却好像害怕他们俩似的。在一排排被围栏围起来的大象跟前，人们点起耀眼的篝火，开始庆祝。小

① toe [təu] *n.* 脚趾
② ram [ræm] *v.* 夯实

③ wit [wit] *n.* 心智

④ fowl [faul] *n.* 家禽
⑤ flour ['flauə] *n.* 粉，谷粉

⑥ hotfoot ['hɔtfut] *ad.* 急忙地

hero of it all. And the big brown elephant catchers, the trackers and drivers and ropers, and the men who know all the secrets of breaking the wildest elephants, passed him from one to the other, and they marked his forehead with blood from the breast of a newly killed jungle-cock, to show that he was a **forester**[1], initiated and free of all the jungles.

And at last, when the flames died down, and the red light of the logs made the elephants look as though they had been dipped in blood too, Machua Appa, the head of all the drivers of all the Keddahs — Machua Appa, Petersen Sahib's other self, who had never seen a made road in forty years: Machua Appa, who was so great that he had no other name than Machua Appa, — leaped to his feet, with Little Toomai held high in the air above his head, and shouted: "Listen, my brothers. Listen, too, you my lords in the lines there, for I, Machua Appa, am speaking! This little one shall no more be called Little Toomai, but Toomai of the Elephants, as his great-grandfather was called before him. What never man has seen he has seen through the long night, and the favor of the elephant-folk and of the Gods of the Jungles is with him. He shall become a great tracker. He shall become greater than I, even I, Machua Appa! He shall follow the new trail, and the **stale**[2] **trail**[3], and the mixed trail, with a clear eye! He shall take no harm in the Keddah when he runs under their **bellies**[4] to rope the wild tuskers; and if he slips before the feet of the charging bull elephant, the bull elephant shall know who he is and shall not crush him. Aihai! my lords in the chains," — he whirled up the line of **pickets**[5] — "here is the little one that has seen your dances in your hidden places, — the sight that never man saw! Give him honor, my lords! Salaam karo, my children. Make your salute to Toomai of the Elephants! Gunga Pershad, ahaa! Hira Guj, Birchi Guj, Kuttar Guj, ahaa! Pudmini, — thou hast seen him at the dance, and thou too, Kala Nag, my pearl among elephants! — ahaa! Together! To Toomai of the Elephants. Barrao!"

And at that last wild yell the whole line flung up their trunks till the tips

图迈则是这场庆祝的主角。那些棕色皮肤的大个子捕手、猎人、象夫和套象人，还有那些最了解如何驯化最凶蛮的大象的人，他们一个接一个地托着小图迈，用刚杀的一只丛林鸡胸口取的血在他的额头上做个记号，表示他已经成为一个合格的丛林居民，从此被丛林正式接纳，但又独立于所有丛林之外。

最后，当篝火渐渐熄灭，余烬的红光把大象们映得好似也浸过鲜血一般。这时，马楚阿·阿帕，所有象圈驭象人的头领——马楚阿·阿帕，也是皮特森·萨黑布的另一个化身，他有四十年没有见过任何人造的道路；马楚阿·阿帕，他是如此不凡以至于人们只用马楚阿·阿帕这个名字来称呼他——一跃而起，双手将小图迈高高举过头顶，然后大喊道："听着，我的兄弟们。象栏里我的主人们，你们也请听着，因为是我，马楚阿·阿帕在说话！这个小孩再也不叫小图迈了，他叫象群的图迈，就像他的曾祖父那样，因为他在长夜里看到了从来没有人见过的景象。从此以后，大象和丛林众神都将保佑他。他会成为一个伟大的猎人。他会比我，马楚阿·阿帕，还要厉害！他的眼睛会把所有的象径看得清清楚楚，无论是新鲜的、陈旧的，还是半老半新的。他在象圈里钻到大象肚子底下用绳索去套那些野象时，永远也不会受伤；如果他在进攻的公象面前摔倒了，他也会被公象认出来，不会被踩死。啊嗨依！身披铁链的我的主人们啊——"他一边说一边沿着象栏一股风似的跑过去——"这就是亲眼看见你们在秘地里舞蹈的小孩——人们从未见过的舞蹈！赐予他荣耀吧，我的主人！向他致敬吧，我的孩子们，跟象群的图迈敬礼！岗加·帕夏德，啊哈！希拉·古奇，伯奇·古奇，库塔·古奇，啊哈！帕德米妮——你在跳舞时见过他的，还有你，卡拉·纳格，我象群里的珍珠！——啊哈！大家一齐！跟象群的图迈敬礼！好啊！"

随着他最后一声狂呼，整个象群都一齐猛地举起他

① forester ['fɔristə] n. 林中民民，林中动物

② stale [steil] a. 不新鲜的
③ trail [treil] n. 痕迹
④ belly ['beli] n.（人或动物的）腹，腹部，肚子

⑤ picket ['pikit] n. 桩，尖桩

touched their foreheads, and broke out into the full salute—the crashing trumpet-peal that only the Viceroy of India hears, the Salaamut of the Keddah.

But it was all for the **sake**[①] of Little Toomai, who had seen what never man had seen before—the dance of the elephants at night and alone in the heart of the Garo hills!

们的鼻子直至鼻尖触到额头，然后爆发出长长的巨吼
——这是只有印度总督才能听到的铿锵如雷的象号，象
圈最高的敬礼。

但是现在这敬礼都归于小图迈，因为他看见了从来
没有人见过的景象——群象之舞，而且是在暗夜里，独
自一人在伽罗群山的怀抱中见到的！

① sake [seik] *n.* 理由，缘故

Shiv and the Grasshopper

(The song that Toomai's mother sang to the baby)

Shiv, who poured the **harvest**① and made the winds to blow,
Sitting at the doorways of a day of long ago,
Gave to each his **portion**②, food and toil and **fate**③,
From the King upon the guddee to the Beggar at the gate.
　All things made he—Shiva the Preserver.
　Mahadeo! Mahadeo! He made all,—
　Thorn for the **camel**④, fodder for the **kine**⑤,
　And mother's heart for sleepy head, O little son of mine!

Wheat he gave to rich folk, **millet**⑥ to the poor,
Broken scraps for holy men that beg from door to door;
Battle to the tiger, carrion to the kite,
And rags and bones to wicked wolves without the wall at night.
Naught he found too lofty, none he saw too low—
Parbati beside him watched them come and go;
Thought to cheat her husband, turning Shiv to **jest**⑦—
Stole the little grasshopper and hid it in her breast.

湿婆与蚱蜢

（图迈的母亲唱的摇篮曲）

① harvest ['hɑːvist] *n.*（谷
物等的）收割,采收,收
获
② portion ['pɔːʃən] *n.* 一部
分（尤指一份）
③ fate [feit] *n.* 命运

湿婆啊，是他予我们丰收，是他让大风呼啸，
很久很久以前的一天，他坐在门口，
赐予众生各自应得的一份食物、劳动还有命运，
无论是宝座上的国王还是门口的乞丐。
　　湿婆，万物的保护者，他创造了万物。
　　马哈迪奥！马哈迪奥！是他创造了一切。
　　荆棘给骆驼，草料给黄牛，
　　母亲的胸口给犯困的小脑袋，哦，我的小宝贝
　　哟！

④ camel ['kæməl] *n.*【动物】
骆驼
⑤ kine [kain] *n.*［复数］牛,
母牛

⑥ millet ['milit] *n.*【植物】
小米,谷子

他把小麦给富人，小米给穷人，
碎渣渣给挨户乞讨的圣人；
争斗给老虎，腐肉给鸢鹰，
骨头和残渣给深夜徘徊在墙外的恶狼。
在他眼里没有高贵和低贱之分。
帕尔瓦蒂在他身旁看着众生来来去去，
想要骗骗她的丈夫，和他开个玩笑——

⑦ jest [dʒest] *n.* 笑柄,笑料

她偷偷拿走小蚱蜢，把它藏在自己的怀里。

So she tricked him, Shiva the Preserver.
Mahadeo! Mahadeo! Turn and see.
Tall are the camels, heavy are the kine,
But this was Least of Little Things, O little son of mine!

When the **dole**① was ended, laughingly she said,
"Master, of a million mouths, is not one unfed?"
Laughing, Shiv made answer, "All have had their part,
Even he, the little one, hidden 'neath thy heart."
From her breast she plucked it, Parbati the thief,
Saw the Least of Little Things gnawed a new-grown leaf!
Saw and feared and wondered, making prayer to Shiv,
Who hath surely given meat to all that live.
All things made he—Shiva the Preserver.
Mahadeo! Mahadeo! He made all,—
Thorn for the camel, fodder for the kine,
And mother's heart for sleepy head, O little son of mine!

这样子来捉弄他，伟大的保护神湿婆。

马哈迪奥！马哈迪奥！转过头去看看啊。

骆驼个子高，黄牛身子重，

而这个呢却是最小的小家伙，我的小宝贝哟！

当众生都已获得施舍，她笑着问：

"主人啊，这万千张嘴当中，你是否漏掉了一个？"

湿婆大笑着回答说："万物皆有份，

哪怕是他，那个藏在你胸口的小家伙。"

小偷帕尔瓦蒂从怀中掏出小蚱蜢，

这最小的小东西正在嚼着一片新叶！

她眼见这一切，心生畏惧，暗暗称奇，便向湿婆祈祷，

因为确确实实众生都已得到他的赐予。

保护神湿婆，他创造了万物。

马哈迪奥！马哈迪奥！是他创造了一切。

荆棘给骆驼，草料给黄牛，

母亲的胸口给犯困的小脑袋，哦，我的小宝贝哟！

① dole [dəul] n.（定期少量发放的）救济物

Her Majesty's Servants

You can work it out by Fractions or by simple Rule of Three,
But the way of Tweedle-dum is not the way of Tweedle-dee.
*You can **twist**[1] it, you can turn it, you can **plait**[2] it till you drop,*
But the way of Pilly Winky's not the way of Winkie Pop!

It had been raining heavily for one whole month—raining on a camp of thirty thousand men and thousands of camels, elephants, horses, bullocks, and mules all gathered together at a place called Rawal Pindi, to be reviewed by the Viceroy of India. He was receiving a visit from the Amir of **Afghanistan**[3]—a wild king of a very wild country. The Amir had brought with him for a bodyguard eight hundred men and horses who had never seen a camp or a locomotive before in their lives—savage men and savage horses from somewhere at the back of Central Asia. Every night a mob of these horses would be sure to break their heel ropes and stampede up and down the camp through the **mud**[4] in the dark, or the camels would break loose and run about and fall over the ropes of the tents, and you can imagine how **pleasant**[5] that was for men trying to go to sleep. My tent lay far away from the camel lines, and I thought it was safe. But one night a man popped his head in and shouted, "Get out, quick! They're coming! My tent's gone!"

女王陛下的侍从

要么用分数，要么用比例法，

但叮当兄和叮当弟就是不一样。

不管你怎么扭，怎么转，怎么编，直到你筋疲力尽，

但比利·温奇和温基·波普就是不一样！

① twist [twist] v. 扭转, 绞, 缠绕

② plait [plæt] v. 把……编成辫

③ Afghanistan [æfˈɡænistæn] n. 阿富汗

④ mud [mʌd] n. 泥, 泥浆

⑤ pleasant [ˈplezənt] a. 愉快的

大雨下了整整一个月。这里有三万人和几千只骆驼、大象、马匹、公牛和骡子，大家都聚集在一个叫作拉瓦尔品第的营地，等着印度总督来检阅。总督这时正在接见阿富汗埃米尔，那是个来自野蛮国家的野蛮国王。这位埃米尔随身带了八百人马的护卫队，他们这辈子从未见过什么营地，更别提火车了。这些野蛮人和野蛮马来自中亚的一片荒蛮之地。每天晚上，必定会有很多马挣脱绊马索，在泥泞的营地里来回乱窜，要么就是骆驼挣脱缰绳四下乱跑，被固定帐篷的绳索绊倒。可以想象，对于想睡觉的人来说这样的场景是多么美妙。我住的帐篷离骆驼队很远，本来以为还挺安全。但有天晚上，一个人把脑袋伸进我的帐篷，大喊："出来，快点！他们来了！我的帐篷已经没了！"

I knew who "they" were, so I put on my **boots**① and **waterproof**② and scuttled out into the **slush**③. Little Vixen, my **fox**④ terrier, went out through the other side; and then there was a roaring and a grunting and bubbling, and I saw the tent cave in, as the pole snapped, and begin to dance about like a mad ghost. A camel had blundered into it, and wet and angry as I was, I could not help laughing. Then I ran on, because I did not know how many camels might have got loose, and before long I was out of sight of the camp, plowing my way through the mud.

At last I fell over the tail-end of a gun, and by that knew I was somewhere near the artillery lines where the cannon were stacked at night. As I did not want to plowter about any more in the drizzle and the dark, I put my waterproof over the muzzle of one gun, and made a sort of wigwam with two or three **rammers**⑤ that I found, and lay along the tail of another gun, wondering where Vixen had got to, and where I might be.

Just as I was getting ready to go to sleep I heard a jingle of harness and a grunt, and a **mule**⑥ passed me shaking his wet ears. He belonged to a screw-gun battery, for I could hear the rattle of the straps and rings and chains and things on his saddle pad. The screw-guns are tiny little cannon made in two pieces, that are screwed together when the time comes to use them. They are taken up mountains, anywhere that a mule can find a road, and they are very useful for fighting in rocky country.

Behind the mule there was a camel, with his big soft feet squelching and slipping in the mud, and his neck bobbing to and fro like a strayed hen's. Luckily, I knew enough of beast language—not wild-beast language, but camp-beast language, of course—from the natives to know what he was saying.

He must have been the one that flopped into my tent, for he called to the mule, "What shall I do? Where shall I go? I have fought with a white thing that waved, and it took a stick and hit me on the neck." (That was my broken tent pole, and I was very glad to know it.) "Shall we run on?"

"Oh, it was you," said the mule, "you and your friends, that have been

① boot [bu:t] n. （皮革、橡胶、布等制的）长筒靴，靴子

② waterproof ['wɔ:təpru:f] n. 雨衣

③ slush [slʌʃ] n. 半融的雪（或冰）

④ fox [fɔks] n.【动物】狐

⑤ rammer ['ræmə] n. 捣槌，装填器

⑥ mule [mju:l] n. 骡子

我当然知道"他们"是谁，于是穿上靴子和雨衣赶紧跑到了外面的烂泥浆里。我的猎狐犬小威克森从另一边跑出来；接着就传来了咆哮声、咕哝声和低沉的呼噜声，眼看着我的帐篷支架咔啪一下就折了，那帐篷像个发疯的幽灵一样游来游去。原来是一只骆驼跌跌撞撞地跑了过来。尽管我浑身湿透、怒火中烧，但还是忍不住大声笑了出来。我接着往前跑，因为不知道到底有多少骆驼挣脱了缰绳。我在泥泞里艰难前行，过了不久，就看不见营地了。

后来我被一门大炮的炮尾绊倒，这才意识已经跑到了炮兵驻扎的地方。我不想在黑天半夜冒着雨往前跑，把自己浑身弄得脏兮兮，于是就把雨衣搭在炮口上，找了两三根推弹器，搭了个棚子，挨着另一门大炮躺下，一边想威克森去了哪里，一边想我到底是在什么地方。

刚要睡着的时候，我听到了一阵挽具丁零当啷的声音，还夹杂着咕噜声。原来是一头骡子摇着他那湿淋淋的耳朵从我身边走过。这骡子是螺式炮炮兵连的，因为我能听到带子、吊环、铁链和马鞍上各种东西发出的声响。螺式炮个头很小，由两部分组成，使用时把这两部分拧到一起，这炮在崎岖的山地作战很有用。骡子把这些炮运上山，能走多远就运到哪儿。

骡子后面跟着头骆驼，骆驼软软的大蹄子嘎吱嘎吱踩进泥里，他的脖子左摆右摆，像只迷路的母鸡。幸好我略通兽语，知道他在说什么。我懂的当然不是野兽的语言，我只懂些营地里兽类的语言。这本事是我从当地人那里学来的。

这骆驼肯定就是把我帐篷踩塌的那位，他对骡子喊道："我该怎么办？我该去哪里？刚才我和一个摇摇晃晃的白家伙干了一架，那家伙用根棍子打了我的脖子。"（那棍子自然是我断掉的帐篷柱子，听他说这个我很高兴。）"咱们该继续跑吗？"

"原来是你啊，"骡子说道，"把营地搞得一团糟的

disturbing the camp? All right. You'll be beaten for this in the morning. But I may as well give you something on account now."

I heard the harness jingle as the mule backed and caught the camel two kicks in the ribs that rang like a drum. "Another time," he said, "you'll know better than to run through a mule battery at night, shouting 'Thieves and fire!' Sit down, and keep your silly neck quiet."

The camel doubled up camel-fashion, like a two-foot rule, and sat down whimpering. There was a regular beat of hoofs in the **darkness**①, and a big troop-horse **cantered**② up as steadily as though he were on parade, jumped a gun tail, and landed close to the mule.

"It's disgraceful," he said, blowing out his nostrils. "Those camels have racketed through our lines again—the third time this week. How's a horse to keep his condition if he isn't allowed to sleep. Who's here?"

"I'm the breech-piece mule of number two gun of the First Screw Battery," said the mule, "and the other's one of your friends. He's waked me up too. Who are you?"

"Number Fifteen, E troop, Ninth Lancers—Dick Cunliffe's horse. Stand over a little, there."

"Oh, beg your pardon," said the mule. "It's too dark to see much. Aren't these camels too sickening for anything? I walked out of my lines to get a little peace and quiet here."

"My lords," said the camel **humbly**③, "we dreamed bad dreams in the night, and we were very much afraid. I am only a **baggage**④ camel of the 39th Native **Infantry**⑤, and I am not as brave as you are, my lords."

"Then why didn't you stay and carry baggage for the 39th Native Infantry, instead of running all round the camp?" said the mule.

"They were such very bad dreams," said the camel. "I am sorry. Listen! What is that? Shall we run on again?"

"Sit down," said the mule, "or you'll snap your long stick-legs between the guns." He cocked one ear and listened. "Bullocks!" he said. "Gun bullocks. On

就是你和你那些朋友们啊？得了。明天一早你们肯定会挨顿揍。不过我得先教训你一下。"

我听见挽具叮当作响，骡子后退了几步，朝骆驼的肋骨位置狠狠踢了两脚，那声音好像闷声闷气的敲鼓声。骡子说："记牢了，下次你们可别大半夜一边喊'着火啦！有小偷啊！'，一边从我们骡子炮兵连穿过去了啊！坐下！别再晃你那傻脖子了！"

① darkness ['dɑːknis] *n.* 暗，黑暗，阴暗

② canter ['kæntə] *v.* 使（马）慢跑

那骆驼像把折尺那样弓着身子缩成一团，坐在那儿哼哼唧唧。黑暗中传来一阵有规律的马蹄声，一匹高头大马步伐稳健地慢慢跑过来，好像是在接受检阅。他纵身跃过炮尾，在骡子旁边站稳。

"太过分了，"他从鼻孔里发出重重的叹息，"那些骆驼又在我们的部队里搅和了一回，七天里这已经是第三次了。如果马得不到应有的休息，那还怎么保持我们的体力呢？你们是谁呀？"

"我是第一螺式炮炮兵连二号炮炮尾的骡子，"那骡子说道，"另一个是你的朋友。他也把我吵醒了。你是谁？"

"第九骑兵团戊连第十五号，迪克·坎利夫的马。往旁边站过去一点儿。"

"噢，抱歉，"骡子说道，"天太黑，看不清。这些骆驼是不是太讨厌了？我也是从部队里跑出来的，想到这里找点儿清静。"

③ humbly ['hʌmbli] *ad.* 谦逊地

④ baggage ['bægidʒ] *n.* 行李

⑤ infantry ['infəntri] *n.* 步兵

"大人，"那骆驼谦卑地说道，"我们晚上做了噩梦，吓坏了。鄙人是第三十九本地步兵团驮行李的骆驼，我可没你们那么英勇，大人。"

"你为什么不好好给第三十九本地步兵团运行李，干吗要在军营里捣乱？"那骡子说。

"我们做的噩梦太可怕啦，"骆驼说道，"真的很抱歉。听啊！那是什么声音？我们是不是又该往前跑了？"

"坐下！"骡子说道，"要不然你那四条像长棍子一样的腿就要被这些大炮给别折了。"他竖起一只耳朵

my word, you and your friends have waked the camp very thoroughly. It takes a good deal of **prodding**① to put up a gun-bullock."

I heard a chain dragging along the ground, and a **yoke**② of the great sulky white bullocks that drag the heavy **siege guns**③ when the elephants won't go any nearer to the firing, came shouldering along together. And almost stepping on the chain was another battery mule, calling wildly for "Billy."

"That's one of our **recruits**④," said the old mule to the troop horse. "He's calling for me. Here, youngster, stop squealing. The dark never hurt anybody yet."

The gun-bullocks lay down together and began chewing the **cud**⑤, but the young mule huddled close to Billy.

"Things!" he said. "Fearful and horrible, Billy! They came into our lines while we were asleep. D'you think they'll kill us?"

"I've a very great mind to give you a number-one kicking," said Billy. "The idea of a fourteen-hand mule with your training disgracing the battery before this gentleman!"

"Gently, gently!" said the troop-horse. "Remember they are always like this to begin with. The first time I ever saw a man (it was in Australia when I was a three-year-old) I ran for half a day, and if I'd seen a camel, I should have been running still."

Nearly all our horses for the English **cavalry**⑥ are brought to India from Australia, and are broken in by the troopers themselves.

"True enough," said Billy. "Stop shaking, youngster. The first time they put the full harness with all its chains on my back I stood on my forelegs and kicked every bit of it off. I hadn't learned the real science of kicking then, but the battery said they had never seen anything like it."

"But this wasn't harness or anything that jingled," said the young mule. "You know I don't mind that now, Billy. It was Things like trees, and they fell up and down the lines and bubbled; and my head-rope broke, and I couldn't find my

① prod [prɔd] v. 刺, 戳, 捅
② yoke [jəuk] n. 轭, 牛轭
③ siege gun【军事】攻城用加农炮

④ recruit [ri'kru:t] n. 新兵

⑤ cud [kʌd] n. 反刍的食物

⑥ cavalry ['kævəlri] n.［总称］骑兵

听着，"是公牛！是炮兵公牛。说实话，你和你的朋友们把整个军营搅了个底朝天。把炮兵公牛给弄醒可是要费老鼻子劲呢。"

我听见一根铁链在地上拖动的声音，一对怒气冲冲的白色大公牛肩并肩走过来。在战场上，当大象不愿意再接近交火点时，就要靠这一对一对的公牛把沉重的攻城加农炮拖到城前。还有一只炮兵骡子差点儿踩到铁链，一遍疯狂地喊着："比利！"

"那是我们连的一个新兵蛋子，"老骡子对战马说道，"他在叫我呢。这儿呢，小子，别嚷嚷了。这大半夜的，还没人受伤呢。"

这时候，两头公牛趴下来，开始反刍，那头年轻的骡子紧紧靠着比利。

"有东西！"他说道，"让人心惊胆战的东西，比利！我们正在睡觉呢，这些东西冲进我们的队伍。他们会把我们杀了吗？"

"我真想狠狠踢你一顿，"比利说道，"没想到你这头受过正规训练、身长十四只手的骡子竟然在这位绅士面前丢尽我们炮兵连的脸！"

"消消气，消消气！"那战马说道，"新兵刚来的时候都这样。我第一次见到人是三岁时在澳大利亚，那时候吓得跑了大半天。要是我那会儿见到头骆驼，说不定会吓得一直跑到现在呢。"

英国骑兵所用的马匹几乎都是从澳大利亚运到印度来的，而且都是由骑兵自己训练的。

"有道理，"比利说道，"别抖了，小子。他们第一次把整副带着铁链的挽具套到我背上时，我跃起后腿把它们全部蹬掉了。我那时还没学会怎么把挽具蹬掉，但炮兵连的人说他们从没见过像我那样的。"

"但这不是挽具啊，也不是什么叮叮当当的东西啊，"年轻的骡子说道，"我现在不害怕那些了，比利。我怕的是像树一样的东西啊，他们在营地里起起伏伏，

driver, and I couldn't find you, Billy, so I ran off with——with these gentlemen."

"H'm!" said Billy. "As soon as I heard the camels were loose I came away on my own account. When a battery——a screw-gun mule calls gun-bullocks gentlemen, he must be very badly shaken up. Who are you fellows on the ground there?"

The gun bullocks rolled their cuds, and answered both together: "The seventh yoke of the first gun of the Big Gun Battery. We were asleep when the camels came, but when we were trampled on we got up and walked away. It is better to lie quiet in the mud than to be disturbed on good **bedding**①. We told your friend here that there was nothing to be afraid of, but he knew so much that he thought otherwise. Wah!"

They went on **chewing**②.

"That comes of being afraid," said Billy. "You get laughed at by gun-bullocks. I hope you like it, young un."

The young mule's teeth snapped, and I heard him say something about not being afraid of any **beefy**③ old bullock in the world. But the bullocks only clicked their horns together and went on chewing.

"Now, don't be angry after you've been afraid. That's the worst kind of **cowardice**④," said the troop-horse. "Anybody can be forgiven for being scared in the night, I think, if they see things they don't understand. We've broken out of our pickets, again and again, four hundred and fifty of us, just because a new recruit got to telling tales of whip snakes at home in Australia till we were scared to death of the loose ends of our head-ropes."

"That's all very well in camp," said Billy. "I'm not above **stampeding**⑤ myself, for the fun of the thing, when I haven't been out for a day or two. But what do you do on active service?"

"Oh, that's quite another set of new shoes," said the troop horse. "Dick Cunliffe's on my back then, and drives his knees into me, and all I have to do is to watch where I am putting my feet, and to keep my hind legs well under me, and be bridle-wise."

还发出低沉的呼噜声；我头上的缰绳断了，找不到牵我的人了，连你都找不到了，比利。所以我就和这些，这些绅士一起跑出来了。"

"嗯！"比利说道，"一听见这些骆驼挣脱了缰绳，我就自己跑了出来。当一头炮兵骡，一头螺式炮炮兵连的骡子管炮兵连公牛叫绅士，那他一定是吓得魂儿都没了。嘿，躺在地上的家伙，你们是谁？"

炮兵连公牛一边反刍，一边齐声答道："大炮兵连第一门炮的第七对牛。本来我们睡得好好的，后来骆驼来了，踩着我们了，我们就起身走了。我们宁愿清清静静躺在泥地里，也不要在舒服的床上被吵醒。我们跟你这位朋友说了，没什么好怕的，但他懂得多，不听我们的。哼！"

说罢，他们接着嚼反刍上来的草料了。

"那是因为害怕，"比利说道，"你被炮兵连公牛笑话了。小子，希望你喜欢这样啊。"

年轻的骡子把牙齿咬得吱咯响，我听见他说了什么不害怕这世上任何健壮的老公牛之类的话。那两头公牛只是碰了碰牛角，继续咀嚼。

"小伙子，恐惧之后不要再发怒。那可是最最怯懦的表现了，"战马说道，"不管谁在夜里看见自己不知道的东西而感到害怕，我看都是可以原谅的。就因为一个新来的家伙讲起澳大利亚家乡鞭蛇的故事，我们四百五十匹战马吓得一次又一次挣脱拴住我们的木桩。后来我们一看见头顶松下来的绳子就吓得要死。"

"军营里什么都好，"比利说道，"我倒并没被吓着，一两天没出来了，出来找找乐子也不错。你打仗的时候具体干些什么呀？"

"噢，那我可就是另一副模样了，"战马说道，"打仗时迪克·坎利夫骑在我的背上，两个膝盖夹紧我，我只管找到前进的方向，前腿迈开，后腿跟上，注意缰绳的指令。"

① bedding ['bediŋ] *n.* 寝具

② chew [tʃuː] *v.* 嚼，咀嚼

③ beefy ['biːfi] *a.* 结实的

④ cowardice ['kauədis] *n.* 懦弱，胆小

⑤ stampede [stæm'piːd] *v.* 使惊逃，使逃窜

"What's bridle-wise?" said the young mule.

"By the Blue Gums of the Back Blocks," snorted the troop-horse, "do you mean to say that you aren't taught to be bridle-wise in your business? How can you do anything, unless you can spin round at once when the rein is pressed on your neck? It means life or death to your man, and of course that's life and death to you. Get round with your hind legs under you the instant you feel the rein on your neck. If you haven't room to swing round, rear up a little and come round on your hind legs. That's being bridle-wise."

"We aren't taught that way," said Billy the mule **stiffly**[1]. "We're taught to **obey**[2] the man at our head: step off when he says so, and step in when he says so. I suppose it comes to the same thing. Now, with all this fine fancy business and rearing, which must be very bad for your hocks, what do you do?"

"That depends," said the troop-horse. "Generally I have to go in among a lot of yelling, hairy men with knives—long shiny knives, worse than the farrier's knives—and I have to take care that Dick's boot is just touching the next man's boot without crushing it. I can see Dick's **lance**[3] to the right of my right eye, and I know I'm safe. I shouldn't care to be the man or horse that stood up to Dick and me when we're in a hurry."

"Don't the knives hurt?" said the young mule.

"Well, I got one cut across the chest once, but that wasn't Dick's fault—"

"A lot I should have cared whose fault it was, if it hurt!" said the young mule.

"You must," said the troop horse. "If you don't trust your man, you may as well run away at once. That's what some of our horses do, and I don't **blame**[4] them. As I was saying, it wasn't Dick's fault. The man was lying on the ground, and I stretched myself not to **tread**[5] on him, and he slashed up at me. Next time I have to go over a man lying down I shall step on him—hard."

"缰绳的指令是什么？"年轻的骡子问。

"我得以内陆蓝桉树的名义起个誓了，"战马轻蔑地哼了一声，"难道你从没有被教过在执行任务时要注意听缰绳的指令？当缰绳在你脖子上勒紧的时候，你要是不立刻转过身来，怎么能做事呢？要是你反应慢，你主人活不成，你的小命自然也难保。一感觉到脖子上缰绳勒紧，你就得立刻用后腿的力量掉转身子。如果地方不够大，你就稍微跳起来一点儿，再用后腿掉头。这就叫听缰绳的指令。"

"我们可不是这么教的，"骡子比利语气很坚定，"我们教的是要听牵我们走的人：他说齐步走，我们就齐步走，他说走进去，我们就走进去。我想这跟你们的缰绳指令差不多。你们要做这么些复杂的动作，还要跳起来，我看肯定对蹠关节不好。你们具体都干些什么啊？"

"那要看情况了，"战马说道；"一般情况下，我得冲进一群大喊大叫、浑身长毛、带着大刀的士兵中间，他们的刀又长又亮，可比给马钉蹄铁时用的刀还可怕。我还得小心让迪克的靴子刚好碰到旁边那个人的靴子，不能踩上去。我要是能用右眼看见迪克的长矛，就知道自己安全了。当我们一团忙乱的时候，我可不会想当迪克和我面前的那个人或那匹马。"

"大刀不会伤到你吗？"年轻的骡子问。

"嗯，有一次我胸口被划了一刀，但那不是迪克的错——"

"如果很疼的话我肯定会在乎是谁的错！"年轻的骡子说。

"没错，"战马说道，"如果你不信任自己的主人，那最好还是立刻逃跑吧。我们有些马就是这样做的，我也不怪他们。就像我说的，那次不是迪克的错。当时有个人躺在地上，我小心地跨过去，不想踩到他，结果他举起刀向我划过来。以后我再经过躺在地上的人时，肯定会从他身上踩过去——狠狠踩。"

① stiffly ['stifli] *ad.* 生硬地
② obey [ə'bei] *v.* 服从，顺从

③ lance [lɑːns] *n.* 长矛

④ blame [bleim] *v.* 责备，谴责

⑤ tread [tred] *v.* 践踏

"H'm!" said Billy. "It sounds very foolish. Knives are dirty things at any time. The proper thing to do is to climb up a mountain with a well-balanced **saddle**[1], hang on by all four feet and your ears too, and creep and crawl and wriggle along, till you come out hundreds of feet above anyone else on a ledge where there's just room enough for your hoofs. Then you stand still and keep quiet—never ask a man to hold your head, young un—keep quiet while the guns are being put together, and then you watch the little **poppy**[2] shells drop down into the tree-tops ever so far below."

"Don't you ever trip?" said the troop-horse.

"They say that when a mule trips you can split a hen's ear," said Billy. "Now and again perhaps a badly packed saddle will upset a mule, but it's very **seldom**[3]. I wish I could show you our business. It's beautiful. Why, it took me three years to find out what the men were driving at. The science of the thing is never to show up against the sky line, because, if you do, you may get fired at. Remember that, young un. Always keep hidden as much as possible, even if you have to go a mile out of your way. I lead the battery when it comes to that sort of climbing."

"Fired at without the chance of running into the people who are firing!" said the troop-horse, thinking hard. "I couldn't stand that. I should want to charge—with Dick."

"Oh, no, you wouldn't. You know that as soon as the guns are in position they'll do all the charging. That's scientific and neat. But knives—pah!"

The baggage-camel had been **bobbing**[4] his head to and fro for some time past, anxious to **get a word in edgewise**[5]. Then I heard him say, as he cleared his throat, nervously:

"I—I—I have fought a little, but not in that climbing way or that running way."

"No. Now you mention it," said Billy, "you don't look as though you were made for climbing or running—much. Well, how was it, old Hay-bales?"

"The proper way," said the camel. "We all sat down—"

① saddle ['sædl] n. 鞍

② poppy ['pɔpi] n.【植物】罂粟

③ seldom ['seldəm] ad. 很少，难得

④ bob [bɔb] v. 使来回（或上下）快速移动（或摆动）

⑤ get a word in edgewise 伺机插嘴

　　"嗯！"比利说道，"这听上去很蠢。大刀无论什么时候都很脏。让我来告诉你应该怎么做吧！你要架上平衡的马鞍，靠着四条腿和两只耳朵沿着弯弯曲曲的山路一路向上爬，爬到你比底下的那些人高出几百英尺，之后找到一块突出的岩石，那里只能容下你的四只蹄子。然后你就一动不动地站着，保持安静——永远也别让马夫抓住你的头，小子——别出声儿，等大炮组装好，你会看见小小的红色弹壳远远地落进山下的树林。"

　　"你难道没有绊倒过？"战马问。

　　"有句俗话是这么说的：要是骡子绊倒了，你就能把母鸡的耳朵撕开，"比利回答，"有时候，要是马鞍没装好，骡子可能会失去平衡，但这种情况很少见。我真希望能向你展示我们的工作。真是很了不起。嗨！我花了三年时间才搞清楚我们背上驮的是什么。我们这工作的秘诀就是永远不要暴露在天际线下，要是暴露了，我们可就要挨枪子儿了。可得记牢啊，小子。一定要隐蔽行动，哪怕会大大偏离预定的路线。爬山架炮时，总是由我来带领整个炮兵连。"

　　"被敌人瞄准但却没法冲进敌人阵营里还击！"战马把自己的想法说了出来，"我可受不了。我还是想冲锋——和迪克一起。"

　　"别别别，可没人想去冲锋。你看，大炮一旦就位，士兵就会装填弹药。整个过程干脆利落。大刀可不一样了——呸！"

　　那驮行李的骆驼之前一直在摇头晃脑，急着想插句话。这会儿我听见他说话了，他清了清嗓子，紧张地说：

　　"我——我——我也算是打过仗的，但不是爬山打，也不是跑着打。"

　　"那当然是不可能的，"比利说道，"你长得可不像能爬山或是能跑步的。跟我们说说你是怎么打仗的吧，老草包！"

　　"最合适的方式是，"骆驼说道，"我们集体蹲下——"

"Oh, my **crupper**① and **breastplate**②!" said the troop-horse under his breath. "Sat down!"

"We sat down—a hundred of us," the camel went on, "in a big square, and the men piled our packs and saddles, outside the square, and they fired over our backs, the men did, on all sides of the square."

"What sort of men? Any men that came along?" said the troop-horse. "They teach us in riding school to lie down and let our masters fire across us, but Dick Cunliffe is the only man I'd trust to do that. It tickles my girths, and, besides, I can't see with my head on the ground."

"What does it matter who fires across you?" said the camel. "There are plenty of men and plenty of other camels close by, and a great many clouds of smoke. I am not frightened then. I sit still and wait."

"And yet," said Billy, "you dream bad dreams and upset the camp at night. Well, well! Before I'd lie down, not to speak of sitting down, and let a man fire across me, my heels and his head would have something to say to each other. Did you ever hear anything so awful as that?"

There was a long silence, and then one of the gun bullocks lifted up his big head and said, "This is very foolish indeed. There is only one way of fighting."

"Oh, go on," said Billy. "Please don't mind me. I suppose you fellows fight standing on your tails?"

"Only one way," said the two together. (They must have been twins.) "This is that way. To put all twenty yoke of us to the big gun as soon as Two Tails trumpets." ("Two Tails" is camp **slang**③ for the elephant.)

"What does Two Tails trumpet for?" said the young mule.

"To show that he is not going any nearer to the smoke on the other side. Two Tails is a great coward. Then we **tug**④ the big gun all together—Heya—Hullah! Heeyah! Hullah! We do not climb like cats nor run like calves. We go across the level plain, twenty yoke of us, till we are **unyoked**⑤ again, and we graze while the big guns talk across the plain to some town with mud walls, and pieces of the wall fall out, and the dust goes up as though many cattle were coming home."

① crupper ['krʌpə] *n.*（马的）臀部

② breastplate ['brestpleit] *n.* 胸铠，胸护甲

③ slang [slæŋ] *n.* 行业用语

④ tug [tʌg] *v.* 用力拉（或拖）

⑤ unyoke [ʌn'jəuk] *v.* 卸除（牲口等的）轭（或挽具）

"妈妈咪呀！"战马压着嗓子哼了一声，"蹲下！"

"我们就这么蹲着——总共有一百只呢，"骆驼继续说道，"蹲在一个大空地上，然后人们把我们驮的东西和鞍具堆在空地外头，然后他们就开枪射击，子弹朝着各个方向飞过我们的背，他们就是这么打仗的。"

"都是些什么人啊？他们这次也来了吗？"战马问道，"在骑术学校，教官教我们如何卧倒，让我们的主人隔着我们开枪。不过我只信任迪克·坎利夫一个人。枪碰到我的腹带，我就痒痒。而且我的头躺在地上，什么也看不见。"

"谁隔着你开枪有那么大关系吗？"骆驼说道，"周围有许多人，还有许多其他骆驼，还有大片浓烟。我一点都不害怕，只是静静地坐着等。"

"可是，"比利说道，"你们晚上会做噩梦，然后把整个营地搅个天翻地覆。呵呵！如果让我趴着，更别提让我蹲着，然后让个人隔着我开枪，那我的脚后跟肯定要和这个人的脑袋好好说句话呢！你们听过这样可怕的事吗？"

大家很长时间都没说话。然后一只炮兵连公牛抬起他巨大的脑袋说："这可真够傻的。打仗只有一种方式。"

"噢，你接着说呀，"比利说道，"我要是说错你们别见怪啊，我猜你们是站在尾巴上打仗的吧？"

"只有一种方法，"那两头牛一齐（他们肯定是双胞胎）说道，"方法是这样的。当'双尾'吼起来，就把我们全部二十对公牛赶到攻城加农炮边上。"（"双尾"是军营里对大象的称呼。）

"双尾为什么吼呢？"年轻的骡子问。

"吼是表明他不想再往火线靠近了。双尾是个胆小鬼。然后我们就一起拖着那门大炮——嘿呀——呼啦！嘿呀！呼啦！我们不像猫那样爬，也不像小牛那样跑。我们穿过平地，一共有二十对公牛，直到士兵把轭具从我们身上卸下来，然后我们就在旁边吃草，大炮开始朝某个围有泥墙的城镇开火，泥墙一块块掉落，漫漫黄沙席卷战场，那场景仿佛是牛群冲回家一样。"

"Oh! And you choose that time for grazing?" said the young mule.

"That time or any other. Eating is always good. We eat till we are yoked up again and tug the gun back to where Two Tails is waiting for it. Sometimes there are big guns in the city that speak back, and some of us are killed, and then there is all the more grazing for those that are left. This is Fate. None the less, Two Tails is a great coward. That is the proper way to fight. We are brothers from Hapur. Our father was a sacred bull of Shiva. We have spoken."

"Well, I've certainly learned something tonight," said the troop-horse. "Do you gentlemen of the screw-gun battery feel inclined to eat when you are being fired at with big guns, and Two Tails is behind you?"

"About as much as we feel inclined to sit down and let men sprawl all over us, or run into people with knives. I never heard such stuff. A mountain **ledge**[①], a well-balanced load, a driver you can trust to let you pick your own way, and I'm your mule. But—the other things—no!" said Billy, with a stamp of his foot.

"Of course," said the troop horse, "everyone is not made in the same way, and I can quite see that your family, on your father's side, would fail to understand a great many things."

"Never you mind my family on my father's side," said Billy **angrily**[②], for every mule hates to be **reminded**[③] that his father was a donkey. "My father was a Southern gentleman, and he could pull down and bite and kick into **rags**[④] every horse he came across. Remember that, you big brown Brumby!"

Brumby means wild horse without any breeding. Imagine the feelings of Sunol if a car-horse called her a "skate," and you can imagine how the Australian horse felt. I saw the white of his eye glitter in the dark.

"See here, you son of an imported Malaga jackass," he said between his teeth, "I'd have you know that I'm related on my mother's side to Carbine, winner of the Melbourne Cup, and where I come from we aren't **accustomed**[⑤] to being ridden over roughshod by any parrot-mouthed, pig-headed mule in a pop-gun pea-shooter battery. Are you ready?"

"啊！你们挑这个时候吃草？"那年轻的骡子说。

"是啊，只要有时间我们就吃草。能吃东西总是好事。我们就这么一直吃，直到脖子上又套上轭具，然后就把大炮拖回到双尾等着的地方去。有时城里也有大炮反击，有些牛就被炸死了。不过活着的牛就有更多的草吃了。这就是命运。不管怎么说，双尾都是胆小鬼。这是最合适的作战方式。我们是从哈普尔而来的兄弟。我们的父亲是湿婆的神牛。我们说过话的。"

"今天晚上我可是学到了好多啊，"战马说道，"你们这些螺式炮炮兵连的绅士，当有大炮在向你们开火，后面还跟着双尾的时候，你们有心思吃东西吗？"

"哪还有心思啊，这就和让我们蹲下，让士兵横七竖八地躺在我们身上，或是让我们冲进一群拿着大刀的敌人时一样。我还从没听过这种事情呢。山上的岩壁，稳稳放好的货物，让你自己选路走的马夫，有了这些我就是你的骡子。其他的事情我可坚决不干！"比利说边跺了跺脚。

"当然了，"战马说，"大家生而不同，我非常理解你的家人，尤其是你爹那边的家人，是不可能明白太多事情的。"

"不许说我父亲那边的亲戚！"比利很生气。骡子的父亲是驴子，这事没有一头骡子愿意别人说。"我父亲可是一位南方的绅士，他能放倒他碰到的每匹马，把他们踢咬成碎块。你给我记着，你这匹大野马！"

野马可是没有经过任何驯化的。想想看吧，如果一匹拉车的马管苏诺尔叫"不中用的老家伙"，她会是什么感受，你就能想象这匹澳大利亚马此刻的感受了。我看见他的眼白在黑暗中闪闪发光。

"你这马拉加进口公驴的儿子，"他从牙齿缝儿里挤出几句话，"我得让你知道卡宾是我母亲那边的亲戚，他可是墨尔本杯赛马冠军。在我们老家，我们可不会让嘴巴长得像鹦鹉，脑袋蠢得像头猪，背着豌豆玩具枪的骡子骑在我们脖子上撒野。你准备好了吗？"

---

① ledge [ledʒ] *n.* （自峭壁突出的）岩架

② angrily ['æŋgrili] *ad.* 愤怒地

③ remind [ri'maind] *v.* 提醒

④ rag [ræg] *n.* 碎片

⑤ accustom [ə'kʌstəm] *v.* 使习惯于

"On your hind legs!" squealed Billy. They both reared up facing each other, and I was expecting a furious fight, when a gurgly, rumbly voice, called out of the darkness to the right—"Children, what are you fighting about there? Be quiet."

Both beasts dropped down with a snort of **disgust**①, for neither horse nor mule can bear to listen to an elephant's voice.

"It's Two Tails!" said the troop-horse. "I can't stand him. A tail at each end isn't fair!"

"My feelings exactly," said Billy, **crowding into**② the troop-horse for company. "We're very alike in some things."

"I suppose we've inherited them from our mothers," said the troop horse. "It's not worth quarreling about. Hi! Two Tails, are you tied up?"

"Yes," said Two Tails, with a laugh all up his trunk. "I'm picketed for the night. I've heard what you fellows have been saying. But don't be afraid. I'm not coming over."

The bullocks and the camel said, half aloud, "Afraid of Two Tails—what **nonsense**③!" And the bullocks went on, "We are sorry that you heard, but it is true. Two Tails, why are you afraid of the guns when they fire?"

"Well," said Two Tails, rubbing one hind leg against the other, exactly like a little boy saying a poem, "I don't quite know whether you'd understand."

"We don't, but we have to pull the guns," said the bullocks.

"I know it, and I know you are **a good deal**④ braver than you think you are. But it's different with me. My **battery**⑤ captain called me a Pachydermatous Anachronism the other day."

"That's another way of fighting, I suppose?" said Billy, who was recovering his spirits.

"You don't know what that means, of course, but I do. It means **betwixt**⑥ and between, and that is just where I am. I can see inside my head what will happen when a shell bursts, and you bullocks can't."

"你给我站起来！"比利嘶叫一声。他们俩都跳了起来，面对着面。我本来还以为要有场激战呢，没想到从右边暗处传来一声低沉的咯咯声："孩子们，你们在那儿打什么呢？安静。"

他们俩都放下蹄子，嫌恶地哼了一声，因为不管是马还是骡子都不能忍受大象的声音。

"是双尾！"战马说道，"我真受不了他。两头都有尾巴真不公平！"

"这话可是说到我心窝里了，"比利边说边挤到战马那儿靠着，"我们在某些方面还真是很像。"

"我猜因为我们的母亲都是马吧，"战马说道，"咱俩吵架不值得。嘿！双尾，你被拴着吗？"

"是的，"双尾说着把鼻子整个仰起来大笑，"今晚我被拴住了。我听见你们这几个家伙说的话了。不过别害怕啊。我可不过去。"

公牛和骆驼低声说："害怕双尾——真是一派胡言！"公牛们继续说："很抱歉你听见了我们的谈话，但我们说的都是实话。双尾，士兵交火时，你为什么害怕大炮呢？"

"嗯，"双尾说着用一条后腿蹭另一条后腿，就像个小男孩在念诗，"我不知道你们能不能明白。"

"我们的确不明白，但我们得拖着大炮往前走。"公牛们说。

"我知道，我也知道你们比自己想象中的要勇敢多了。不过我可不一样。有一次，我的炮兵连连长说我是个厚脸皮、不合时宜的家伙。"

"我猜，那是另一种作战方式？"比利说，他慢慢回过神来。

"你当然不懂那是什么意思，但是我懂。大象就是要在战场的中间，不能太往前，也不能太靠后，那就是我的位置。我非常清楚炮弹爆炸了会发生什么，但你们公牛就不懂了。"

① disgust [dis'gʌst] n. 厌恶，憎恶

② crowd into 涌入

③ nonsense ['nɔnsəns] n. 胡说，废话

④ a good deal 非常，很，极其

⑤ battery ['bætəri] n. 炮兵连

⑥ betwixt [bi'twikst] ad. 在中间（的）

"I can," said the troop-horse. "At least a little bit. I try not to think about it."

"I can see more than you, and I do think about it. I know there's a great deal of me to take care of, and I know that nobody knows how to cure me when I'm sick. All they can do is to stop my driver's pay till I get well, and I can't trust my driver."

"Ah!" said the troop horse. "That explains it. I can trust Dick."

"You could put a whole **regiment**① of Dicks on my back without making me feel any better. I know just enough to be uncomfortable, and not enough to go on in spite of it."

"We do not understand," said the bullocks.

"I know you don't. I'm not talking to you. You don't know what **blood**② is."

"We do," said the bullocks. "It is red stuff that soaks into the ground and smells."

The troop-horse gave a kick and a bound and a snort.

"Don't talk of it," he said. "I can smell it now, just thinking of it. It makes me want to run—when I haven't Dick on my back."

"But it is not here," said the camel and the bullocks. "Why are you so stupid?"

"It's **vile**③ stuff," said Billy. "I don't want to run, but I don't want to talk about it."

"There you are!" said Two Tails, waving his tail to explain.

"Surely. Yes, we have been here all night," said the bullocks.

Two Tails stamped his foot till the iron ring on it **jingled**④. "Oh, I'm not talking to you. You can't see inside your heads."

"No. We see out of our four eyes," said the bullocks. "We see straight in front of us."

"If I could do that and nothing else, you wouldn't be needed to pull the big guns at all. If I was like my captain—he can see things inside his head

"我懂,"战马说道,"至少懂一点儿,不过我尽量不去想它。"

"我比你懂得多,而且我还要去想。我知道得好好照顾自己,我还明白万一我生了病,谁也不知道怎么治好我。他们只会停发象夫的薪水,直到我恢复健康,而且我也不信任我的象夫。"

"啊!"战马说道,"原来如此。我相信迪克。"

① regiment ['redʒimənt] n. 【军事】团

"你把一整个团的迪克放到我背上也不会让我舒服一丁点儿。我知道在战场上什么时候就不该再往前走了,我也不会明知有危险还继续往前冲。"

"我们没听懂。"公牛们说。

"我就知道你们听不懂。我压根儿没在跟你们讲。你们根本不知道血是什么。"

② blood [blʌd] n.（脊椎动物的）血,血液

"我们知道,"两只公牛说道,"就是红色的东西,会渗进地里,还有腥味。"

战马踢了踢腿,跳了一下,鼻子喷出一口气。

"别说了,"他说道,"光是想想,我就能闻到那味道了。如果迪克没在我背上,我要是闻到那味道肯定想跑。"

"但咱们这儿又没血,"骆驼和公牛们说,"你怎么这么蠢?"

"那是脏东西,"比利说道,"我不想跑,但我也不想提它。"

③ vile [vail] a. 无价值的

"对了吧!"双尾边解释边摇着尾巴。

"当然了。是啊,我们在这儿待了整个晚上了。"公牛们说。

双尾跺着脚,脚环叮当作响:"嘿,我没和你们说话。你们根本看不到脑子里在想什么。"

④ jingle ['dʒiŋgl] v. 发出叮当声

"是看不见。我们是用四只眼睛看,"公牛们说道,"我们用眼睛看我们面前的东西。"

"如果我只能看见眼前的东西,别的什么都不会,那就根本用不着你们去拉大炮了。我的连长在开火之前就能看见他脑子里的东西,他会吓得浑身发抖,不过他

before the firing begins, and he shakes all over, but he knows too much to run away—if I was like him I could pull the guns. But if I were as **wise**① as all that I should never be here. I should be a king in the forest, as I used to be, sleeping half the day and bathing when I liked. I haven't had a good bath for a month."

"That's all very fine," said Billy. "But giving a thing a long name doesn't make it any better."

"H'sh!" said the troop horse. "I think I understand what Two Tails means."

"You'll understand better in a minute," said Two Tails angrily. "Now you just explain to me why you don't like this!"

He began trumpeting furiously at the top of his trumpet.

"Stop that!" said Billy and the troop horse together, and I could hear them stamp and shiver. An elephant's trumpeting is always **nasty**②, especially on a dark night.

"I shan't stop," said Two Tails. "Won't you explain that, please? Hhrrmph! Rrrt! Rrrmph! Rrrhha!" Then he stopped suddenly, and I heard a little whimper in the dark, and knew that Vixen had found me at last. She knew as well as I did that if there is one thing in the world the elephant is more afraid of than another it is a little barking dog. So she stopped to bully Two Tails in his pickets, and **yapped**③ round his big feet. Two Tails **shuffled**④ and squeaked. "Go away, little dog!" he said. "Don't snuff at my ankles, or I'll kick at you. Good little dog—nice little doggie, then! Go home, you yelping little beast! Oh, why doesn't someone take her away? She'll bite me in a minute."

"Seems to me," said Billy to the troop horse, "that our friend Two Tails is afraid of most things. Now, if I had a full meal for every dog I've kicked across the parade-ground I should be as fat as Two Tails nearly."

I whistled, and Vixen ran up to me, muddy all over, and **licked**⑤ my nose, and told me a long **tale**⑥ about hunting for me all through the camp. I never let her know that I understood beast talk, or she would have taken all sorts of liberties. So I buttoned her into the breast of my overcoat, and Two Tails

知道的很多，明白自己不能逃跑。如果我像他那样，我也能拉大炮往前冲。但是，如果我要真有他那么聪明，就不会落到今天这个境地了。我会在森林里接着当我的大王，一睡就是半天，想洗澡就去洗澡。我可一个月没好好洗过澡了。"

"你说得真好听，"比利说道，"但是给一个东西取个很长的名字并不会让它变得更好啊。"

"嘘！"战马说道，"我想我听懂双尾的话了。"

"再过一小会儿你就会更明白的，"双尾愤怒地说道，"现在，你跟我说说你为什么不喜欢这样！"

他开始扯着最大的嗓门吼叫起来。

"别吼了！"比利和战马一起说，我能听见他们跺着脚，浑身颤抖。大象的吼声总是令人不快，尤其是在黑暗的夜里。

"我不停，"双尾说道，"你不解释一下吗？请啊。呼啦噗！啦特！啦噗！啦哈！"然后他突然停下，我听见黑暗中有声呜咽，知道是威克森总算是找到了我。她和我一样清楚，如果这世界上有什么东西是大象最害怕的，那就是只吠叫的小狗。于是她停下来，去欺负拴在木桩上的双尾，围着双尾的大脚狂吠。双尾一边抬脚一边尖叫。"走开，你这小狗！"他说道，"别在我的脚边上嗅来嗅去的，不然我可要踢你了。好小狗，乖乖狗！回家去吧。你这叫个不停的小东西！为什么没人来把她带走啊？她马上就要咬我了。"

"我看，"比利对战马说道，"让我们的朋友双尾害怕的东西可真不少。如果我在阅兵场上每踢一条狗就能饱餐一顿，那现在我恐怕是要和双尾差不多肥了。"

我吹了声口哨，威克森就朝我跑来。她浑身是泥，舔着我的鼻子，告诉我她是怎么找遍了整个军营。我从没跟她说我听得懂兽语，否则她就会没规没矩了。我把她紧紧按在我的胸口，双尾慢吞吞地抬起脚，跺下去，愤愤不平地抱怨着。

① wise [waiz] a. 聪明的

② nasty ['nɑːsti] a. 烦人的

③ yap [jæp] v.（狗）狂吠
④ shuffle ['ʃʌfl] v. 拖着脚走

⑤ lick [lik] v. 舔，舐
⑥ tale [teil] n. 传说

shuffled and stamped and growled to himself.

"Extraordinary! Most extraordinary!" he said. "It runs in our family. Now, where has that nasty little beast gone to?"

I heard him feeling about with his trunk.

"We all seem to be affected in various ways," he went on, blowing his nose. "Now, you gentlemen were alarmed, I believe, when I trumpeted."

"Not alarmed, exactly," said the troop-horse, "but it made me feel as though I had **hornets**① where my saddle ought to be. Don't begin again."

"I'm frightened of a little dog, and the camel here is frightened by bad dreams in the night."

"It is very lucky for us that we haven't all got to fight in the same way," said the troop-horse.

"What I want to know," said the young mule, who had been quiet for a long time—"what I want to know is, why we have to fight at all."

"Because we're told to," said the troop-horse, with a snort of **contempt**②.

"Orders," said Billy the mule, and his teeth **snapped**③.

"Hukm hai!" (It is an order!), said the camel with a gurgle, and Two Tails and the bullocks repeated, "Hukm hai!"

"Yes, but who gives the orders?" said the recruit-mule.

"The man who walks at your head—Or sits on your back—Or holds the nose rope—Or twists your tail," said Billy and the troop-horse and the camel and the bullocks one after the other.

"But who gives them the orders?"

"Now you want to know too much, young un," said Billy, "and that is one way of getting kicked. All you have to do is to obey the man at your head and ask no questions."

"He's quite right," said Two Tails. "I can't always obey, because I'm betwixt and between. But Billy's right. Obey the man next to you who gives the order, or you'll stop all the battery, besides getting a **thrashing**④."

The gun-bullocks got up to go. "Morning is coming," they said. "We will

"过分！真是过分！"他说道。"我们家族都这样。那个讨厌的小东西跑哪儿去了？"

我听见他用自己的鼻子四下摸索着。

"我们每个人都有自己害怕的东西，"他边说边擤了擤鼻涕，"我猜，刚才我吼叫的时候，你们这些绅士也都被吓到了吧。"

"其实我们没被吓到，"战马说道，"但你这声音让我感觉好像背上有群大黄蜂。你可别再叫了。"

"我害怕小狗，骆驼夜里害怕噩梦。"

"我们不必用同样的方式作战，这可是够幸运的。"战马说。

"我想知道，"那年轻的骡子说道，他很长时间没有说话了，"我想知道的是，我们到底为什么要打仗呢？"

"因为命令。"战马不屑地哼了一声。

"命令。"骡子比利说，他咬紧牙关。

"呼克姆——嗨！"（这是一个命令！）骆驼咯咯叫着，双尾和公牛重复道，"呼克姆——嗨！"

"没错，但是命令是谁下的？"新来的骡子问。

"在你前面走的人，骑在你背上的人，牵着你鼻子缰绳的人，拧你尾巴的人。"比利、战马、骆驼和公牛们一个接一个说。

"但是又是谁向他们发出命令呢？"

"你问得太多了，小子，"比利说道，"这就该挨踢了。你要做的就是服从你前面的人说的话，什么问题也别问。"

"他说得很对，"双尾说道，"我不总是服从命令，因为我就是个中间派。但比利说得对，照你身边发号施令的人说的做，不然你会让整个连队都停下来，而且还会挨抽。"

拖大炮的公牛们起身要走了。"天快亮了，"他们说道，"我们得回我们的部队了。我们确实只用眼睛看外面的世界，也的确不是很聪明。但今晚，只有我们没有

① hornet ['hɔ:nit] n. 【昆虫】大黄蜂

② contempt [kən'tempt] n. 轻蔑，鄙视

③ snap [snæp] v.（牙齿等）咯咯作响

④ thrashing ['θræʃiŋ] n. 鞭打，鞭笞，痛打

go back to our lines. It is true that we only see out of our eyes, and we are not very clever. But still, we are the only people to-night who have not been afraid. Good-night, you brave people."

Nobody answered, and the troop-horse said, to change the **conversation**①, "Where's that little dog? A dog means a man somewhere about."

"Here I am," yapped Vixen, "under the gun tail with my man. You big, **blundering**② beast of a camel you, you upset our tent. My man's very angry."

"Phew!" said the bullocks. "He must be white!"

"Of course he is," said Vixen. "Do you suppose I'm looked after by a black bullock-driver?"

"Huah! Ouach! Ugh!" said the bullocks. "Let us get away quickly."

They plunged forward in the mud, and managed somehow to run their yoke on the pole of an **ammunition**③ **wagon**④, where it jammed.

"Now you have done it," said Billy calmly. "Don't struggle. You're hung up till daylight. What **on earth's**⑤ the matter?"

The bullocks went off into the long hissing snorts that Indian cattle give, and pushed and crowded and slued and stamped and slipped and nearly fell down in the mud, grunting savagely.

"You'll break your necks in a minute," said the troop-horse. "What's the matter with white men? I live with 'em."

"They—eat—us! Pull!" said the near bullock. The yoke snapped with a twang, and they lumbered off together.

I never knew before what made Indian cattle so scared of Englishmen. We eat beef—a thing that no cattle-driver touches—and of course the cattle do not like it.

"May I be flogged with my own pad-chains! Who'd have thought of two big lumps like those losing their heads?" said Billy.

"Never mind. I'm going to look at this man. Most of the white men, I know, have things in their pockets," said the troop-horse.

"I'll leave you, then. I can't say I'm over-fond of 'em myself. Besides, white

害怕。晚安，你们这些勇敢的家伙。"

谁也没有接茬儿，战马转移了下话题："那只小狗在哪儿？有狗意味着附近有人。"

"我在这儿，"威克森叫道，"和我的主人一起在炮尾下面。你这只鲁莽的骆驼，是你把我们的帐篷弄翻的。我的主人很生气。"

"哎哟！"公牛说道，"他肯定是白人吧！"

"那当然了，"威克森说道，"难道你以为我是由黑人牛倌照看的？"

"啊！嘿呦！呃！"公牛说道，"咱们赶紧离开这个鬼地方。"

他们在泥浆里使劲儿往前冲，没想到牛轭卡在一辆弹药车的柱子上了。

"这下好了，"比利平静地说道，"别使劲儿了。你们到天亮都走不了。你们要干吗啊？"

公牛们爆发出一阵长长的嘶叫喘气声，印度的牛就这么叫，使劲往前拱，挤到一起，扭动身体，蹄子蹬地，脚下一滑，差点摔倒在泥浆里，狂喊个不停。

"你们的脖子要扯断啦，"战马说道，"白人怎么了？我就和白人住在一起呢。"

"他们——吃——牛肉！使劲儿！"近处的那头公牛说道。牛轭"啪"的一声断了，两头牛"轰"的一下倒在地上。

我以前完全不知道印度牛为什么害怕英国人。我们吃牛肉（当然牛倌不吃），牛自然不喜欢我们。

"我真想让人用我挽具上的铁链抽自己一顿！谁会想到这两个大块头就这样丢了自己的脑袋？"比利说。

"别担心。我倒是要去看看这个人。我知道大部分白人口袋里是有东西的。"战马说。

"那你自己去吧。我对白人可没那么深的感情。再说，连睡觉地方都没有的白人说不定是小偷，我身上可是驮着好多公家的财产呢。走吧，小子，咱们回去吧。

men who haven't a place to sleep in are more than likely to be thieves, and I've a good deal of Government **property**① on my back. Come along, young un, and we'll go back to our lines. Good-night, Australia! See you on parade to-morrow, I suppose. Good-night, old Hay-bale! — try to control your feelings, won't you? Good-night, Two Tails! If you pass us on the ground tomorrow, don't trumpet. It spoils our **formation**②."

Billy the Mule stumped off with the swaggering limp of an old campaigner, as the troop-horse's head came nuzzling into my breast, and I gave him **biscuits**③, while Vixen, who is a most **conceited**④ little dog, told him **fibs**⑤ about the scores of horses that she and I kept.

"I'm coming to the parade to-morrow in my dog-cart," she said. "Where will you be?"

"On the left hand of the second **squadron**⑥. I set the time for all my troop, little lady," he said politely. "Now I must go back to Dick. My tail's all muddy, and he'll have two hours' hard work dressing me for parade."

The big parade of all the thirty thousand men was held that afternoon, and Vixen and I had a good place close to the Viceroy and the Amir of Afghanistan, with high, big black hat of **astrakhan**⑦ wool and the great diamond star in the center. The first part of the review was all sunshine, and the regiments went by in wave upon wave of legs all moving together, and guns all in a line, till our eyes grew **dizzy**⑧. Then the cavalry came up, to the beautiful cavalry canter of "Bonnie Dundee," and Vixen cocked her ear where she sat on the dog-cart. The second squadron of the Lancers shot by, and there was the troop-horse, with his tail like spun silk, his head pulled into his breast, one ear forward and one back, setting the time for all his squadron, his legs going as smoothly as waltz music. Then the big guns came by, and I saw Two Tails and two other elephants harnessed in line to a forty-pounder siege gun, while twenty yoke of oxen walked behind. The seventh pair had a new yoke, and they looked rather stiff and tired. Last came the screw guns, and Billy the mule carried himself as though he commanded all the troops, and his harness was oiled and polished till it winked.

晚安，澳大利亚马！咱们明天阅兵场上见。晚安，老草包！学着控制一下你的情绪，行吗？晚安，双尾！明天你要是在场上经过我们的方阵，可别再吼了，那样会把我们的队形搞乱的。"

骡子比利像个趾高气扬的老兵那样，迈开步子一脚深一脚浅地走了。战马把头拱到我的胸口，我给了他几块饼干。我那自以为是的小狗威克森骗他说我俩养了几十匹马。

"明天，我要坐着我的狗车来阅兵，"小狗说，"你会在哪儿？"

"在第二骑兵中队的左手边。整个方阵得随着我的步子走，小女士，"他彬彬有礼地说道，"现在我得回到迪克身边了。我的尾巴上都是泥，他得帮我好好打扮一番，参加阅兵仪式，要花两个小时呢。"

有三万人参加的大阅兵将在那天下午举行，威克森和我占了个绝佳位置，离总督和阿富汗埃米尔很近。那位埃米尔戴着俄国羔羊毛的黑色高礼帽，帽子中间还镶着颗硕大的钻石星星。阅兵仪式的第一个环节天气很晴朗，一个个方阵依次通过，步伐整齐、铿锵有力，大炮排成一行，看得我们眼花缭乱。接着骑兵团在《邦妮·杜迪》乐曲的伴奏下迈着小碎步走过来，威克森坐在她的小车上支起耳朵听。第二长矛骑兵中队走过来了，其中就有那匹战马。他的尾巴打了结，就像一个纺锤，脑袋被拽到胸部，一只耳朵向前，一只耳朵向后，腿脚的动作就像在跳华尔兹一样流畅，为整个中队设定步速。现在大炮来了，我看见双尾和另外两头大象排成一排，拖着一门能发射四十磅重炮弹的攻城炮，他们身后是二十对公牛。第七对公牛的牛轭是新的，这两只牛看上去行动僵硬、疲惫不堪。最后通过的是螺式炮连，骡子比利忘我的样子就像是他在统领整个军队。他的挽具上了油，擦得铮铮发亮。我一个人为骡子比利喝起了彩，可他没往左看，也没往右看。

---

① property ['prɔpəti] *n.* 资产

② formation [fɔːˈmeiʃ(ə)n] *n.* 编队

③ biscuit ['biskit] *n.* 饼干
④ conceited [kənˈsiːtid] *n.* 自高自大的
⑤ fib [fib] *n.* 无关紧要（或无伤大雅）的谎言

⑥ squadron ['skwɔdrən] *n.* 骑兵中队

⑦ astrakhan [ˌæstrəˈkæn] *n.* （产于阿斯特拉罕的）俄国羔皮

⑧ dizzy ['dizi] *a.* 眩晕的

I gave a cheer all by myself for Billy the mule, but he never looked right or left.

The rain began to fall again, and for a while it was too misty to see what the troops were doing. They had made a big half circle across the plain, and were spreading out into a line. That line grew and grew and grew till it was three-quarters of a mile long from wing to wing—one solid wall of men, horses, and guns. Then it came on straight toward the Viceroy and the Amir, and as it got nearer the ground began to shake, like the deck of a steamer when the **engines**① are going fast.

Unless you have been there you cannot imagine what a frightening effect this steady come-down of troops has on the **spectators**②, even when they know it is only a **review**③. I looked at the Amir. Up till then he had not shown the shadow of a sign of astonishment or anything else. But now his eyes began to get bigger and bigger, and he picked up the reins on his horse's neck and looked behind him. For a minute it seemed as though he were going to draw his sword and slash his way out through the English men and women in the **carriages**④ at the back. Then the advance stopped dead, the ground stood still, the whole line saluted, and thirty bands began to play all together. That was the end of the review, and the regiments went off to their camps in the rain, and an infantry band struck up with—

> *The animals went in two by two,*
>   *Hurrah!*
> *The animals went in two by two,*
> *The elephant and the battery mul',*
>   *and they all got into the Ark*
>   *For to get out of the rain!*

Then I heard an old **grizzled**⑤, long-haired Central Asian chief, who had come down with the Amir, asking questions of a native officer.

"Now," said he, "in what manner was this wonderful thing done?"

雨又开始下了，有段时间视线非常模糊，完全看不清队伍在做什么。受阅部队在平地上组成一个大大的半圆形，接着这个半圆展开成一条线，这条线不断延长，直到两端的距离达到四分之三英里，形成了一面由人、马和大炮组成的铜墙铁壁。接着，这面铜墙铁壁径直向总督和埃米尔走来，队伍离观众更近一些时，就能感觉到地面开始颤抖，就好像蒸汽船发动机加速时站在甲板上的那种感觉。

你要是没有亲临现场，肯定无法想象军队这样稳健地朝观众走过来会给他们带来怎样的震撼，尽管观众知道这只是阅兵而已。我看了看埃米尔。在此之前，他都没有露出任何惊讶或什么别的表情。但在此刻，他的眼睛越睁越大，他拉起马颈上的缰绳，朝身后看了看。有那么一小会儿，他看起来好像准备要拔出剑，在自己后面马车里的英国人中间杀出一条逃生路。就在这时，部队停止前进，大地恢复平静，所有士兵一起敬礼，三十支乐队开始齐声演奏。阅兵结束了，各个方阵在雨中返回自己的营地，一支步兵团乐队开始演奏——

> 动物们进去了，成双成对，
> 万岁！
> 动物们进去了，成双成对，
> 大象和炮兵连的骡子，
> 他们全都进了那个方舟
> 为了躲避这场雨！

接着我听见一位留着花白长发的中亚老酋长问一个本地官员，这位老酋长是随埃米尔一起来的。

"那么，"他问道，"这么精彩的阅兵是怎么做到的？"

那官员答道："命令下达，士兵服从。"

---

① engine ['endʒin] *n.* 引擎，发动机

② spectator [spek'teitə] *n.* 观察者，目击者

③ review [ri'vju:] *n.* 检查

④ carriage ['kæridʒ] *n.* 四轮马车

⑤ grizzled ['grizld] *a.* 头发灰白的

And the officer answered, "An order was given, and they obeyed."

"But are the beasts as wise as the men?" said the chief.

"They obey, as the men do. Mule, horse, elephant, or bullock, he obeys his driver, and the driver his **sergeant**①, and the sergeant his **lieutenant**②, and the lieutenant his captain, and the captain his major, and the major his **colonel**③, and the colonel his **brigadier**④ commanding three regiments, and the brigadier the general, who obeys the Viceroy, who is the servant of the Empress. Thus it is done."

"Would it were so in Afghanistan!" said the chief, "for there we obey only our own wills."

"And for that reason," said the native officer, twirling his mustache, "your Amir whom you do not obey must come here and take orders from our Viceroy."

"动物难道也和人一样聪明不成？"酋长问。

"他们和人一样也服从命令。骡子、马、大象，还有公牛，他们服从自己主人的命令，他们的主人服从中士，中士服从中尉，中尉服从上尉，上尉服从少校，少校服从上校，上校服从统领三个团的准将，准将服从将军，将军又服从总督，总督是女王的侍从。就是这么做到的。"

"要是在阿富汗也是这样就好了！"酋长说道，"因为在阿富汗，我们只听自己的。"

"正因为这样，"那位本地的官员捻着胡子说道，"你们不服从埃米尔的命令，但埃米尔必须来这里听从我们总督的命令啊。"

① sergeant ['sɑ:dʒənt] *n.* 军士，中士
② lieutenant [lef'tenənt] *n.* 陆军中尉
③ colonel ['kɜːnəl] *n.* （英国陆军及海军陆战队的）上校
④ brigadier [ˌbrɪɡə'dɪə] *n.* 【英军】（陆军或海军陆战队）准将

Parade Song of the Camp Animals

ELEPHANTS OF THE GUN TEAMS

*We lent to Alexander the **strength**① of Hercules,*
The wisdom of our foreheads, the cunning of our knees;
*We **bowed**② our necks to service: they ne'er were loosed again,—*
Make way there—way for the ten-foot teams
    Of the Forty-Pounder train!

GUN BULLOCKS

*Those heroes in their **harnesses**③ avoid a cannon-ball,*
*And what they know of **powder**④ upsets them one and all;*
Then we come into action and tug the guns again—
Make way there—way for the twenty yoke
    Of the Forty-Pounder train!

CAVALRY HORSES

*By the brand on my shoulder, the finest of **tunes**⑤*

军营动物的阅兵歌

炮兵连大象

我们把大力神的力量借给亚历山大，
我们有聪明的头脑，灵活的腿脚；
我们弯下腰使劲拉：他们再也不会松开——
往前冲——为十条腿的队伍开路，
为四十磅重的炮车开路！

炮兵连公牛

那些套着挽具的英雄躲闪炮弹，
因为他们知道炮弹的威力；
于是我们开始行动，接着把大炮往前拖——
开路——为二十对公牛开路，
为四十磅重的炮车开路！

骑兵团战马

凭我肩上的记号起誓，最动听的曲调
是枪骑兵、轻骑兵、龙骑兵演奏的，

① strength [streŋθ] *n.*
力，气力

② bow [bəu] *v.* 使弯曲

③ harness ['hɑ:nis] *n.* 马具，挽具

④ powder ['pɑudə] *n.* 粉，火药

⑤ tune [tju:n] *n.* 歌曲

Is played by the Lancers, Hussars, and Dragoons,
And it's sweeter than "Stables" or "Water" to me—
The Cavalry Canter of "Bonnie Dundee"!

Then feed us and break us and handle and groom,
And give us good riders and plenty of room,
And launch us in column① of squadron and see
The way of the war-horse to "Bonnie Dundee"!

SCREW-GUN MULES

As me and my companions were scrambling up a hill,
The path was lost in rolling stones, but we went forward still;
For we can wriggle and climb, my lads, and turn up everywhere,
Oh, it's our delight on a mountain height②, with a leg or two to spare③!
    Good luck to every sergeant, then, that lets us pick our road;
Bad luck to all the driver-men that cannot pack a load:
For we can wriggle and climb, my lads, and turn up everywhere,
Oh, it's our delight on a mountain height, with a leg or two to spare!

COMMISSARIAT CAMELS

We haven't a camelty tune of our own
To help us trollop④ along,
But every neck is a hair trombone⑤
(Rtt-ta-ta-ta! is a hair trombone!)
And this our marching-song:
Can't! Don't! Shan't! Won't!
Pass it along the line!

对于我，这可比"清理马厩"和"饮水"的号声听着还要美妙——

就是轻骑兵舒缓的《邦妮·杜迪》！

喂我们吧，驯服我们吧，驾驭我们吧，打扮我们吧，
给我们优秀的骑手和开阔的场地，
把我们排成纵列，看吧！
战马踏着《邦妮·杜迪》的节奏行进的模样！

螺式炮骡子

当我和伙伴们在攀爬一座高山，
道路消失在翻滚的石块中，可是我们依然头也不回；
因为我们能挪动步子往上爬，我的小伙子们，到处都是我们的身影，
噢，能爬上只能容下一两条腿的山顶我们很高兴！

祝每位让我们自己选路的中士好运；
祝每位捆不好行李的赶骡人倒霉：
因为我们能挪动步子往上爬，我的小伙子们，到处都是我们的身影，
噢，能爬上只能容下一两条腿的山顶我们很高兴！

军需部骆驼

我们没有自己的骆驼歌
伴着我们一路懒散前行，
可每个脖子都是长毛的喇叭
（利特——嗒——嗒——嗒！都是长毛的喇叭！）

① column ['kɔləm] *n.*（部队的）纵列，纵队

② height [hait] *n.* 高，高度
③ spare [spɛə] *v.* 剩下，余下

④ trollop ['trɔləp] *v.* 懒散地闲逛
⑤ trombone [trɔm'bəun] *n.* 长号

Somebody's pack has slid from his back,
Wish it were only mine!
Somebody's load has tipped off in the road—
Cheer for a **halt**① and a **row**②!
Urrr! Yarrh! Grr! Arrh!
Somebody's catching it now!

ALL THE BEASTS TOGETHER

Children of the Camp are we,
Serving each in his degree;
Children of the yoke and goad,
Pack and harness, pad and load.
See our line across the plain,
Like a heel-rope bent again,
Reaching, writhing, rolling far,
Sweeping③ all away to war!
While the men that walk beside,
Dusty④, silent, heavy-eyed,
Cannot tell why we or they
March and suffer day by day.
   Children of the Camp are we,
   Serving each in his degree;
   Children of the yoke and goad,
   Pack⑤ and harness, pad and load!

① halt [hɔ:lt] *n.* 暂停前进，
停住
② row [rəu] *n.* 排，行

③ sweep [swi:p] *v.* 扫，打
扫

④ dusty ['dʌsti] *a.* 满是灰
尘的

⑤ pack [pæk] *n.* 包

我们这支行军歌：
不能！不要！不行！不会！
沿着队伍传唱！
谁的货物从背上滑下来了，
希望是我的！
谁的担子又翻倒在路上——
为这片刻的休息欢呼喧闹吧！
呃！呀！咯！啊！
现在有谁跟上了！

所有动物的合唱

我们是军营的孩子，
在自己的岗位上服役；
牛轭和刺棒的孩子，
货物和挽具，衬垫和担子。
看我们的队伍穿过平原，
就像绊马索弯了，
抵达，翻滚，轰轰隆隆走向远方，
把一切都卷入了战场！
而走在旁边的人们，
灰扑扑，静悄悄，眼沉沉，
无法说出为什么我们或他们
日复一日行军，遭罪。
我们是军营的孩子，
在自己的岗位上服役；
牛轭和刺棒的孩子，
货物和挽具，衬垫和担子！